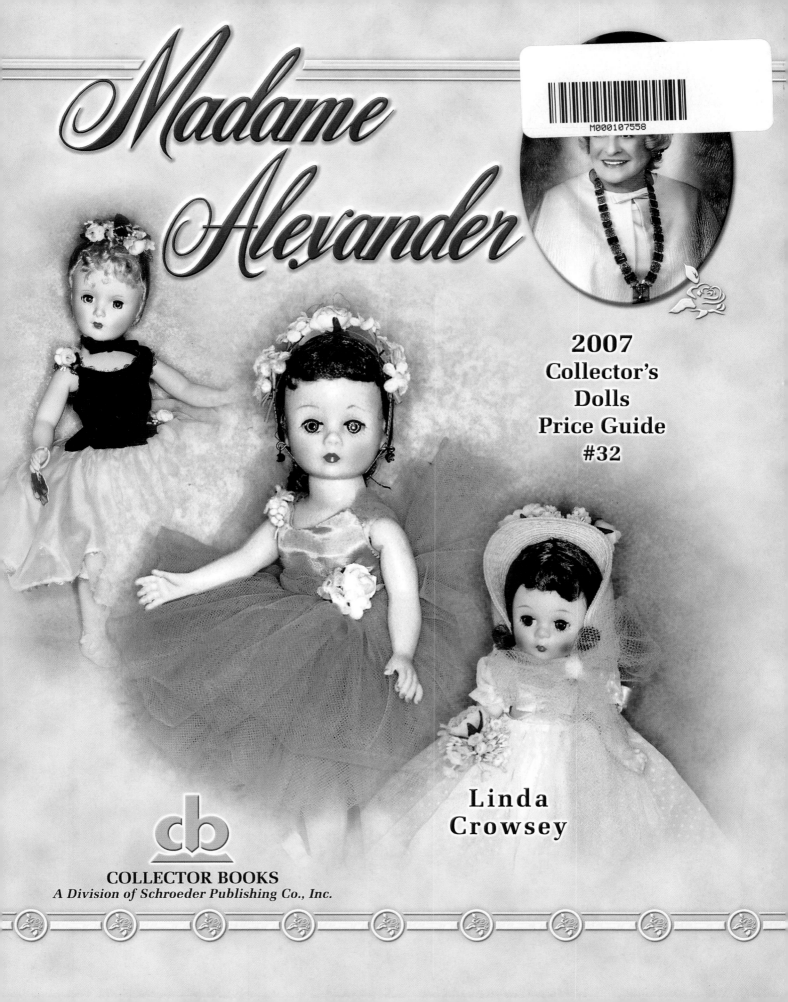

# Madame Alexander

2007
Collector's
Dolls
Price Guide
#32

Linda
Crowsey

**COLLECTOR BOOKS**
*A Division of Schroeder Publishing Co., Inc.*

On the front cover: Top left, Nina Ballerina, 14", 1949 – 1951, $1,500.00. Middle, Cissette Ballerina, 10", 1962, $850.00. Right, Wendy Bridesmaid, 8", 1957, $750.00.

On the back cover: Top left, Lissy Kelly, 12", 1959, $700.00. Middle, McGuffey Ana, 18", 1949, $2,000.00. Right, Maggie, 21", 1948 – 1949, $1,200.00.

Cover design by Beth Summers
Book design by Terri Hunter

COLLECTOR BOOKS
P.O. Box 3009
Paducah, Kentucky 42002-3009

www.collectorbooks.com

Copyright © 2007 Linda Crowsey

The current values in this book should be used only as a guide. They are not intended to set prices, which vary from one section of the country to another. Auction prices as well as dealer prices vary greatly and are affected by condition as well as demand. Neither the author nor the publisher assumes responsibility for any losses that might be incurred as a result of consulting this guide.

## Searching for a Publisher?

We are always looking for people knowledgeable within their fields. If you feel that there is a real need for a book on your collectible subject and have a large comprehensive collection, contact Collector Books.

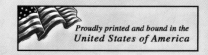
Proudly printed and bound in the United States of America

# *Dedication*

I dedicate *Madame Alexander 2007 Collector's Dolls Price Guide #32* to Madame Alexander Doll Club presidents Margaret Winson, Billie Stevens, and Laura Colpus. Each of these leaders was instrumental in the club becoming a stable organization to continue playing a pivotal role in the research and knowledge of Alexander dolls. Margaret Winson founded M.A.D.C. in 1961 with the permission of Madame Alexander. She nurtured the club through the early years largely at her own expense. Billie Stevens became president in 1995 and helped to bring stability to the club. She and former Alexander CEO Herb Brown greatly expanded the number of dolls and designs available to club members only. Laura Colpus became president in 2002 during a time of instability and financial crisis. Under her leadership and working with Alexander president Gale Jarvis, the club is now financially sound. These three ladies devoted countless hours to a club that continues today to allow members to learn about and enjoy Alexander dolls through the club's publications, events, and conventions. My thanks to each of them!

# *Madame Alexander Doll Club*

For membership information, write to:
Madame Alexander Doll Club (M.A.D.C.)
P.O. Box 2739
New York, NY 10027-9998

## *Photo Credits*

Gary Green, Susan Huey, Hank and Shirley Kronkowski, Ann McCurdy, Lahanta McIntyre, Christene McWilliams, Terri Queen, Carol Strasser, Ben and Helen Thomas, Turn of Century Antiques, and Mike Way.

# The Madame Alexander Doll Company

The first doll hospital in New York City was owned by Maurice Alexander, Madame Alexander's father. He repaired broken dolls and sold new ones as well as fine porcelain pieces. Madame grew up seeing the joy that dolls brought to children. Madame and her sisters began making cloth dolls, and their business shortly outgrew their homes. Madame and her husband, Phillip Behrman, started manufacturing dolls in New York City in 1923. Through the years the Alexander Company made exquisite composition and cloth dolls. Hard plastic became available in 1948, and some of the most highly sought after dolls were made during the 1950s. Madame was inspired by literature, films, plays, fashion, celebrities, history, art, and foreign countries. This golden era produced the Coronation Set, Glamour Girls, Me and My Shadow series, Beaux Arts, Bible characters, 8" Wendy, Cissy, Lissy, Elise, Cissette, and many more.

The Alexander Company continues to be an award-winning company under the leadership of president Gale Jarvis. The company produces a complete line of dolls from high fashion dolls for the discriminating collector to play dolls for children. The Alexander Company added 12" Lissy to the 2006 fall line. Lissy was made originally from 1956 to 1967 which makes this year her fiftieth birthday. President Gale Jarvis and the Alexander Company continue to bring joy to children and adults with their creations.

The Alexander Company is keenly interested in collectors and all areas of collecting. Collectors may contact the Alexander Company and arrange for tours of the Hermitage Gallery where a wide assortment of vintage dolls may be seen. The company also hosts tours of the factory, showroom, doll hospital, and factory store. The Alexander Company is located at 615 West 131st Street, New York City. The company has been located in the same building since the 1950s. I assure you that there is no more exciting place for Alexander collectors to be than the Madame Alexander Doll factory!

Linda Crowsey (left) and daughter, Susan Crowsey Huey (right), with Thomas Jefferson (portrayed by Bill Barker) at the 2006 M.A.D.C. Williamsburg Convention.

Linda Crowsey is dressed in a 1780s era costume and is pictured just before entering the Williamsburg Governor's Ball Banquet. Ms. Crowsey chaired the 2006 M.A.D.C. Convention.

# What Is a Price Guide?

Price guides must be based upon values for a perfect doll, since all collectors need accurate prices for insurance purposes. Insurance companies and postal services must have a way to determine the value of a damaged or stolen doll. Collectors must also have a way to appraise and insure their collections. A price guide, while not the final word, is a starting point to determine the value of a doll. The prices listed are for perfect dolls. Imperfect dolls will bring considerably less than exceptional dolls, which collectors call "tissue mint." Original boxes are important because the information on the box helps determine the age and manufacturer of the doll. The prices quoted are for dolls without their boxes, prior to 1972. Prices for dolls from 1973 to present are for dolls with their original boxes. Prices of these dolls would be adjusted lower if they are missing their boxes. Boxes can be a fire hazard. It is possible to fold most boxes and store them inside a larger box and place the boxes in an airy, dry room. Collectors will pay a higher price for a doll in its original box. Beware of storing dolls for a long time in their boxes — clothing, wigs, and vinyl can fade or change colors. Also, vinyl dolls tend to become greasy or sticky when stored in their boxes.

Marme (right) is a straight leg walker, mint in original box from 1955. Marme (left) is a bend knee doll made from 1966 – 1972. Her clothes are dingy and shelf worn. Elastic in her hat is stretched. Marme (right) is worth $500.00 while Marme (left) is worth $50.00.

## Perfect Dolls

- Complete outfit on correct doll
- Beautiful face color
- Clothes and doll in excellent condition
- Has all accessories, such as hats, etc.
- Clothes not laundered or ironed
- Hair in original set

## Less Than Perfect Dolls

- Re-dressed or has part of original clothes
- Washed, cleaned, ironed clothes
- Stains, soil, faded, shelf dust, holes in fabric
- Faded face color
- Tag cut or missing
- Hair mussed or dirty

## Exceptional Dolls

- Extremely rare doll
- Has wrist tag or original box
- Autographed by Madame Alexander
- Unique outfit or doll
- "Tissue mint" condition
- Has wardrobe or trunk
- Matched set of same year (such as "Little Women")

There is no guarantee that any doll, antique or modern, will appreciate in price year after year. However, prices remain high on exceptional dolls, and always will.

## Mold Marks

Mold marks can be the same for an extended period of time. For example, 14" Mary Ann dolls will be marked "1965" which is the first year the doll was made. From then to now, all Mary Ann dolls will be marked "1965." Another example is the 21" Jacqueline, first introduced in 1961. This doll has been used for the Portraits since 1965 and, up to now, still bears the 1961 date mark on the head. Determining the exact year can be difficult for that reason.

## Doll Names

The dolls named after real people are listed with last name first (example: Bliss, Betty Taylor). Make-believe doll names will be listed with first name first (example: Tommy Snooks).

## Abbreviations

h.p. – hard plastic
compo. – composition
FAD – factory altered dress
SLNW – straight leg non-walker
SLW – straight leg walker
BKW – bend knee walker
BK – bend knee
U.F.D.C. – United Federation of Doll Clubs
M.A.D.C. – Madame Alexander Doll Club
C.U. – Collectors United

## Photo Captions

Listings highlighted in burgundy correspond to a photo shown in the respective section.

## Box Numbers

Order/box numbers for the 8" dolls with "0" prefix (example: 0742) were used in 1973 only. It must be noted the box numbers found with doll's name are from the Madame Alexander catalogs, but many dolls were placed in wrong boxes by the stores from which they were sold.

## Auction Prices

Auction prices have little or no effect on general pricing for Madame Alexander dolls. Dolls often sell at auction for exorbitant prices. It is as simple as two or more people wanting the same item — the bidders just get carried away! Another reason is the rarity or the pristine condition of a doll. This type of doll is extremely difficult to find and warrants the high auction price.

The final word is Madame Alexander dolls have always been collectible and should continue to be. They should endure in time and value. Wise collectors purchase dolls that they really like rather than purchasing dolls that are rumored to go up in value. Then, even if the doll's value doesn't go up, the collector has a beautiful doll that he or she loves. I hope you will continue to build the collections you desire, be they of older dolls or the wonderful current dolls that become available each year.

## 8" Alexander-Kins, Wendy Ann, Wendy, or Wendy-Kin

*1953 – 1976:*
Has "Alex" on back of doll.

*1953:*
First year of production, straight leg, non-walker. Only year Quiz-Kins were produced with two buttons on their backs for the heads to nod "yes" or "no."

*1954:*
Straight leg walker.

*1955:*
Straight leg walker with no painted lashes under the eye.

*1956 – 1965:*
Bend knee walker.

*1965 – 1972:*
Bend knee, does not walk.

*1973 – 1976:*
Straight leg, non-walker with "Alex" on back of doll.

*1977 – Present:*
Has "Alexander" on back.

# The Many Faces of Madame Alexander Dolls

Wendy Ann (composition)

Tiny and Little Betty

Princess Elizabeth

Maggie

Margaret (O'Brien)

Cissy

Elise (1950s – 1960s)

Lissy (1950s)

Cissette

Mary-Bel

Jacqueline

Mary Ann

Elise (1960s – 1980s)

Polly and Leslie

Nancy Drew

Wendy Ann – new 1988 face

Maggie Mixup (1960 – 1961)

Wendy Ann (1953 – 1965)

Alexander-Kin, 8", SLW, 1955, #429. Wendy loves pinafores.

**Active Miss** — 18" h.p., 1954 only (Violet/Cissy)..................................................................$850.00

**Adams, Abigail** — 1976 – 1978, Presidents' Ladies/First Ladies Series, First Set (Mary Ann) ..$125.00

**Adams, Louisa** — 1976 – 1978, Presidents' Ladies/First Ladies Series, First Set (Louisa).......$100.00

**Addams Family** — #31130, 1997 – 1998, set of four dolls (8", 10") and Thing................$225.00

    #31110, 1997 – 1998, 10" Gomez and Morticia..........................................................$125.00

    #31120, 1997 – 1998, 8" Wednesday and Pugsley......................................................$110.00

**Adorable Silk Victorian** — 8", #26875, 2001, white dress .........................................$80.00

**Africa** — 8" h.p., #766, 1966 – 1971, BK (Wendy Ann) .................................................$250.00

    8" h.p., straight leg, reissued, #523 – 583, 1988 – 1992 (Wendy Ann) ....................$50.00

**African Bride** — 10", #28600, 2001, includes broom.................................................$80.00

**African Safari** — 8", #33501, Caucasian, 2002, tan costume with lion ........................$70.00

    8", #33500, African-American, 2002 ...........................................................................$70.00

**Agatha** — 18" h.p. (Cissy)

    1954 only, Me and My Shadow Series, rose taffeta dress, excellent face color................. $1,900.00 up

    8" h.p. (Wendy Ann), #00308, 1953 – 1954, black top and floral gown ......................... $1,900.00 up

    21" Portrait, #2171, 1967, red gown (Jacqueline) .....................................................$650.00

        #2297, 1974, rose gown with full length cape (Jacqueline) ...............................$450.00

        #2291, 1975, blue with white sequin trim (Jacqueline)....................................$350.00

        #2294, 1976, blue with white rickrack trim (Jacqueline) ................................$275.00

        #2230, 1979, 1980, lavender; #2230, 1981, turquoise blue (Jacqueline) ..............$250.00

        #2230, 1981, turquoise blue (Jacqueline) .........................................................$250.00

  10" Portrette, #1171, 1968 only, red velvet (Cissette)..................................................$400.00

**Age of Innocence** — 10", #28400, 2001, dark blue vintage gown ...............................$100.00

**Agnes** — cloth/felt, 1930s.............................................................................................$750.00

**Aladdin** — 8" h.p., #482, 1993; #140482, 1994 only, Storybook Series ..........................$50.00

**Alaska** — 8", #302, 1990 – 1992, Americana Series (Maggie smile face)..........................$50.00

**Albania** — 8", straight leg, #526, 1987 only (Wendy Ann) ...........................................$60.00

**Alcott, Louisa May** — 14", #1529, 1989 – 1990, Classic Series (Mary Ann) .............$80.00

    8" h.p., #409, 1992 only, Storyland Series (Wendy Ann) ............................................$85.00

    8" h.p., #36760, 2003, long brown dress with black trim, book ...................................$85.00

**Alegria** — 10" h.p., #20118, 1996 Cirque du Soleil, silver outfit .....................................$80.00

**Alex** — 16" plastic/vinyl, 2000, Fashion Doll Editor-in-Chief, 2000, #25570,

        brown skirt, white sweater, camel coat......................................................$80.00

    Millennium Ball, 2000, #25580, ball gown with beading ............................................$125.00

    Museum Gala, 2000, #27280, gray sweater, beaded taffeta skirt................................$100.00

    Runway Review, 2000 – 2002, #27275, black evening dress.........................................$85.00

    Magazine Launch, 2000, #27285, beaded jet black suit ..............................................$85.00

    Alexandra Fairchild Ford, 2000, #26930, pink chiffon and taffeta dress.....................$85.00

    Lunch at 2, 2000, #27290, gray crepe dress ..............................................................$75.00

    Woman of the Year, 2001 – 2002, #30640, stunning gold gown ................................$125.00

    Tides, #30630, 2001 – 2002, BK, redhead..................................................................$65.00

Alexander-Kin, 8", 1953, SLNW. Wendy Gift Set.

Alexander-Kin, 8", SLW. Navy coat over red taffeta dress.

Alexander-Kin, Wendy, 8", SLW, #576, sailor. Mint with box.

Tides, #30620, 2001 – 2002, BK, blonde..................................................$65.00
Tides, #30625, 2001 – 2002, BK, brunette..............................................$65.00
Book Tour, #31625, 2001 ......................................................................$150.00
Mardi Gras, #31155, 2001 – 2002 .......................................................$200.00
Cyber Launch, #31215, 2001 ..................................................................$80.00
Sunset Grille, #31165, 2001 – 2002 ......................................................$80.00
Milano, #31221, 2001 ............................................................................$90.00
New Year's Eve, #28455, 2001 – 2002 .................................................$150.00
Music Video Awards, #31220, 2001.......................................................$80.00
Santa Baby, #30635, 2001, red dress, coat with Christmas room................$250.00
Paris, 16", 2001 African-American Fashion Doll Grand Entrance, #31170, 2001 – 2002,
    stunning orange gown with lavender accents.......................................$180.00
La Concorde, #31175, 2001 ..................................................................$100.00
Crocus, 16", long gown, #33260, 2002 .................................................$100.00
Newport, 16", #33255, 2002 ..................................................................$90.00
Breakfast at the Breakers, 16", brunette, #33246; blonde, #33245;
    honey blonde, #33247, striped p.j's, white robe, 2002 .......................$80.00
Graphic Impact, 16", #33605, 2002, two-piece black checked dress (Jadde) ..........$80.00
VIP, 16", #33265, 2002 (Paris), limited to 1,000 ...................................$80.00
Backstage Pass, 16", #33270, 2002 (Paris) ............................................$85.00
Cherry Blossom, 16", #33275, 2002 (Jadde) ..........................................$80.00
Sedona, 16", #33205, 2002 (Alex)...........................................................$80.00
Houston Blues, 16", #32181, 2002 (Alex).................................................$85.00
Denver Days, 16", #33210, 2002 (Alex) ..................................................$85.00
Arabesque, 16", #33215, 2002 (Alex), black silk and velvet gown...............$135.00
Twilight, 16", #33225, 2002 (Alex), blue formal silk ball gown.................$150.00
Blue Maxe Jadde Lee, 16", 2003, #36530, blue dress, limited to 750.........$90.00
Sold Out Show Paris Williams, 16", 2003, #36535, long lacy dress, limited to 750 ...............$180.00
Back to the Basic Alexandra Fairchild Ford, 16", #36250, black dress, hat, limited to 750..............$85.00
Cheongsam Jadde Lee, 16", 2003, #36520, pink short kimono, limited to 500 ...........$120.00
Spotlight Paris Williams, 16", #36235, black and white ball gown, limited to 500..................$150.00
Dancing Til Dawn Alexandra Fairchild Ford, 16", 2003, #37995, long ball gown .................$135.00
Bordeaux Alex, 16", 2003, #36190, long wine gown, limited to 750 .........................$110.00
Breathtaking Jadde, 16", 2003, #36525, tan gown trimmed in faux fur, limited to 750..........$125.00
Dots Alex, 16", #36225, 2003, black dress with big dots at hem, limited to 750 .....................$100.00
Bouquet Alex, 16", 2003, #36210, pink sequin gown, limited to 750 ........................$165.00
Dinner for Two Paris, 16", 2003, #36545, black pants, cream suede jacket, limited to 750 .............$100.00
Firecracker Alex, 16", 2003, #36195, red skirt, black top, limited to 750....................$150.00
Red Label Alex, 16", 2003, #36200, two outfits with red coat, limited to 750 ..........................$200.00
Fuchsia Jadde, 16", 2003, #36740, fuchsia and black gown, limited to 750............................$150.00
Camellia Paris, 16", 2003, #36730, pink ball gown, limited to 750...........................................$120.00

Alexander-Kin, 8", BKW, 1957, #380. Wendy feels so grown up.

Alexander-Kin, 8", BKW, 1960, #335. Wendy dressed for any occasion.

Alexander-Kin, 8", SLW, 1954, #318.

Alexander-Kin, 8", SLW, 1955, #444. Wendy in a school outfit.

Alexander-Kin, 8", BKW, 1956, #593. Wendy goes shopping.

# Alex

Alexander-Kin, 8", BKW, 1957. Blue taffeta dress and straw hat.

Betrayal Alex, 16", 2003, #36755, long black gown and cape, limited to 750 .......................... $125.00
Greed Paris, 16", 2003, #36715, ball gown, tiara, and candlestick, limited to 750 .................. $125.00
Desire Jadde, 16", 2003, #36720, red ball gown, dagger, limited to 750 ................................ $125.00
Red Carpet Alex, 16", 2003, #36390, black sequin gown, limited to 750 .............................. $125.00
Amanda Fairchild, 16", 2003, #36220, ball gown, limited to 500 ......................................... $135.00
Strike a Pose, 2004, six hair colors, body suits ........................................................................ $70.00
Alexandra Fairchild Ford, 16", denim bathing suit, 2004 ......................................................... $60.00
Straight Cuts Jadde Lee, 19", #40185, 2005, silk top, skirt, architect's bag ............................. $100.00
Flirting with the Fifties Amanda Fairchild Ford, 16", #40205, 2005, white hat,
    purse, sheath dress ............................................................................................................. $100.00
Elan's "It" Girl Suzette Morgan, 16", #40225, 2005, jacket, pants, portfolio ............................ $85.00
Set for Style Alexandra Fairchild Ford, 16", #40180, 2005, suit with dress coat .................... $100.00
Fashion Fix Paris Williams, 16", #40195, 2005, blue sweater dress with fringe ..................... $100.00
Power Play Sophia Cruz, 16", #40190, 2005, white and red suit dress ..................................... $100.00
Miami Modern Alexandra Fairchild Ford, 16", #42285, 2006, pants, white coat, scarf ......... $100.00
Looks and Luxury Amanda Fairchild, 16", #42310, 2006, brown dress ................................. $120.00
Elegant Sunset Sofia Cruz, 16", #42300, 2006, orange long gown ........................................ $120.00
Flawless Finish Jadde Lee, 16", #42290, 2006, silk dress, floral coat ..................................... $120.00
World Class Suzette Morgan, 16", #42305, 2006, pink print dress .......................................... $110.00
Cocktail Chic Sienna Evans, 16", #42295, 2006, black dress .................................................. $110.00
True Romance Alexandra Fairchild Ford, 16", bride gown ...................................................... $150.00

Alexander-Kin, 8", BKW, 1956, #606. First long dancing dress.

**Alexander-Kins** — 7½" – 8" h.p., must have excellent face color (also referred to as Wendy, Wendy Ann, or Wendy-Kin). If doll is not listed here, see regular listing for name. (Add more for mint or mint in box dolls. Special hairdos are higher priced.)

Straight leg non-walker, 1953 (Add more for Quiz-Kins.)

| | |
|---|---|
| Coat/hat (dress) | $650.00 up |
| Cotton dress, organdy or cotton pinafore, hat | $550.00 up |
| Dresser, doll, wardrobe, mint | $3,200.00 up |
| Easter doll | $950.00 up |
| Felt jackets, pleated skirt dresses | $550.00 up |
| Garden Party long gown | $1,400.00 up |
| Jumper, one-piece bodysuit | $400.00 |
| Nightgown | $275.00 |
| Nude, perfect doll (excellent face color) | $375.00 |
| Organdy dress, cotton or organdy pinafore, hat | $575.00 up |
| Satin dress, organdy or cotton pinafore, hat | $650.00 |
| Sleeveless satin dress, organdy or cotton pinafore | $475.00 |
| Taffeta dress, cotton pinafore, hat | $650.00 |
| Robe, nightgown or p.j.'s | $300.00 |
| Wendy Gift Set, window box, extra clothes | $2,800.00 up |

Straight leg walker, 1954 – 1955, must have good face color.
    (Add more for mint or mint in box dolls.)

Alexander-Kin, BKW, 1957, #376. Variation of first long party dress.

Alexander-Kin, 8", BKW, 1957, #368. Wendy wears a school frock.

Alexander-Kin, Wendy, 8", BKW, 1957, #376, Wendy's first long party dress.

12

Basic doll in box, panties, shoes, socks ................................................................$525.00

Coat, hat (dress) ...........................................................$475.00 up

Cotton or taffeta dress, pinafore, hat ..............................$475.00 up

Cotton school dress........................................................$375.00 up

Day in Country ...............................................................$975.00 up

Garden Party, long gown ............................................$1,400.00 up

Maypole Dance............................................................$600.00

Nightgown, robe, or p.j.'s ...........................................$300.00

Jumper dress with blouse effect, any material...............$450.00 up

Organdy party dress, hat...............................................$500.00 up

Riding Habit ...................................................................$375.00 up

Sailor dress....................................................................$950.00 up

Sleeveless organdy dress ............................................$375.00

Swimsuits (mint) ...........................................................$375.00 up

Taffeta/satin/nylon party dress/hat...............................$575.00 up

Bend knee walker, 1956 – 1965, must have good face color.

(Add more for mint or mint in box dolls.)

"Alexander-Kin" dropped in 1963 and "Wendy Ann" used through 1965.

Nude (excellent face color) ..........................................$175.00

Basic doll in box, panties, shoes, and socks (mint in box)................$475.00

Car coat set...................................................................$1,700.00

Cherry Twin ...................................................................$1,500.00 up

Coat, hat, dress.............................................................$450.00 up

Cotton dress, cotton pinafore, hat.................................$450.00

Cotton, taffeta, or satin dress, organdy pinafore, hat....$475.00 up

Easter Egg, doll, 1965, 1966 only .................................$1,500.00 up

Felt jacket, pleated skirt, dress, cap or hat ...................$425.00 up

First Dancing Dress (gown) ...........................................$800.00 up

Flower girl......................................................................$900.00 up

French braid, cotton dress, 1965...................................$650.00

June Wedding.................................................................$900.00 up

Long party dress ............................................................$800.00 up

Nightgown, robe .............................................................$275.00

Neiman-Marcus (clothes must be on correct doll with correct hairdo)

Doll in case with all clothes ..........................................$1,400.00 up

Name of store printed on dress material........................$750.00

Two-piece playsuit, navy with red trim ..........................$650.00 up

Robe, navy (no doll) .......................................................$100.00

Red coat, lined with blue stripe (no doll) .......................$125.00

Nude, perfect doll with excellent face color, bend knee, non-walker .....$85.00

Organdy dress, hat, 1965...............................................$475.00 up

Organdy dress, organdy pinafore, hat ...........................$500.00 up

Riding habit, boy or girl ..................................................$375.00 up

Devon Horse Show ........................................................$900.00

Riding habit, checked pants, girl, 1965, boy, 1965........$375.00

Sewing Kit, doll, 1965, 1966 only ..................................$950.00 up

Skater ............................................................................$750.00 up

Sundress .......................................................................$375.00

Swimsuits, beach outfits ...............................................$325.00

Taffeta or nylon party dress, hat ...................................$475.00 up

Tennis ............................................................................$450.00

**Alexander Rag Time Dolls** — cloth, 1938 – 1939 only .........................$850.00 up

**Algeria** — 8" straight leg, #528, 1987 – 1988 only (Maggie) ...............$55.00

**Alice** — 18" h.p., 1951 only, saran wig to waist (Maggie) ...................$750.00

**Alice and Her Party Kit** — 1965 only, included case, wardrobe,
and wigs, mint (Mary Ann) ..........................................$700.00

Alexander-Kin, Wendy, 8",
BKW, 1960s organdy dress
and hat trimmed in lace.

Alexander-Kin, Wendy, 8", BKW,
1959, #444. Wendy dressed in
organdy with pinafore.

Alexander-Kin, 8", BKW.
Early 1960s. Roller skater.
Felt jacket, pleated skirt.

13

Alexander-Kin, Wendy Goes Ice Skating, 8", BKW, #535, felt bonnet and skirt.

Alexander-Kin, 8", BKW, #587, 1956. Sunday School.

**Alice (in Wonderland)** — 16" cloth, 1930 flat face, eyes painted to side ................................... $875.00

1933 formed mask face .................................................................. $675.00

7" compo., 1930s (Tiny Betty) .......................................................... $425.00

9" compo., 1930s (Little Betty) ........................................................ $425.00

11" – 14" compo., 1936 – 1940 (Wendy Ann) ................................ $425.00 – 525.00

13" compo., 1930s, has swivel waist (Wendy Ann) ......................................... $425.00

14½" – 18" compo., 1948 – 1949 (Margaret) ................................. $450.00 – 850.00

21" compo., 1948 – 1949 (Margaret, Wendy Ann) ........................................ $950.00

14" h.p., 1950 (Maggie) ................................................................ $750.00

17" – 23" h.p., 1949 – 1950 (Maggie and Margaret) ........................ $600.00 – 950.00

15", 18", 23" h.p., 1951 – 1952 (Maggie and Margaret) ................... $450.00 – 950.00

14" h.p. with trousseau, 1951 – 1952 (Maggie) ............................... $1,600.00 up

15" h.p., 1951 – 1952 (Maggie and Margaret) ......................................... $600.00

17" h.p., 1949 – 1950 (Maggie and Margaret) ......................................... $700.00

23" h.p., 1942 – 1952 (Maggie and Margaret) ...................................... $850.00 up

29" cloth/vinyl, 1952 (Barbara Jane) ............................................... $700.00 up

8" h.p., #465 – #590, 1955 – 1956 (Wendy Ann) ................................... $800.00 up

8", #494, Storyland Series, blue/white eyelet pinafore, 1990 – 1992 ................... $65.00

#492, 1993, #140492, 1994 blue/white with red trim ........................... $65.00

8" h.p., 1972 – 1976, Disney crest colors (Disneyland, Disney World) ................. $325.00

8" h.p., blue with lace trim, organdy pinafore, 1995 ................................ $65.00

8" h.p., #13000, 1997 – 1998, Alice with calendar, blue party dress,

gold crown, #13001, 1999 – 2000 ............................................. $65.00

12", Prom Party Set, 1963 (Lissy) ................................................. $950.00 up

14" plastic/vinyl, #1452 to 1974, #1552, 1966 – 1992,

Literature & Classic Series (Mary Ann) ...................................... $75.00

14" plastic/vinyl, #87001, 1996 Storyland Friends ................................. $85.00

14" h.p., #25905 (Margaret), 2000 – 2001, blue with white dot dress, organdy pinafore ........ $125.00

10", 1991, with white rabbit (see Disney under Special Events/Exclusives)

18", #16001, 1996 Rag Doll Series (cloth doll) ...................... not available for sale

8", #30665, 2001 – 2005, includes plush rabbit, eyelet pinafore, blue dress ............... $50.00

5", #36295, 2004, vinyl, with rabbit ............................................... $25.00

8", #33545, 2005, Wendy-Kin Wood with white rabbit .............................. $260.00

**All-American Wendy** — 8", #35600, 2003, patriotic outfit, bear ...................... $70.00

**Allison** — 18" cloth/vinyl, 1990 – 1991 ......................................... $60.00

**All My Love** — 8", #40945, 2006, white dress, red heart box ........................ $75.00

8", #42425, 2006, blue dress, eyelet trimmed pinafore ............................. $50.00

**All Star** — 8" h.p., #346 – 346-1, Americana Series, 1993 white or black, 1994 white only ........ $50.00

**All Wrapped Up Christmas** — 8", #45345, 2006, red and gold dress .................. $60.00

**Aloha** — 8", #38870, 2004 – 2005, Latin doll, grass skirt, surfboard ................... $85.00

**Alpine Boy and Girl** — 1992 (see Christmas Shoppe under Special Events/Exclusives)

**Altar Boy** — 8" h.p., #311, 1991 only, Americana Series ........................... $55.00

**Amanda** — 8" h.p., #489, 1961 only, Americana Series, burnt orange, lace trim (Wendy Ann). $2,000.00 up

**American Babies** — 16" – 18" cloth, 1930s .............................. $150.00 – 375.00

**American Beauty** — 10" Portrette, #1142, 1991 – 1992, all pink ...................... $65.00

**American Farm Couple** — 8", 1997, #22160, 1930s rural America ................... $100.00

**American Flag Wendy** — 8", 2001, Caucasian, African-American ..................... $65.00

**American Girl** — 7" – 8" compo., 1938 (Tiny Betty) ............................... $385.00

9" – 11" compo., 1937 (Little Betty, Wendy Ann) .......................... $325.00 – 550.00

8" h.p., #388, #788, 1962 – 1963, became "McGuffey Ana" in 1964 – 1965 (Wendy Ann) ..... $350.00

**American Indian** — 9" compo., 1938 – 1939 (Little Betty) .......................... $375.00

**American Legend, An** — 10", #12510, 1999, with hardcover book with doll (Cissette) .......... $200.00

#17330, 1999 – 2002, hardcover book, no slipcase ................................ $40.00

#12520, 1999 – 2002, deluxe book, slipcase ..................................... $55.00

**American Parade** — 8", #36465, 2003, black and red checked dress, with bear on tricycle ...... $80.00

**American Sweetheart** — 8", #39110, 2004, red skirt ................................ $50.00

**American Tots** — 16" – 21" cloth, dressed in child's fashions .........................................$275.00 – 550.00

**American Women's Volunteer Service (A.W.V.S.)** — 14" compo., 1942 (Wendy Ann).. $850.00 up

**Amish Boy** — 8" h.p., BK, #727, 1966 – 1969, Americana Series (Wendy Ann) ...............................................$375.00

**Amish Girl** — 8" h.p., BK, #726, 1966 – 1969, Americana Series (Wendy Ann) .........................$375.00

**Amy** — (see Little Women)

**Amy Goes to Paris Trunk Set** — 8", #14635, 1996.............................................$200.00

**Amy the Bride** — 10", #14622, 1996, ivory lace dress.........................................$85.00

**Anastasia** — 10" Portrette, #1125, 1988 – 1989 (Cissette) .........................................$75.00

    14" (see M.A.D.C. under Special Events/Exclusives)

    8" h.p., 2003 – 2004, #35695, white dress, blue bodice, gold locket .........................................$80.00

**Anatolia** — 8" straight leg, #524, 1987 only .........................................$60.00

**Angel** — 8", in pink, blue, off-white gowns (Wendy and Maggie) .........................$950.00 up

    Baby Angel — 8" h.p., #480, 1955, multi-layered chiffon wings (Wendy Ann)............ $975.00 up

    Guardian Angel — 8", #480, 1954 only (Wendy Ann) .........................................$800.00 up

    Guardian Angel — 8", #618, 1961 (Maggie smile face) .........................................$800.00 up

    Guardian Angel — 10", #10602, 1995, first in series, all pink with white wings.................$100.00

    Pristine Angel — 10", #10604, 1995, second in series, white with gold trim........................$100.00

    Angel of Bliss — 10", #32155, 2000, long pink dress, white wings ........................................$100.00

**Angel and 8" Music Box Créche** — 8", #19530, 1997 – 2000, Nativity set ........................$200.00

**Angel Face** — (see Shirley's Doll House under Special Events/Exclusives)

**Alexander-Kin, 8", BKW, 1958, #566. Wendy adores a party.**

**Angel Harmony Tree Topper** — 8", #39465, 2005, gold wings .........................................$110.00

**Angelique Innocence Angel** — 10", #35855, 2003, white gown, wings .......................................$150.00

**Angel Tree Topper** — (see Tree Topper)

**Anglund, Joan Walsh** — Joy, 10", #28805 .........................................$35.00

**Anna and the King of Siam** — 8", 1996, #14656, sold as set.........................................$125.00

**Anna Ballerina** — 18" compo., 1940, Pavlova (Wendy Ann) .........................................$950.00 up

**Annabelle** — 14" – 15" h.p., 1951 – 1952 only, Kate Smith's stories of Annabelle (Maggie) ......$700.00

    14" – 15" trousseau/trunk, 1952 only, FAO Schwarz (Maggie) .........................................$1,500.00 up

    18" h.p., 1951 – 1952 (Maggie) .........................................$725.00 up

    20" – 23" h.p., 1951 – 1952 (Maggie).........................................$750.00 – 1,000.00

**Annabelle at Christmas** — (see Belk & Leggett under Special Events/Exclusives)

**Anna Karenina** — 21" Portrait, #2265, 1991 (Jacqueline) .........................................$300.00

    10", #21900 (Cissette) bustle dress, 1998 – 1999 .........................................$90.00

    10", #21910 (Cissette) trunk set, doll, three outfits, 1998 – 1999 .........................................$200.00

**Anne of Green Gables** — 14", #1530, 1989 – 1990 only (Mary Ann) .........................................$100.00

    14", #1579, 1992 – 1994, Goes to School, with trunk/wardrobe (Louisa/Jennifer)................$150.00

    14", #1570 in 1993 only, #261501 in 1995, Arrives at Station .........................................$85.00

    14", 1993, Becomes the Teacher .........................................$85.00

    8" h.p., 1994 – 1995, #260417, At the Station (Wendy Ann) .........................................$85.00

    8" h.p., #260418, 1994, puff sleeve dress .........................................$90.00

    8" h.p., #26423, 1995, concert dress .........................................$100.00

    8" h.p., #26421, 1995, trunk playset .........................................$225.00

    8" h.p., #13830, 1998 – 1999, floral dress, drawstring bag, straw hat.........................................$75.00

    8" h.p., #36115, 2003 – 2004, brown print dress, straw hat .........................................$80.00

**Ann Estelle** — 8", #17600, 1999 – 2001, Mary Engelbreit sailor outfit.........................................$70.00

**Annette** — 1993 (see Disney Annual Showcase of Dolls under Special Events/Exclusives)

**Annie Laurie** — 14" compo., 1937 (Wendy Ann) .........................................$650.00

    17" compo., 1937 (Wendy Ann) .........................................$925.00

**Annie the Artist** — 20", #35001, 1996, artist outfit, crayons .................................not available for sale

**Antiqua** — 8", #45215, 2006, African-American, blue skirt, hat .........................................$55.00

**Antique Chaos the Bear and Wendy** — 8", #36420, 2003 – 2004, 5" bear .........................................$95.00

**Antoinette** — 21" compo., 1946, extra make-up, must be mint (Wendy Ann) .................$2,300.00 up

**Antoinette, Marie** — 21", 1987 – 1988 only, multi-floral with pink front insert .......................$350.00

**Antony, Mark** — 12", #1310, 1980 – 1985, Portraits of History (Nancy Drew) .........................$60.00

**Ants Go Marching, The** — 8", #39920, 2005 – 2006, with two ants .........................................$75.00

**Apple a Day, An** — 8", #38530, 2004 – 2005, doctor outfit with chart, etc .................................$85.00

**Alexander-Kin, Wendy, 8", BKW, early 1960s, nylon party dress.**

Alice in Wonderland, 1950, hard plastic (Maggie). Mint and all original.

Annabelle, 15", hard plastic, 1951 – 1952 only. All original.

**Apple Annie of Broadway** — 8" h.p., 1953 – 1954 (Wendy Ann) .................................... $1,100.00 up

**Apple of Madame's Eye** — 8", #41980, 2006, apple dress, basket of apples ................. $95.00

**Apple Picking** — 8", #33025, 2002 (Maggie), denim dress, basket of apples ............... $60.00

**Apple Pie** — 14", #1542, 1991 only, Doll Classics (Mary Ann).................................... $65.00

**Apple Tree** — 8", #13290, 2000 – 2001, dressed as a tree trunk with leaves and apples ...... $80.00

**April** — 14", #1533, 1990 – 1991, Doll Classics (Mary Ann and Jennifer)................... $75.00

**April in Paris** — 8", #42530, 2006, pink outfit, beret ............................................... $70.00

**April Showers Bring May Flowers** — 8", #13480, 1998 – 1999, pink taffeta and lace, parasol ......... $80.00

**Aquarius** — 8", #21310, 1998, orange and gold mermaid costume ............................. $80.00

**Argentine Boy** — 8" h.p., BKW and BK, #772, 1965 only (Wendy Ann) .................... $450.00

**Argentine Girl** — 8" h.p., BK, #0771-571, 1965 – 1972 (Wendy Ann)....................... $125.00

    BKW, #771 (Wendy Ann) .......................................................... $150.00

    8" h.p., straight legs, #571, 1973 – 1976, marked "Alex"................... $55.00

    8" h.p., straight legs, #571, 1976 – 1986 (1985 – 1986 white face).................. $50.00

**Argyle Twist Total Moves Wendy** — 8", 2004, #38800 ...................................... $85.00

**Ariel** — 9", #37810, 2005 – 2006, vinyl, mermaid outfit, ball gown ........................... $35.00

**Aries** — 8", #21330, 1998, gray furry ram outfit ..................................................... $85.00

**Armenia** — 8", #507, 1989 – 1990 (Wendy Ann) .................................................... $60.00

**Arriving in America** — 8" h.p., #326, 1992 – 1993 only, Americana Series (Wendy Ann)........ $65.00

**Artie** — 12" plastic/vinyl, 1962, sold through FAO Schwarz (Smarty) ....................... $275.00

**Artiste Wendy** — 8", #31250, 1998 – 1999, pink smock and black beret .................... $70.00

**Asakusa Ichimaru** — 10", #42090, 2006, Japanese kimono ..................................... $150.00

**Ashley** — 8", #628, 1990 only, Scarlett Series, tan jacket, hat .................................. $125.00

    8" h.p., #633, 1991 – 1992 only, Scarlett Series, as Confederate officer................ $150.00

**Ashley Rose** — 14", #34335, 2002 – 2003, African-American, print dress ................... $80.00

**Astor** — 9" early vinyl toddler, 1953 only, gold organdy dress and bonnet................... $150.00

**Astrological Month Dolls** — 14" – 17" compo., 1938 (Wendy) ............................. $525.00

**A-Tisket-A-Tasket** — 8", #34315, 2002 – 2003, pink dress, white pinafore, basket ....... $75.00

**Aunt Agatha** — 8" h.p., #434, 1957 (Wendy Ann), checked taffeta gown......................... $1,400.00 up

**Aunt Betsy** — cloth/felt, 1930s................................................................................. $900.00

**Auntie Em** — 8" h.p., #14515, 1995 only, Wizard of Oz Series................................. $60.00

    8" h.p., #39910, 2006, Wizard of Oz Series ................................................ $60.00

**Aunt March** — 8", #14621, 1996 .......................................................................... $70.00

**Aunt Pitty Pat** — 14" – 17" compo., 1939 (Wendy Ann), from *Gone with the Wind* ............ $1,500.00 up

    8" h.p., #435, 1957 (Wendy Ann), from *Gone with the Wind*........................ $1,600.00 up

    8" h.p., straight leg, #636, 1991 – 1992, Scarlett Series ............................... $85.00

    8" h.p., #33465, 2002, blue dress, black lace trim........................................ $90.00

**Australia** — 8" only (Wendy Ann) ........................................................................ $55.00

    8" h.p., #35965, 2003 – 2005, kangaroo skirt, binoculars, plush kangaroo................ $90.00

**Austria Boy\*** — 8" h.p., 1974 – 1989 (Wendy Ann), straight legs, #599 – #533, 1973 – 1975,

    marked "Alex"......................................................................................... $65.00

    #599, 1976 – 1989, marked "Alexander" ..................................................... $55.00

**Austria Girl\*** — 8" h.p., 1974 – 1993 (Wendy Ann) straight legs, #598, 1973 – 1975,

    marked "Alex"......................................................................................... $65.00

    #598 – #532, 1976 – 1990, marked "Alexander"........................................... $55.00

    Reintroduced, #110539 (Maggie), 1994 only .............................................. $55.00

**Autumn** — 14", 1993, Changing Seasons doll with four outfits ................................. $90.00

    5" porcelain, #25860, 2000, brown dress and jacket, black hat ........................ $50.00

**Autumn in N.Y.** — (see First Modern Doll Club under Special Events/Exclusives)

**Autumn Leaves** — 14", 1994, Classic Dolls........................................................... $80.00

    8", #42840, 2006, brown dress, Chaos bear ............................................... $95.00

**Avril, Jane** — 10" (see Marshall Fields under Special Events/Exclusives)

**Baa Baa Black Sheep** — 8", #34020, 2002 – 2003, black polka dot outfit, white hat................ $75.00

**Babbie** — cloth with long thin legs, inspired by Katharine Hepburn ................................ $1,000.00 up

    16" cloth child doll, 1934 – 1936................................................................ $800.00 up

\*Formerly Tyrolean Boy and Tyrolean Girl.

14" h.p. (Maggie) ........................................................................ $800.00 up

**Babette** — 10" Portrette, #1117, 1988 – 1989, short black dress
(Cissette) ........................................................................ $65.00

**Babs** — 20" h.p., 1949 (Maggie) ........................................................................ $850.00

**Babsie Baby** — compo./cloth, moving tongue ........................................................................ $550.00

**Babsie Skater (roller)** — 15", 1941 (Princess Elizabeth) ........................................................................ $850.00

**Babs Skater** — 18" compo. (Margaret) ........................................................................ $1,300.00 up

15" h.p., 1948 – 1950 (Margaret) ........................................................................ $1,200.00 up

17" – 18" h.p. ........................................................................ $1,300.00 up

21" h.p. ........................................................................ $1,500.00 up

**Baby Betty** — 10" – 12" compo., 1935 – 1936 ........................................................................ $300.00

**Baby Brother and Sister** — 20" cloth/vinyl, 1977 – 1979 (Mary Mine) ...... $125.00 ea.

14", 1979 – 1982 ........................................................................ $70.00 ea.

14", reintroduced 1989 only ........................................................................ $65.00 ea.

**Baby Clown** — (see Clown)

**Baby Ellen** — 14", 1965 – 1972 (black Sweet Tears) ........................................................................ $125.00

**Baby Genius** — 11" all cloth, 1930s ........................................................................ $425.00

11" – 12" compo./cloth, 1930s – 1940s ........................................................................ $250.00 up

16" compo./cloth, 1930s – 1940s ........................................................................ $250.00

22" compo./cloth, 1940s ........................................................................ $475.00

15", 18" h.p. head, vinyl limbs, 1949 – 1950 (some get sticky or turn dark) ............. $100.00 – 225.00

21" h.p. head, vinyl limbs, 1952 – 1955 ........................................................................ $350.00

8" h.p./vinyl, 1956 – 1962 (see Little Genius)

**Baby in Louis Vuitton** — trunk/wardrobe or wicker basket with legs, any year ............... $900.00 up

**Baby Jane** — 16" compo., 1935 ........................................................................ $950.00 up

**Baby Lynn** — 20" cloth/vinyl, 1973 – 1976 ........................................................................ $125.00

14" cloth/vinyl, 1973 – 1976 ........................................................................ $100.00

**Baby Madison** — 14", #29750, 1999, vinyl, with layette ........................................................................ $75.00

**Baby McGuffey** — 22" – 24" compo., 1937 ........................................................................ $350.00

20" cloth/vinyl, 1971 – 1976 ........................................................................ $125.00

14" cloth/vinyl, 1972 – 1978 ........................................................................ $100.00

**Baby Precious** — 14" cloth/vinyl, 1975 only ........................................................................ $125.00

21" cloth/vinyl, 1974 – 1976 ........................................................................ $150.00

**Baby's Breath Flower Girl** — 8", #42500, 2006, white dress with flowers ................................ $75.00

**Baby Shaver** — 12" cloth h.p., 1941 – 1943, yellow floss wig, round painted eyes
(Little Shaver) ........................................................................ $650.00 up

**Baby Sister** — 18", #30300, cloth, 2001 –2002, pink checked dress ........................................................................ $40.00

**Baby Snoopy Huggums** — 8", #26440, 2002, Snoopy booties ........................................................................ $50.00

**Bad Little Girl** — 16" cloth, 1966 only, blue dress, eyes and mouth turned down, looking sad ... $250.00

**Bali** — 8" h.p., #533, 1993 only ........................................................................ $55.00

**Ballerina** — (Also see individual dolls – Leslie, Margaret, etc.)

9" compo., 1935 – 1941 (Little Betty) ........................................................................ $375.00

11" – 13", 1930s (Betty) ........................................................................ $400.00

11" – 14" compo., 1936 – 1938 (Wendy Ann) ........................................................................ $425.00

17" compo., 1938 – 1941 (Wendy Ann) ........................................................................ $700.00 up

21" compo., 1947, "Debra" ("Deborah") Portrait ballerina in mint condition
(Wendy Ann) ........................................................................ $8,500.00 up

(Also see Enchanted Doll House under Special Events/Exclusives)

(Also see M.A.D.C. under Special Events/Exclusives)

SLNW, 8" h.p., #354, 1953 – 1954, lavender, yellow, pink, or blue (Wendy Ann) .......................... $750.00 up

SLW, #454, 1955, lavender, yellow, pink, or white ........................................................................ $675.00 up

BKW, #564, 1954 – 1960, golden yellow ........................................................................ $550.00 up

#454, 1955, white ........................................................................ $475.00 up

#564, 1956, rose ........................................................................ $650.00

Ballerina, 8", BKW, #730, mint in box, hard to find yellow ballerina.

#564 – 631, 1956, yellow.............................................................................$700.00

#364, 1957, blue......................................................................................$400.00

#544, 1958, pink......................................................................................$375.00

#420, 1959, gold......................................................................................$750.00

#420, 1961, lavender...............................................................................$700.00

#640, 1964, pink......................................................................................$375.00

BK, #620 – 730, 1965 – 1972, yellow (BKW #730 1965 only)............................$375.00

#440 – 730, 1962 – 1972, blue................................................................$275.00

#440 – 730, 1962 – 1972, pink................................................................$250.00

8" straight leg, #0730, #530, #430, 1973 – 1992 (1985 – 1987 white face)............$60.00

SLNW, #330, 1990 – 1991 (black or white dolls, 1991), Americana Series,

     white/gold outfit (Wendy Ann)...........................................................$60.00

#331 – 331-1, 1992, black or white doll in pink/silver outfit (Wendy Ann)........$60.00

#331, 1993, white doll only, pink/silver outfit.........................................$60.00

#100331, 1994 – 1995, white doll, pink tutu............................................$60.00

#13900, 1998, lace tutu over pink tulle....................................................$65.00

#17640, 1999 – 2000, blue Ballet Recital, wears silver crown.....................$60.00

#17660, 2000 – 2001, pink Ballet Class...................................................$60.00

#17650, 1999 – 2000, lilac Ballet Recital, lilac and silver.........................$65.00

#17690, 1999 – 2000, pink Ballet Recital, pink knit outfit.........................$65.00

#25030, 2000, Irish Dream, green bodice, white tutu with shamrocks..........$70.00

#26810, 2000, pink petal, light pink costume.............................................$65.00

#35075, 8", Twirling Confetti Ballerina, 2004 – 2005, lavender tutu.............$50.00

#35635, 8", The Red Shoes, 2004, white tutu, red shoes..........................$70.00

#38560, 8", Plie Total Moves Wendy, 2004 – 2005, pink tutu....................$95.00

#38620, 8", Land of Sweets Ballerina, 2004, gold tutu.............................$85.00

#38855, 8", 2004 – 2005, Caucasian, Ballet Lessons, with dog, bear, and cat.....$90.00

#38856, 8", 2004 – 2005, African-American, Ballet Lessons, with dog, bear, and cat........$90.00

#39100, 8", Tutu Cute, 2004 – 2006, white tutu, pastel top.......................$75.00

#38857, 8", 2004 – 2005, Asian, Ballet Lessons, with dog, bear, and cat.............$90.00

#38875, Enchanted Garden Ballernia, 2005, pink petal costume....................$75.00

#40175, Encore Performance, 2005 – 2006, blue and white costume.............$75.00

#40285, Polka Dot Plié, 2005 – 2006, pink costume.................................$70.00

#45485, Marzipan Ballerina, 8", 2006, pink, green tutu.............................$75.00

#42635, 8", 2006, pink tutu, hippo, ostrich..............................................$90.00

Autumn Ballerina, #30445, 5", 2002, porcelain, white tutu.............................$60.00

Spring Ballerina, #30435, 5", 2002, porcelain, pink tutu................................$60.00

Summer Ballerina, #30440, 5" porcelain, 2002, green ballet costume....................$60.00

Winter Ballerina, #30450, 5" porcelain, 2002, white ballet costume....................$60.00

10" – 11" h.p., #813, 1957 – 1960, must have excellent face color (Cissette)...........$385.00 up

12", 1964 only (Janie).....................................................................................$275.00

12", 1989 – 1990, "Muffin" (Janie).................................................................$75.00

12", 1990 – 1992 only, Romance Collection (Nancy Drew)................................$60.00

12", 1993 only, lavender (Lissy).......................................................................$135.00

14", 1963 only (Melinda)................................................................................$325.00

15" – 18" h.p., 1950 – 1952, must have good face color (Margaret).............$625.00 – 900.00

16½" h.p., 1957 – 1964, jointed ankles, knees, and elbows, must have good

     face color (Elise)...........................................................................$475.00 up

1957, yellow, rare........................................................................................$900.00

1958, white................................................................................................$425.00

1959, gold.................................................................................................$450.00

1960, pink.................................................................................................$425.00

1961, upswept hairdo, pink..........................................................................$500.00

1962, blue.................................................................................................$425.00

1963 – 1964 only, small flowers in 1963; large flowers in 1964 (Mary-Bel)

(18" also Elise) ............................................................................................... $400.00 up

16" plastic/vinyl, #38350, Principal Ballerina, 2004, white/gold tutu..................$200.00

16" plastic/vinyl, #38355, Dance Under the Stars, 2004, blue tutu........................$200.00

17" plastic/vinyl, 1967 – 1989, discontinued costume (Elise) .................................$95.00

17" plastic/vinyl, 1990 – 1991, "Firebird" and "Swan Lake" (Elise) .....................$100.00

17", 1966 – 1971 only (Leslie – black doll) ............................................................$450.00

16", #22700, 2000 only, Classic Ballerina .............................................................$125.00

16", #40410, 2005, Standing Ovation Ballerina, pink and green............................$220.00

16", #38350, 2005, Principal Ballernia, eyelet and organdy .................................$220.00

16", #42355, 2006, Ballet Imperial, white and red ballet outfit............................$220.00

**Bandstand Swing Set** — 8", girl, boy, #39610, 2004 – 2005, poodle skirt .............$135.00

**Barbara Jane** — 29" cloth/vinyl, 1952 only, mint...............................................$500.00

**Barbara Lee** — 8", 1955, name given by FAO Schwarz.........................................$650.00

**Barton, Clara** — 10", #1130, 1989 only, Portrette, wears nurse's outfit (Cissette) ....$110.00

10", #42070, 2006, green vintage dress and hat........................................................$130.00

**Baseball Boy** — 8", #16313, 1997, red and white baseball outfit ...........................$50.00

**Baseball Girl** — 8", #16300, baseball outfit with ball glove....................................$50.00

**Bathing Beauty** — (see U.F.D.C. under Special Events/Exclusives)

**Bathing Beauty Coca-Cola** — 10", red vintage bathing suit, life preserver ...........$125.00

**Beary Best Friends** — 8" with 2½" bear, #32160, 2000, white dress.....................$65.00

8", #32161, 2002, with 3½" bear, 100th Anniversary Edition .................................$75.00

**Beast** — 12", #1317, 1992 only, Romance Series (Nancy Drew)............................$90.00

8", #140487, Storyland Series – 1994, Fairy Tales Series – 1995 ...........................$70.00

**Beatrice** — 18", 2005, vinyl baby dolls, assorted outfits ....................................$100.00

**Beau Brummel** — cloth, 1930s ...........................................................................$800.00

**Beauty** — 12", #1316, 1992 only, Romance Series (Nancy Drew)...........................$90.00

8", #140486, Storyland Series – 1994, Fairy Tales Series – 1995 ...........................$75.00

**Beauty Queen** — 10" h.p., 1961 only (Cissette) .................................................$400.00

**Beaux Arts Dolls** — 18" h.p., 1953 only (Margaret, Maggie) ........................ $2,750.00 up

**Beddy-Bye Brenda** — (Brooke's sister) (see FAO Schwarz under Special Events/Exclusives)

**Beddy-Bye Brooke** — (see FAO Schwarz under Special Events/Exclusives)

**Bee My Friend** — 8", #38125, 2004 – 2005, dress with bees on it.................................$85.00

**Being Prom Queen** — (see Wendy)

**Being Just Like Mommy** — (see Wendy Loves)

**Belgium** — 8" h.p., BK, #762, 1972 only (Wendy Ann) .......................................$100.00

8" straight legs, #0762, #562, 1973 – 1975, marked "Alex".....................................$60.00

8" straight legs, #562, 1976 – 1988, marked "Alexander" .......................................$55.00

7" compo., 1935 – 1938 (Tiny Betty) .....................................................................$300.00

9" compo., 1936 only (Little Betty)........................................................................$325.00

**Belk & Leggett Department Stores** — (see Special Events/Exclusives)

**Belle** — 14", #18402, 1996 Dickens, red jacket, long skirt......................................$100.00

9", #36375, 2004 – 2006, vinyl, yellow dress ..........................................................$35.00

**Belle Brummel** — cloth, 1930s...........................................................................$800.00

**Belle of the Ball** — 10", #1120, 1989 only, Portrette, deep rose gown (Cissette) ......$100.00

**Belle's Enchanted Christmas** — 10", #34945, 2002, red satin ball gown with plastic Angelique $125.00

**Belle Watling** — 10", 1992 only, Scarlett Series (Cissette) ................................$125.00

21", #16277, 1995 only, red outfit with fur trim (Jacqueline) ...............................$325.00

10", #30820, 2001, gold satin dress, brown trim......................................................$100.00

**Bellows' Anne** — 14" plastic/vinyl, #1568, 1987 only, Fine Arts Series ..................$75.00

**Bernhardt, Sarah** — 21", #2249, 1987 only, dressed in all burgundy .....................$300.00

**Berries and Cream** — 8", #28475, 2001 – 2002, pink stripe dress, hat ...................$75.00

**Bessy Bell** — 14" plastic/vinyl, #1565, 1988 only, Classic Series (Mary Ann) ...........$75.00

**Bessy Brooks** — 8", #487, 1988 – 1991, Storybook Series (Wendy Ann)....................$60.00

8", 1990 (see Collectors United/C. U., Bride under Special Events/Exclusives)

**Best Friend** — 8", #26090, 2000, blue silk dress with smocking .......................................$90.00

    8", #26085, 2000 – 2001, pink silk dress with smocking ..........................................$90.00

**Best Friends** — 8", #36895, 2003 – 2004, doll, 18" Chaos bear, toy box....................$150.00

**Best Man** — 8" h.p., #461, 1955 only (Wendy Ann) ...............................................$875.00

**Beth** — (see Little Women) 10" (see Spiegel's under Special Events/Exclusives)

**Betty** — 14" compo., 1935 – 1942..................................................................................$425.00

    12" compo., 1936 – 1937 only....................................................................................$350.00

    16" – 18" compo., 1935 – 1942....................................................................................$425.00

    19" – 21" compo., 1938 – 1941....................................................................................$550.00

    14½" – 17½" h.p., 1951 only, made for Sears (Maggie) ..........................................$575.00

    30" plastic/vinyl, 1960 only .........................................................................................$400.00

**Betty Bag** — 23" all cloth, holds clothes back of head ...............................................$225.00

**Betty Blue** — 8" straight leg, #420, 1987 – 1988 only, Storybook Series (Maggie) .....................$55.00

**Betty Boop** — 10", #17500 (Cissette), red dress, 1999 – 2001 ..................................$125.00

    21", #25125, 2000, doll with two outfits.................................................................$225.00

    10", #26450, 2000 – 2001, Razzle Dazzle, long white dress, hat ..........................$125.00

**Betty, Little** — 9" compo., 1935 – 1943............................................................$350.00 up

**Betty, Tiny** — 7" compo., 1934 – 1943................................................................$350.00 up

**Bible Character Dolls** — 8" h.p., 1954 only (Wendy Ann) (Mary of Bethany, David,

    Martha, Ruth, Timothy, Rhoda, Queen Esther, and Joseph) .........................$7,500.00 up

    1995 (see Delilah, Joseph, Queen Esther, and Samson)

**Big Sister Wendy** — 8", #36550, 2003 – 2004, blue dress, stuffed doll, book ...........$90.00

**Bike Riding Wendy** — 8", #41580, 2006, pink checked outfit, bike.......................$90.00

**Bill/Billy** — 8" h.p., #320, #567, #420, 1955 – 1963, has boy's clothes and hairstyle

    (Wendy Ann) ..........................................................................................$450.00 up

    #577, #464, #466, #421, #442, #488, #388, 1953 – 1957, as groom ...................$450.00 up

**Billie Holiday** — 10", #22070, 1997, long silver gown ..............................................$90.00

**Billy-in-the-Box** — 8" jester, 1996, Alexander signature box......................................$100.00

**Binah** — 8", #39450, 2004 – 2005 (Wendy), with mouse.............................................$85.00

    5", #39440, 2004 – 2005, petite, red skirt....................................................................$25.00

    9", #39435, 2004 – 2005, vinyl, with mouse ..............................................................$35.00

    12", #39160, posable cloth doll, 2006 ........................................................................$25.00

    6", #39445, 2004, cloth, red skirt................................................................................$10.00

**Binnie** — 18" plastic/vinyl toddler, 1964 only ............................................................$350.00

**Binnie Walker** — 15" – 18" h.p., 1954 – 1955 only (Cissy) ...........................$250.00 – 425.00

    15", 1955 only, in trunk with wardrobe ...................................................................$750.00

    15", 1955 only, h.p. skater.......................................................................................$700.00 up

    18", toddler, plastic/vinyl, 1964 only .....................................................................$350.00 up

    25", 1955 only, in formals........................................................................................$550.00 up

    25" h.p., 1954 – 1955 only, dresses .........................................................................$400.00 up

**Birds, The** — 10", #14800, green dress, fur coat, pictured 1998 catalog, 2005 .........................$130.00

    10", #40720, 2006, dress, fur coat with birds attached............................................$130.00

**Birthday Dolls** — 7" compo., 1937 – 1939 (Tiny Betty)........................................$375.00 up

**Birthday, Happy** — 1985 (see M.A.D.C. under Special Events/Exclusives)

**Bitsey** — 11" – 12" compo., 1942 – 1946................................................................................$22500

    11" – 16", with h.p. head, 1949 – 1951 ......................................................................$250.00

    19" – 26", 1949 – 1951.........................................................................$150.00 – 375.00

    12" cloth/vinyl, 1965 – 1966 only ..............................................................................$150.00

**Bitsey, Little** — 9" all vinyl, 1967 – 1968 only .........................................................$125.00

    11" – 16"..............................................................................................$75.00 – 250.00

**Black and White Ball** — 10", #38735, 2004, white gown, black flowers...................$135.00

**Black Forest** — 8", #512, 1989 – 1990 (Wendy Ann)................................................$55.00

**Blast Off 2000** — 8", #17830, 2000 only (Maggie), silver and gold costume .............................$80.00

**Bless the Night Tree Topper** — 8", #38710, 2004 – 2005, wine and beige angel costume ......$100.00
**Bliss, Betty Taylor** — 1979 – 1981, second set Presidents' Ladies/First Ladies Series
   (Mary Ann) ................................................................................................$100.00
**Blooming Rose** — 8", #28470, 2001 – 2002, pink stripe dress, hat................$80.00
**Blue Bird Shadow Wendy** — 8", #37135, African-American or Caucasian, 2004,
   white dress, straw hat................................................................................$90.00
**Blue Boy** — 16" cloth, 1930s.................................................................$650.00
   7" compo., 1936 – 1938 (Tiny Betty) .......................................................$350.00
   9" compo., 1938 – 1941 (Little Betty) .......................................................$375.00
   12" plastic/vinyl, #1340, 1972 – 1983, Portrait Children (Nancy Drew)...................$60.00
      1985 – 1987, dressed in blue velvet..........................................................$65.00
   8", #22130, 1997  – 1998, blue satin outfit ................................................$65.00
**Blue Danube** — 18" h.p., 1953 only, pink floral gown (#2001B – blue floral gown)
      (Maggie) ................................................................................. $1,800.00 up
   18" h.p., 1954 only, Me and My Shadow Series, blue taffeta dress (Margaret)............. $1,900.00 up
**Blue Edwardian Lady** — 5" porcelain, #27025, long blue gown, 2000 .......................$65.00
**Blue Fairie** — 10", #1166, 1993; #201166, 1994, Portrette, character from Pinocchio (Cissette)..$100.00
**Blue Fairy** — 8", #32135, 2000, blue gown, wings................................................$80.00
   10", #31760, 2003 – 2004 and 10" wooden Pinocchio, long blue ball gown............................$200.00
**Blue Gingham Chloe** — 14" vinyl, #25350, 2001 ................................................$70.00
**Blue Hat Doll** — 8", #25310, 2000, Maud Humphrey design ...................................$65.00
**Blue Mist Angel** — 10", #25290, 2000 – 2001, Caucasian doll, blue costume ...........................$125.00
   10", #25291, 2000 – 2001, African-American doll, blue costume ...........................................$125.00
**Blue Moon** — 14", #1560, 1991 – 1992 only, Classic Series (Louisa) ................................$85.00
**Blue Skies Angel** — 8", #37900, 2003 – 2004, blue and white dress................................$90.00
**Blue Zircon** — 10", #1153, 1992 only, Birthday Collection, gold/blue flapper............................$125.00
**Blynkin** — (see Dutch Lullaby)
**Bobby** — 8" h.p., #347, 1957 only (Wendy Ann) ...............................................$575.00
   8" h.p., #361, #320, 1960 only (Maggie Mixup)...............................................$625.00
**Bobby Q.** — cloth, 1940 – 1942 ....................................................................$750.00
**Bobby (Bobbie) Soxer** — 8" h.p., 1990 – 1991 (see Disney under Special Events/Exclusives)
**Bobo Clown** — 8", #320, 1991 – 1992, Americana Series (Wendy Ann)....................$70.00
**Bohemia** — 8", #508, 1989 – 1991 (Wendy Ann) ............................................$50.00
**Bolivia** — 8" h.p., BK and BKW, #786, 1963 – 1966 (Wendy Ann) ..............................$350.00
**Bonnet Top Wendy** — 8", #14487, 1995, Toy Shelf Series, yarn braids and large bonnet .........$55.00
**Bonnie (Baby)** — 16" – 19" vinyl, 1954 – 1955....................................$125.00 – 250.00
   24" – 30", 1954 – 1955................................................................$125.00 – 250.00
**Bonnie Blue** — 14", #1305, 1989 only, Jubilee II (Mary Ann)....................................$150.00
   8" h.p., #629, #630, 1990 – 1992 (Wendy Ann) ...............................................$100.00
   8", #16649, 1995, side-saddle riding outfit................................................$100.00
   8", #42280, 2006, blue party dress....................................................................$80.00
**Bonnie Goes to London** — 8", #640, 1993, Scarlett Series, #160640 – 1994............................$125.00
**Bonnie Toddler** — 18" cloth/h.p. head/vinyl limbs, 1950 – 1951................................$175.00
   19" all vinyl, 1954 – 1955..............................................................................$225.00
   23" – 24"....................................................................................................$275.00
**Bon Voyage** — 8" and 10" (see I. Magnin under Special Events/Exclusives)
**Bon Voyage Paris Wendy Trunk Set** — 8", #39730, 2005 – 2006, six outfits,
   bear and mini doll ..............................................................................$290.00
**Boone, Daniel** — 8" h.p., #315, 1991 only, Americana Series, has no knife (Wendy Ann) .........$60.00
**Bo Peep, Little** — 7" compo., 1937 – 1941, Storybook Series (Tiny Betty) ............................$375.00
   9" – 11" compo., 1936 – 1940 (Little Betty, Wendy Ann).........................................$350.00
   7½" h.p., SLW, #489, 1955 only (Wendy Ann) ................................................$675.00
   8" h.p., BKW, #383, 1962 – 1964 (Wendy Ann) ................................................$325.00
   8" h.p., BK, #783, 1965 – 1972 (Wendy Ann) ................................................$125.00

8" h.p., straight leg, #0783 – 483, 1973 – 1975, marked "Alex" (Wendy Ann)............................$75.00
8" h.p., 1976 – 1986, #483 – #486, marked "Alexander" (Wendy Ann)......................................$60.00
14", #1563, 1988 – 1989, Classic Series (Mary Ann)..............................................................$80.00
14", #1567, 1992 – 1993 only, candy stripe pink dress (Mary Ann) ..........................................$90.00
12" porcelain, #009, 1990 – 1992.......................................................................................$135.00
10" Portrette Series, 1994 ..................................................................................................$80.00
8" (see Dolly Dears under Special Events/Exclusives)
8", #25960, 2000 – 2003, long blue dress and hat with staff ...................................................$80.00
8", #42570, 2006, pink dress, staff and sheep .....................................................................$80.00

**Born to Ride** — 10", #40695, 2005, black leather coat, boots ............................................$130.00
**Boston Tea Party** — 8", #45480, 2006, blue coat, tea box ..............................................$85.00
**Bowl-O-Rama** — 8", #39720, 2005, pants outfit, bowling bag and ball ..............................$75.00
**Boys Choir of Harlem** — 8", #20170, 1997 – 1998, maroon blazer, Kufi hat.............$75.00 each
**Brazil** — 7" compo., 1937 – 1943 (Tiny Betty) .................................................................$350.00
9" compo., 1938 – 1940 (Little Betty) ...........................................................................$375.00
8" h.p., BKW, #773, 1965 – 1972 (Wendy Ann) ............................................................$125.00
BK, #773.......................................................................................................................$100.00
8" h.p., straight leg, #0773, #573, 1973 – 1975, marked "Alex" (Wendy Ann)..........................$65.00
8" h.p., straight leg, #573, #547, #530, 1976 – 1988, marked "Alexander" ..............................$60.00
#573, #547, #530, 1985 – 1987 ....................................................................................$55.00
8" straight leg, #11564, 1996 International, carnival costume ..................................................$55.00

**Breakfast in Bed** — 8", #34040, 2003, white dress, tray with coffee, glasses ............................$65.00
**Brenda Starr** — 12" h.p., 1964 only (became "Yolanda" in 1965) ....................................$350.00
Bride ..........................................................................................................................$375.00
Street dresses................................................................................................................$375.00
Ball gown....................................................................................................................$450.00
Beach outfit .................................................................................................................$275.00
Raincoat/hat/dress.........................................................................................................$350.00

**Briar Rose** — (see M.A.D.C. under Special Events/Exclusives)
10", #14101, 1995, Brothers Grimm Series, blue floral with apron (Cissette) ...........................$90.00
8", #42540, 2006, blue skirt, red shawl ..............................................................................$65.00

**Brick Piggy** — 12", #10010, 1997, denim overalls, maize felt cap ....................................$85.00
**Bride** — Tiny Betty: 7" compo., 1935 – 1939 ................................................................$325.00
9" – 11" compo., 1936 – 1941 (Little Betty)...................................................................$350.00
Wendy Ann: 13", 14", 15" compo., 1935 – 1941 (Wendy Ann) .................................$300.00 – 550.00
17" – 18" compo., 1935 – 1943 (Wendy Ann) ............................................................$475.00
21" – 22" compo., 1942 – 1943 (Wendy Ann) ............................................................ $650.00 up
In trunk/trousseau (Wendy Ann) .............................................................. $1,650.00 up
21" compo., 1945 – 1947, Royal Wedding/Portrait (Wendy Ann)........................... $2,400.00 up
Margaret, Maggie: Hard plastic
15" h.p., 1951 – 1955 (Margaret) ............................................................................. $675.00 up
17" h.p., 1950, in pink (Margaret) ............................................................................ $850.00 up
18" h.p., tagged "Prin. Elizabeth" (Margaret)...............................................................$750.00
18" h.p., 1949 – 1955 (Maggie, Margaret) ................................................................ $700.00 up
21" h.p., 1949 – 1953 (Margaret, Maggie) ............................................................. $1,200.00 up
18" – 21", pink bride, 1953 (Margaret)..................................................................... $1,200.00 up
23" h.p., 1949, 1952 – 1955 (Margaret)................................................................... $850.00 up
25" h.p., 1955 only (Margaret)................................................................................. $875.00 up
Elise: 16½" h.p., 1957 – 1964, jointed ankles, elbows, and knees, must have good face
color, 1957, nylon tulle, chapel length veil............................................................. $475.00 up
1958, wreath pattern on hem of skirt............................................................................$550.00
1959, tulle puffed sleeves, long veil (pink) ..................................................................$800.00
1960, satin gown, lace bodice with sequins and beads.....................................................$475.00
1961, short bouffant hair, tulle with puff sleeves ...........................................................$475.00

1962, lace pattern bodice and trim on tulle skirt.................................................................$425.00

1963, tulle, rows of lace on bodice .........................................................................................$475.00

1964, lace bodice and sleeves, lace on skirt, chapel length veil ........................................$425.00

2000, 16", Classic Bride, white lace and tulle gown ..........................................................$125.00

Cissy: 20" h.p., 1955 – 1958

1955 only, Dreams Come True Series, brocade gown with floor length veil............ $1,500.00 up

1956 only, tulle gown, tulle cap and chapel length veil, Fashion Parade Series....... $1,200.00 up

1957 only, Models Formal Gowns Series, nylon tulle with double train of satin........ $950.00 up

1958 only, Dolls to Remember Series, lace circles near hem (wreath pattern), #2280. $1,400.00 up

1959 only, tulle over white satin...............................................................................................$850.00

Cissette: 10" h.p., 1957 – 1963, must have good face color

1957, tulle gown, short veil or lace and tulle cap veil.........................................................$375.00

1958, lace wreath pattern, matches Elise and Cissy..............................................................$575.00

1959 – 1960, tulle gown, puff sleeves......................................................................................$450.00

1961, tulle, rhinestones on collar and veil...............................................................................$450.00

1962, lace bodice and trim on skirt, long veil .......................................................................$400.00

1963, tulle, rows of lace on bodice and at hem (matches Elise from the same year).........$475.00

In trunk/trousseau, various years............................................................................... $950.00 up

#1136, 1990 – 1991, Portrette .................................................................................................$75.00

#14103, 1995, 1920s style ......................................................................................................$100.00

#22470, 10" Empire Bride, 1998, lace gown, straw bonnet ................................................$100.00

#22460, 10" Rococo Bride, 1998, peach gown, lace train ....................................................$100.00

#22480, 10" Victorian Bride, 1998, blue satin gown .........................................................$100.00

#26880, 10", Contemporary Bride, blonde ...........................................................................$100.00

#26881 (brunette), 2000 ..........................................................................................................$100.00

#32990 (blonde), 2002, white gown, pink trim, limited to 1,000......................................$100.00

#33325 (blonde), #33326 (brunette), Down the Aisle, 2002 – 2003...................................$100.00

#33327, African-American, 2002 – 2003, Down the Aisle....................................................$100.00

#38750, 10", 2004, My Special Day, blonde, white dress, lace trim.....................................$140.00

#38751, 10", 2004, My Special Day, brunette, white dress, lace trim....................................$140.00

#38752, 10", 2004, My Special Day, African-American, white dress, lace trim ................$140.00

#40355, 10", 2005, blonde, Lasting Memories Bride .............................................................$90.00

#40356, 10", 2005, brunette, Lasting Memories Bride..........................................................$90.00

#40357, 10", 2005, African-American, Lasting Memories Bride..........................................$90.00

#42480, 10", 2006, brunette, Visions of Love .......................................................................$100.00

#42475, 10", 2006, blonde, Visions of Love ..........................................................................$100.00

#42485, 10", 2006, Visions of Love Bride ..............................................................................$100.00

#42490, 10", 2006, African-American ....................................................................................$100.00

Lissy: 12" h.p., 1956 – 1959

1956, jointed knees and elbows, tulle, tulle cap veil.............................................. $650.00 up

1957, same as 1956 except long veil..........................................................................................$675.00

1958 – 1959, dotted net, tulle veil ........................................................................... $675.00 up

1991 – 1992 only, porcelain (version of 14" head) ...........................................................$140.00

Jacqueline: 21" Portrait

#2151, 1965, full lace, wide lace edge on veil (Jacqueline) .................................................$950.00

#2192, 1969, full lace overskirt and plain veil .....................................................................$750.00

Alexander-Kin (Wendy Ann): 8" h.p. or plastic/vinyl

8" h.p., #315, 1953 only, Quiz-Kin ........................................................................................$700.00

8" h.p., 1954............................................................................................................... $650.00 up

SLW, BKW, #735 in 1955, #615 in 1956, #410 in 1957,  #582 in 1958 ..................... $375.00 up

BKW, #482, 1959, pink.......................................................................................... $1,000.00 up

BKW, #735, 1960 ....................................................................................................................$425.00

BKW, #480, 1961 ....................................................................................................................$375.00

BKW, #760 (#630 in 1965), 1963 – 1965.............................................................................$350.00

BK, #470 in 1966, #735 in 1967 – 1972 ..............................................................$175.00
Straight legs, #0735-435, 1973 – 1975, marked "Alex" .............................$85.00
Straight legs, #435, 1976 – 1994, marked "Alexander" ............................$70.00
#337, white doll; #336-1, black doll, 1991 – 1992 ..................................$65.00
#337, 1993, white only ..........................................................................$60.00
#435, 1985 – 1987 ................................................................................$55.00
Collectors United (see under Special Events/Exclusives)
  #10395, 1995, Special Occasions Series, African-American .....................$65.00
  #10392, 1995, Special Occasions Series, three hair colors .......................$60.00
  #17016, 1996 white lace and satin gown...................................................$60.00
  #21030, 1997 – 1998, white gown, comes with cake top, #21033 – African-American...$100.00
  #21171, 1999, blonde or brunette, satin ribbon at hem .........................$60.00
  #25015 (blonde), #25016 (brunette), 2000 ...........................................$70.00
  #25017, 2000, African-American ............................................................$65.00
  #30650 (blonde), #30652 (brunette), 2001 – 2002, white dress, sequin trim .....................$65.00
  #30651, African-American, 2001 – 2002, Memories of a Lifetime................$65.00
  #36275, blonde, 2003 – 2004, Rosette Dreams, white dress, pink roses...........$80.00
  #36276, brunette, 2003 – 2004, Rosette Dreams.......................................$80.00
  #36277, African-American, 2003 – 2004, Rosette Dreams............................$80.00
  #39065, 8", 2005 – 2006, blonde, Honeymoon Sweet Dreams.....................$80.00
  #39066, 8", 2005 – 2006, brunette, Honeymoon Sweet Dreams...................$80.00
  #39067, 8", 2005 – 2006, African-American, Honeymoon Sweet Dreams .........$80.00
Mary Ann, Jennifer, Louisa: 14" plastic/vinyl
  #1465 (#1565 in 1974, #1565 in 1977, #1570 in 1976), 1973 – 1977
    (Mary Ann)....................................................................................$90.00
  #1589 in 1987 – 1988; #1534 in 1990, Classic Series (Mary Ann, Jennifer)..........$90.00
  #1566, reintroduced 1992 only, ecru gown (Louisa, Jennifer) .....................$90.00
Elise, Leslie, Polly: 17" plastic/vinyl or 21" porcelain
  1966 – 1988 (Elise) .............................................................................$150.00
  1966 – 1971 (Leslie) ............................................................................$250.00
  1965 – 1970 (Polly).............................................................................$250.00
  Porcelain, 1989 – 1990, satin and lace look like bustle ............................$200.00
  Porcelain, Portrait Series, 1993 – 1994....................................................$200.00
**Bridesmaid** — 9" compo., 1937 – 1939 (Little Betty) ...............................$350.00
11" – 14" compo., 1938 – 1942 (Wendy Ann)..............................$325.00 – 475.00
15" – 18" compo., 1939 – 1944 (Wendy Ann)..............................$375.00 – 600.00
20" – 22" compo., 1941 – 1947, Portrait (Wendy Ann)..................... $1,800.00 up
21½" compo., 1938 – 1941 (Princess Elizabeth) ............................. $950.00 up
15" – 17" h.p., 1950 – 1952 (Margaret, Maggie) ..................$400.00 – 550.00
15" h.p., 1952 (Maggie) ......................................................................$650.00
18" h.p., 1952 (Maggie) .................................................................. $700.00 up
21" h.p., 1950 – 1953, side part mohair wig, deep pink or lavender gown
  (Margaret)..................................................................................... $800.00 up
19" rigid vinyl, in pink, 1952 – 1953 (Margaret)............................... $600.00 up
15" h.p., 1955 only (Cissy, Binnie)........................................................$450.00
18" h.p., 1955 only (Cissy, Binnie)........................................................$475.00
25" h.p., 1955 only (Cissy, Binnie) .................................................. $475.00 up
20" h.p., 1956 only, Fashion Parade Series, blue nylon tulle and net (Cissy)........ $1,500.00 up
10" h.p., 1957 – 1963 (Cissette)............................................................$475.00
12" h.p., 1956 – 1959 (Lissy) ........................................................... $750.00 up
16½" h.p., 1957 – 1959 (Elise) ........................................................ $475.00 up
8" h.p., SLNW, 1953, pink, blue, or yellow ...................................... $900.00 up
8" h.p., SLW, #478, 1955 (Wendy Ann)............................................ $800.00 up
BKW, #621, 1956 ............................................................................ $750.00 up

BKW, #408, #583, #445, 1957 – 1959 ..............................................$700.00 up

8", 2000, Little Gardenia, #26855 (Wendy), white tulle and satin ........................ $65.00

8", 2000, Little Pearl, #26800 (Wendy), lace bodice ................................................. $75.00

17" plastic/vinyl (Elise) 1966 – 1987 ...................................................... $125.00

17" plastic/vinyl, 1966 – 1971 (Leslie) ................................................... $325.00

**Brigitta** — 11" and 14" (see Sound of Music)

**Brooke** — (see FAO Schwarz under Special Events/Exclusives)

**Bubbles the Clown** — 8" h.p., #342, 1993 – 1994, Americana Series..................... $100.00

**Buck Rabbit** — cloth/felt, 1930s ........................................................$700.00 up

**Bud** — 16" – 19", 1952 only, cloth/vinyl (Rosebud head) ........................................ $175.00

19" and 25", 1952 – 1953 only ................................................ $175.00 – 350.00

**Bulgaria** — 8", #557, 1986 – 1987, white face (Wendy Ann) ..................................... $55.00

**Bumble Bee** — 8" h.p., #323, 1992 – 1993 only, Americana Series ........................... $60.00

**Bunny** — 18" plastic/vinyl, 1962 only, mint ................................................ $275.00

**Bunny Tails** — 8", #28200, 2000 – 2003, yellow dress, bunny pinafore, basket of eggs ...$75.00

**Burma** — 7" compo., 1939 – 1943 (Tiny Betty)................................................ $350.00

**Butch** — 11" – 12" compo./cloth, 1942 – 1946 ............................................... $175.00

14" – 16" compo./cloth, 1949 – 1951 ........................................................ $185.00

14" cloth, vinyl head and limbs, 1950 only................................................... $175.00

12" cloth/vinyl, 1965 – 1966 only .......................................................... $125.00

**Butch, Little** — 9" all vinyl, 1967 – 1968 only.............................................. $125.00

**Butch McGuffey** — 22" compo./cloth, 1940 – 1941 ........................................$275.00

**Butterfly Queen** — 8", #25670, 2000 – 2001 (Wendy), lavender costume ...................$75.00

**C is for Cookie** — 8", #41820, 2006, with Cookie Monster, cookies.........................$80.00

**C.U.** — (see Collectors United under Special Events/Exclusives)

**Cafe Rose and Ivory Cocktail Dress** — 10", #22200 – white, #22203 – black,
1997 – 1998 ..........................................................................................$90.00

**Caitlin** — 5", #27405, 2003, Petite, checked sundress........................................$20.00

**Cake Topper** — 6", Caucasian, 2002, bride and groom, #33570 ............................$80.00

6", #33571, 2002, African-American bride and groom.....................................$80.00

**Calamity Jane** — 8" h.p., Americana Series, 1994 only (Wendy Ann)........................$65.00

**Calendar Girls** — 5", #33070 – 33130, Jan. – Dec., 2002 – 2004 ........ set of 12, $320.00, $20.00 each

**Calendar Girls Prepack** — 5", #33065, 2002, 12 dolls, Jan. – Dec.................................$20.00 each

**Calla Lilly** — 10", #22390, 1998 (Cissette), white gown, hand beaded jewels ...........................$175.00

**Camelot** — (see Collectors United/C. U. under Special Events/Exclusives)

**Cameo Lady** — (see Collectors United/C. U. under Special Events/Exclusives)

**Camille** — 21" compo., 1938 – 1939 (Wendy Ann) ........................................... $3,500.00 up

**Canada** — 8" h.p., BK, #760, 1968 – 1972 (Wendy Ann) ....................................$90.00

Straight legs, #0706, 1973 – 1975, marked "Alex".......................................$60.00

Straight legs, #560 (#534 in 1986), 1976 – 1988 (white face 1985 – 1987),
marked "Alexander" ....................................................................$55.00

Straight legs, #24130, 1999, hockey skater................................................$60.00

**Cancer** — 8", #21360, 1998, red crab costume ...........................................$80.00

**Candy Kid** — 11" – 15" compo., 1938 – 1941 (Wendy Ann), red/white
striped dress ......................................................................$275.00 – 450.00

8" h.p., #27060, 2000, Peter Pan series, red coat, black pants....................................$75.00

**Candy Land Game** — Princess Lolly, 8", #25250, 2000, yellow costume ................................$75.00

**Capricorn** — 8", #21300, 1998 (Maggie), fuchsia snakeskin body...............................$75.00

**Captain Hook** — 8" h.p., #478, 1992 – 1993 only, Storyland Series (Peter Pan)
(Wendy Ann) ......................................................................$90.00

8" h.p., #27060, 2000 – 2001, Peter Pan series, red coat, black pants.............................$85.00

**Careen** — (see Carreen)

**Carhop Takes Your Order** — 8", #17710, 2000, black checked dress.......................................$80.00

**Carmen** — Dressed like Carmen Miranda, but not marked or meant as such.

**Bridesmaid, Wendy composition, 1945. Tag: Madame Alexander/New York USA.**

7" compo., 1938 – 1943 (Tiny Betty) ...............................................................................$375.00

9" – 11" compo., 1938 – 1943, boy and girl (see also "Rumbera/Rumbero") (Little Betty)...$325.00 ea.

11" compo., 1937 – 1939, has sleep eyes (Little Betty) ......................................................$350.00

14" compo., 1937 – 1940 (Wendy Ann).............................................................................$450.00

17" compo., 1939 – 1942 (Wendy Ann)..............................................................................$650.00

21" compo., 1939 – 1942, extra make-up, mint (Wendy Ann) ...................................... $1,400.00 up

21" compo., 1939 – 1942, Portrait with extra make-up.........................................$1,900.00 up

14" plastic/vinyl, #1410, 1983 – 1986, Opera Series (Mary Ann)....................................$75.00

10" h.p., #1154, 1993 only, Portrette Series (Miranda), yellow/red...............................$85.00

16", #28395, 2001, red Spanish dress, black lace .........................................................$185.00

**Carmen Miranda Lucy** — 10", #25760, 2000, white dress with ruffles...........................$150.00

**Carnavale Doll** — (see FAO Schwarz under Special Events/Exclusives)

**Carnival in Rio** — 21" porcelain, 1989 – 1990.............................................................$375.00

**Carnival in Venice** — 21" porcelain, 1990 – 1991........................................................$400.00

**Caroline** — 15" vinyl, 1961 – 1962 only, in dresses, pants, jacket.................................$375.00

In riding habit ..............................................................................................................$400.00

In case/wardrobe.................................................................................................. $900.00 up

8", 1993 (see Belk & Leggett under Special Events/Exclusives)

8", 1994 (see Neiman-Marcus under Special Events/Exclusives)

**Caroling with Minnie and Mickey** — 8", #42610, 2006, Minnie, Mickey...........................$120.00

**Carousel Melody** — 8", #42140, 2006, with carousel horse ..........................................$120.00

**Carreen/Careen** — 14" – 17" compo., #1593, 1937 – 1938 (Wendy Ann) ..........................$750.00 up

14" plastic/vinyl, 1992 – 1993 only (Louisa/Jennifer) ....................................................$125.00

8", plaid, two large ruffles at hem, #160646, 1994 only.................................................$90.00

8", #15190, 1999 (Wendy), blue dress, straw hat..........................................................$85.00

**Carrot Kate** — 14", #25506, 1995, Ribbons & Bows Series, vegetable print dress (Mary Ann)....$125.00

**Carrot Top** — 21" cloth, 1967 only..................................................................................$125.00

**Casey Jones** — 8" h.p., 1991 – 1992 only, Americana Series ........................................$60.00

**Casper's Friend Wendy** — 8" (Maggie), #15210, 1999, red costume, broom...........................$75.00

**Catch a Falling Star** — 8", #33060, 2002, white dress.................................................$65.00

**Caterpillar** — 8" h.p., #14594, 1995 – 1996, has eight legs, Alice in Wonderland Series..........$100.00

**Cat on a Hot Tin Roof** — 10", #20011, "Maggie," white chiffon dress .....................................$125.00

**Celebrating America** — 8", #38515, 2004, patch quilt dress, vintage ...............................$90.00

**Celia's Dolls** — (see Special Events/Exclusives)

**Celtic Bride** — 10", #28595, 2001, white gown, gold trim, red rose headpiece and bouquet.....$100.00

**Celtic Dancer** — 8", #40120, 2005, green sweater..................................................$50.00

**Century of Fashion** — 14" and 18" h.p., 1954 (Margaret, Maggie, and Cissy)............... $2,000.00 up

**Champs-Elysées** — 21" h.p., black lace over pink, rhinestone on cheek .........................$6,500.00 up

**Change of Season** — 8", #40120, 2005 – 2006, green sweater ....................................$50.00

**Changing Seasons** — (Spring, Summer, Autumn, Winter) 14", 1993 – 1994 ......................$110.00 ea.

**Chanukah Celebration** — 8", #27330, 2001 – 2002, blue dress, brunette ..................................$85.00

**Charity** — 8" h.p., #485, 1961 only, Americana Series, blue cotton dress (Wendy Ann) ... $1,900.00 up

**Charlene** — 18" cloth/vinyl, 1991 – 1992 only ..........................................................$100.00

**Charlie Brown** — 10", #26425, 2001 – 2003, Peanuts Gang, includes Snoopy and ball glove ...$40.00

10", #33710, 2002 – 2004 Charlie Brown Christmas, tree, Snoopy, blanket ............................$50.00

10", #36055, 2003 – 2004 Trick or Treat, with Snoopy and doghouse.....................................$60.00

10", #38805, Happy Birthday, 2004, with cake and Snoopy ................................................$70.00

**Charlotte's Web** — 8", #41955, 2006, yellow dress, spider, goose, pig.........................$85.00

Trunk set, 8", #45455, 2006, pig, goose, sheep, rat, spider, trunk ...............................$130.00

**Chatterbox** — 24" plastic/vinyl talker, 1961 only.........................................................$250.00

**Cheerleader** — 8", #324, 1990 – 1991 only, Americana Series (Wendy Ann)...........................$60.00

8", 1990 (see I. Magnin under Special Events/Exclusives)

8" h.p., #324, #324-1, 1992 – 1993 only, Americana Series, black or white doll,

royal blue/gold outfit........................................................................................$60.00

**Chef Alex** — 8", #31260, 1998 (Maggie), chef attire.................................................................$70.00

**Cheri** — 18" h.p., 1954 only, Me and My Shadow Series, white satin gown,
    pink opera coat (Margaret) ........................................................$1,800.00 up

**Cherry Blossom** — 14", #25504, 1995, Ribbons & Bows Series, cherry print dress
    (Mary Ann) ......................................................................................$125.00

**Cherry Girl** — 8", #17590, 1999 – 2001, Mary Engelbreit, comes with basket and card...........$80.00

**Cherry Parfait** — 8", #42175, 2006, red skirt with cherry parfait................................$80.00

**Cherry Twins** — 8" h.p., #388E, 1957 only (Wendy Ann).........................................$1,500.00 up, ea.
    8", BK, #17700, 1999, pair, remake of 1957 set ....................................$130.00

**Cherub** — 12" vinyl, 1960 – 1961.................................................................$250.00
    18" h.p. head, cloth and vinyl, 1950s..........................................................$350.00
    26", 1950s.................................................................................................$375.00

**Cherub Babies** — cloth, 1930s.................................................................... $450.00 up

**Cheshire Cat** — 8", #13070, 1997 – 1999 Storyland Series,
    pink velvet cat suit ........................................................................$65.00

**Chicken Little** — 8", #39905, 2005 – 2006, green dress........................................$50.00

**Child at Heart Shop** — (see Special Events/Exclusives)

**Children's Prayer** — 8", #28385, 2001 – 2002, pink gown, bonnet ...........................$85.00

**Child's Angel** — 8", #14701, 1996, gold wings, harp, halo ...................................$70.00

**Chile** — 8" h.p., #528, 1992 only (Maggie) ....................................................$60.00

**China** — 7" compo., 1936 – 1940 (Tiny Betty) .................................................$325.00
    9" compo., 1935 – 1938 (Little Betty) ......................................................$300.00
    8" h.p., BK, #772, 1972 (Wendy Ann) .......................................................$100.00
    8" (Maggie) .............................................................................................$125.00
        Straight legs, #0772 – #572, 1973 – 1975, marked "Alex".................$60.00
        Straight legs, #572, 1976 – 1986, marked "Alexander" (Wendy Ann) ..............$55.00
        #572, 1987 – 1989 (Maggie).................................................$55.00
    8", #11550, 1995 only, three painted lashes at edges of eyes (Wendy Ann) ..............$55.00
    8", #11561, 1996 International, Little Empress costume ........................................$70.00
    8", #26280, 2000 – 2001 (Wendy), red silk costume with panda bear ......................$65.00

**Chinese New Year** — 8", #21040, 1997 – 1998, two dolls.......................................$130.00
    8", #21050, 1997 – 1998, three dolls, dragon ..........................................$200.00
    8", #42250, 2006, red silk Chinese pants outfit, dog............................................$80.00

**Chloe** — Blue gingham, 14", #25350, 2000, dress and hat.......................................$60.00
    Pink gingham, 14", #25345, 2000, white dress with pink check.............................$60.00

**Christening Baby** — 11" – 13" cloth/vinyl, 1951 – 1954.......................................$150.00
    16" – 19"...................................................................................................$175.00

**Christmas Angels** — (see Tree Topper)

**Christmas at Grandma's** — 8", #27445, 2000 – 2002, red coat and hat, black trim .................$80.00

**Christmas Ballerina** — 8", white tulle, red bodice, green leaves, 2003 – 2004......................$80.00

**Christmas Bear with Lenox Ornament** — 8", Wendy, Lenox bear, #38535, 2004 – 2005.....$95.00

**Christmas Candy** — 14", #1544, 1993 only, Classic Series ....................................$90.00

**Christmas Cardinals** — 8", #38850, 2004 – 2005, cardinals on pinafore............................$75.00

**Christmas Carol** — (see Saks Fifth Avenue under Special Events/Exclusives)

**Christmas Caroler** — 8", #19650, 1997, red velvet cape, print skirt ...........................$80.00

**Christmas Caroling** — 10", #1149, 1992 – 1993 only, Portrette, burnt orange/gold dress .......$100.00

**Christmas Cookie** — 14", #1565, 1992 (also see 'Lil Christmas Cookie) (Louisa/Jennifer)........$100.00

**Christmas Eve** — 14" plastic/vinyl, #241594, 1994 only (Mary Ann) .........................$100.00
    8", #10364, 1995, Christmas Series ..........................................................$70.00

**Christmas Holly** — 8", #19680, 1998 – 1999, print dress, red coat ...........................$75.00

**Christmas is Coming** — 8", #42375, 2006, with tree, ornaments...............................$95.00

**Christmas Pudding** — 8", #45510, 2006, Maggie, pudding cake....................................$75.00

**Christmas Shoppe** — (see Special Events/Exclusives)

**Christmas Song** — 10", #33455, 2002, long red dress, limited to 1,000......................$125.00

27

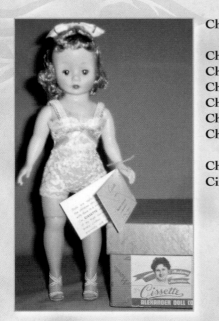

Cissette, 10", 1957 – 1963, mint basic Cissette.

Cissy, 21", wearing a rare 1950s tulle gown with flower trim. Also wears matching panties and slip.

**Christmas Stocking** — Dancing Wendy, 20" stocking, #28530, 2001......................$50.00
 Skating Maggie, 20" stocking, #31255, 2001 ..................................................$50.00
**Christmas Stocking Stuffers** — 8", #38890, 2004 – 2005, stocking with toys.........................$90.00
**Christmas Tea with Ornament** — 8", #38540, 2004 – 2005, with teapot ornament ................$90.00
**Christmas Tree Topper** — (see Spiegel's under Special Events/Exclusives; also Tree Topper)
**Christopher Robin** — 8", #31890, 2003 – 2004, yellow top, blue pants, 4½" Pooh bear ............$85.00
**Chrysanthemum Garden Ball** — 10", #31245, 2001, green and pink ball gown....................$110.00
**Churchill, Lady** — 18" h.p., #2020C, 1953 only, Beaux Arts Series, pink gown
 with full opera coat (Margaret)............................................................ $2,300.00 up
**Churchill, Sir Winston** — 18" h.p., 1953 only, hat (Margaret) ......................................... $1,250.00 up
**Cinderella** — (see also Topsy-Turvy for two-headed version)
 7" – 8" compo., 1935 – 1944 (Tiny Betty) .......................................................$350.00
 9" compo., 1936 – 1941 (Little Betty) .............................................................$375.00
 13" compo., 1935 – 1937 (Wendy Ann) ...........................................................$375.00
 14" compo., 1939 only, Sears exclusive (Princess Elizabeth) ...............................$500.00
 15" compo., 1935 – 1937 (Betty) ...................................................................$450.00
 16" – 18" compo., 1935 – 1939 (Princess Elizabeth) ........................................ $550.00 up
 8" h.p., #402, 1955 only (Wendy Ann) ............................................................$900.00
 8" h.p., #498, 1990 – 1991, Storyland Series (Wendy Ann) .................................$60.00
 8", #476, 1992 – 1993, blue ball gown, #140476, 1994 Storyland Series ..............$70.00
 8" h.p., #475, 1992 only, "Poor" outfit in blue with black stripes........................$65.00
 8" h.p., #14540, 1995 – 1996, pink net gown with roses, Brothers Grimm
  Series, #13400, 1997 – 2000 .................................................................$70.00
 8" h.p., #13410, 1997 – 1999, calico skirt with broom and pumpkin.....................$65.00
 8" h.p., #13490, 1999 – 2001, Cinderella's wedding, white gown......................$90.00
 8", At the Ball, #30670, 2002 – 2003, white dress, long blue cape.......................$80.00
 8", #35625, 2004 – 2006, Stroke of Midnight, blue ball gown .............................$80.00
 5", #36320, vinyl, petite, 2004 – 2005, pink gown ...........................................$25.00
 12" h.p., 1966 only, Literature Series (Classic Lissy) ..................................... $950.00 up
 12" h.p., 1966, "Poor" outfit...................................................................$675.00
 1966, in window box with both outfits .................................................... $1,700.00 up
 14" h.p., 1950 – 1951, ball gown (Margaret).............................................. $900.00 up
 14" h.p., 1950 – 1951, "Poor" outfit (Margaret)......................................... $700.00 up
 14" h.p., #25940, 2000, pink, lace-trimmed long gown ....................................$100.00
 18" h.p., 1950 – 1951 (Margaret)............................................................ $800.00 up
 21", #45501, 1995, pink and blue, Madame's Portfolio Series........................$300.00
 14" plastic/vinyl (#1440 to 1974; #1504 to 1991; #1541 in 1992) 1967 – 1992,
  "Poor" outfit (can be green, blue, gray, or brown) (Mary Ann) .......................$75.00
 14", #140 on box, 1969 only, FAO Schwarz, all blue satin/gold trim, mint (Mary Ann).........$425.00
 14" plastic/vinyl, #1445, #1446, #1546, #1548, 1970 – 1983, Classic Series,
  dressed in pink (Mary Ann)...................................................................$90.00
 #1548, #1549, 1984 – 1986, blue ball gown, two styles (Mary Ann) .....................$100.00
 14", #1546, #1547, 1987 – 1991, Classic Series, white or blue ballgown
  (Mary Ann, Jennifer)..........................................................................$100.00
 14", #1549, 1992 only, white/gold ball gown (Jennifer) .........................................$90.00
 14", 1985, with trunk (see Enchanted Doll House under Special Events/Exclusives)
 14", 1994, has two outfits (see Disney Annual Showcase of Dolls under Special Events/Exclusives)
 14", 1996, #87002, white gown, gold crown (Mary Ann).....................................$100.00
 14", #25940, 2001 (Margaret), long pink ball gown ..........................................$125.00
 10", 1989 (see Disney Annual Showcase of Dolls under Special Events/Exclusives)
 10", #1137, 1990 – 1991, Portrette, dressed in all pink (Cissette) ............................$90.00
 10", #34950, 2002 – 2004, blue ball gown with three mice, long white gloves .......................$150.00
 9", #36240, 2004 – 2006, vinyl, blue satin gown.................................................$35.00
**Cinderella's Carriage** — #13460, 1999 – 2000, white metal carriage.............................$150.00

**Cinderella's Footmouse** — 8", #13470, 1999 – 2000, painted face ...........................................$100.00
**Cinderella's Prince** — 8", #35630, 2003 – 2005, white hat, blue pants.............................$80.00
**Cinderella's Wicked Stepmother** — 8", #38625, 2005, red and black dress...........................$75.00
**Cissette** — 10" – 11" h.p., 1957 – 1963, high heel feet, jointed elbows
    and knees, must have good face color, in various street dresses.
    10", basic Cissette, 1957 – 1963, mint in box...............................................................$450.00
    Rare or fancy outfits, mint in box ................................................................. $600.00 up
    In formals, ball gowns.................................................................................... $550.00 up
    Coats and hats..................................................................................................$350.00
    1961 only, beauty queen with trophy............................................................$375.00
    Special gift set, three wigs...........................................................................$950.00 up
    Doll only, clean with good face color............................................................$125.00
    1957, Queen, trunk, trousseau .................................................................. $1,200.00 up
    Slacks or pants outfits...................................................................................$375.00
**Cissette Barcelona** — 10", Spanish costume, black lace, 1999 ...............................................$110.00
**Cissette Lingerie Trunk** — 10", #40700, 2005, doll, armoire, trunk with
    padded bench, and lingerie............................................................................$150.00
**Cissette Shadow Yardley** — 10", #36605, blonde, blue dress, perfume bottle .......................$150.00
**Cissy** — 20" h.p. (also 21"), 1955 – 1959, jointed elbows and knees, high heel feet,
    must have good face color, in various street dresses .................................... $750.00 up
    Dress and full-length coat ............................................................................ $800.00 up
    In ball gowns................................................................................................ $1,000.00 up
    Trunk, wardrobe .......................................................................................... $1,400.00 up
    Pants set....................................................................................................... $750.00 up
    1950s magazine ads using doll (add $10.00 if framed) .......................................... $30.00 up
    21", reintroduced in the following 1996 MA Couture Collection:
        #67303, aquamarine evening column and coat................................$300.00
        #67302, cafe rose and ivory cocktail dress....................................$325.00
        #67306, cafe rose and ivory cocktail dress, African-American.......................$550.00
        #67301, coral and leopard travel ensemble....................................$350.00
        #67601, ebony and ivory houndstooth suit......................................$650.00
        #67603, ebony and ivory houndstooth suit, African-American...........................$750.00

## *Dating Cissette Dolls*

**Eyelids:** 1975, beige; 1958, pale pink; 1959 – 1963, beige

**Clothes:** 1957 – 1958, darts in bodice; 1959 – 1963, no darts except ball gowns

**Fingernails:** 1962 – 1963, polished

**Eyebrows:** 1957 – 1963, single stroked

**Body and legs:** 1957 – 1963, head strung with hook and rubber band, legs jointed with plastic socket

**Feet:** 1957 – 1963, high heels

**Wigs:** 1957 – 1958, three rows of stitching; 1959 – 1963, zigzag stitches except 1961 – 1962 with fancy hairdos, then three rows; 1963, few have rooted hair in cap, glued to head or removable wigs

**Tags:** 1957 – 1962, turquoise; 1963, dark blue

**Portrette:** 1968 – 1973, two or three stroke eyebrows, blue eyelids, no earrings, strung head with hook, high heels

**Jacqueline:** 1961 – 1962, two or three stroke eyebrows, side seam brunette wig, small curl on forehead, blue eyelids, eyeliner, painted lashes to sides of eyes, polished nails, head strung, socket jointed hips with side seams, high heels

**Sleeping Beauty:** 1959 only, three stroke eyebrows, pink eyelids, no earrings, mouth painted wider, no knee joints, flat feet, jointed with metal hooks

**Sound of Music:** 1971 – 1973 (Brigitta, Liesl, Louisa), two stroke eyebrows, the rest same as Portrettes

**Tinker Bell:** 1969 only, two stroke eyebrows, blue eyelids, painted lashes to side of eyes, no earrings, hair rooted into wig cap, head and legs strung with metal hooks

**Margot:** 1961, same as Jacqueline, except has three stroke eyebrows and elaborate hairdos

Cissy, 21", #2095, 1955. White organdy gown trimmed in lace and red rosebuds. Red satin sash and bag, ruby ring and wrist tag. Large picture hat trimmed in red.

Close-up of 1955 Cissy #2095.

Cissy, 21", #2094, 1955. Slipper satin gown with tulle muff with red roses.

Cleopatra and Marc Anthony, 12", #1315, #1310, 1980 – 1985 (Nancy Drew), Portraits of History series (see page 67).

Clown, Baby, 8", #464, 1955, SLW, painted face. Original dog.

**Clara's Party Dress** — 8", #14570, 1995, Nutcracker Series................................$70.00
**Classic Ballerina** — 16", #22700, white tulle and satin (1999)...........................$110.00
**Classic Bride** — 16", #22690, white tulle and lace gown (1999)..........................$100.00
**Claudette** — 10", #1123 (in peach), 1988 – 1989, Portrette (Cissette).................$85.00
**Claudia** — 14", #34360, 2003, blue dress with lace........................................$90.00
**Cleopatra** — 12", #1315, 1980 – 1985, Portraits of History Series.....................$60.00
   10", #86002, 1996 Platinum Collection ...............................................$90.00
   10", #40830, 2005, white dress .......................................................$100.00
**Cleveland, Frances** — 1985 – 1987, fourth set Presidents' Ladies/First Ladies Series (Mary Ann) .$100.00
**Clover Kid** — 7" compo., 1935 – 1936 (Tiny Betty) .......................................$375.00
**Clown** — 8", #305, 1990 – 1992 only, Americana Series, has painted face (Wendy) .....$70.00
   Baby — 8", #464, 1955, painted face (Wendy Ann), dog ........................ $1,000.00 up
   Bobo — 8" h.p., #310, 1991 – 1992 (Wendy Ann)......................................$90.00
   Pierrot — 8", #561, 1956 only (Wendy Ann) .............................. $1,000.00 up
   14", 1991 only, #1558, white costume with red trim .................................$90.00
   Stilts — 8", #320, 1992 – 1993, doll on stilts.......................................$125.00
**Clue Game Doll** — 8", #25255, 2000, maid costume ......................................$65.00
**Coca-Cola Carhop** — 10", #17400, 1997 – 2000, roller skates, #17401, brunette........$90.00
**Coca-Cola Celebrates American Aviation** — 10", #17380, 1998 – 1999...................$100.00
**Coca-Cola Fantasy** — 10", #31210 – white, #31213 – black, 1997 – 1998................$125.00
**Coca-Cola 1920s** — 10", #28280, 2001, long white dress with lace......................$125.00
**Coca-Cola Nostalgia** — 16", #17490, 1999, white lace dress.............................$125.00
**Coca-Cola Off to the North Pole** — 8", #25245, 2001, with bear.........................$100.00
**Coca-Cola School Days** — 8" #28275, 2001 – 2002, includes lunchbox.....................$100.00
**Coca-Cola Sock Hop** — 10", #26255, 2001, red checked skirt.............................$125.00
**Coca-Cola Victorian Calendar Doll** — 10", #17360, 1998 – 1999.........................$125.00
**Coca-Cola Winter Fun Wendy** — 8", #17370, 1999, red ski outfit.........................$90.00
**Coco** — 21" plastic/vinyl, 1966, in various clothes (other than Portrait)............. $2,000.00 up
   In sheath style ball gown ..................................................... $2,200.00 up
   14", #1558, 1991 – 1992, Classic Series (Mary Ann) .................................$80.00
   10", #1140, 1989 – 1992, Portrette, dressed in all black (Cissette) ................$75.00
   16", #31240, 1997 – 1998, travel wardrobe and dog, Cleo............................$325.00
   16", #22400, 1998, Belle Epoque, includes houndstooth and glitter gown outfits....$275.00
**Collecting Bears, Teddy and Me** — 8", #33020, 2002 – 2003, 8" doll and 5" bear
   in matching blue outfits .............................................................$100.00
**Collecting Butterflies** — 8", #28240, 2001, lavender dress with butterflies ..............$55.00
**Collecting Buttons** — 8", #28245, 2001, white dress trimmed in pink ....................$55.00
**Collecting Dolls** — 8", #30940, 2001 – 2002, pink lacy dress with doll and dollhouse case........$80.00
**Collecting Seashells** — 8", #28250, 2001, yellow dress with seashells...................$55.00
**Collecting Trains** — 8", #28585, 2001 – 2002, striped overalls with Bachmann train .....$100.00
**Collector Pin Series** — 1999, 2½" polyresin miniature doll ..............................$10.00
**Collectors United** — (see Special Events/Exclusives)
**Colleen** — 10", #1121, 1988 only, Portrette, in green (Cissette) .........................$75.00
**Colonial** — 7" compo., 1937 – 1938 (Tiny Betty) .......................................$325.00
   9" compo., 1936 – 1939 (Little Betty).............................................$350.00
   8" h.p., BKW, #389, #789, 1962 – 1964 (Wendy Ann) ...............................$325.00
**Columbian Sailor** — (see U.F.D.C. under Special Events/Exclusives)
**Columbine** — 8", #14575 – 1995, Nutcracker Series ....................................$60.00
**Columbus, Christopher** — 8" h.p., #328, 1992 only, Americana Series ...................$125.00
**Comedienne** — 10", #20120, clown, 1996 Cirque du Soleil Series.........................$90.00
**Computer Age Wendy** — 8", #17820, 1999, comes with laptop and cell phone............$70.00
**Confederate Officer** — 12", 1990 – 1991, Scarlett Series (Nancy Drew) ..................$85.00
   8" h.p., 1991 – 1992, Scarlett Series (see Ashley)

**Contemporary Bride** — 10", 2001 ..................................................................$110.00
**Cookie** — 19" compo./cloth, 1938 – 1940, must be in excellent condition ...................................$650.00
**Coolidge, Grace** — 14", 1989 – 1990, sixth set Presidents' Ladies/First Ladies Series
   (Louisa) ..................................................................$100.00
**Coppelia** — 16", #28390, 2001, pink ballerina ..................................................................$125.00
**Coppertone Beach Set** — 8", #12110, 1998 – 1999, bikini, umbrella, suntan lotion ...............$125.00
**Coquette Cissy** — 10", #39255, pants, sweater, purse, 2004..........................................................$80.00
   10", #39600, red suit, 2004.................................................................$80.00
   10", #40670, 2005, elegant Simplicity Coquete Jacqui, print dress, blue sweater ....................$85.00
   10", #40660, 2005, Dressed to Thrill Coquette Cissy, Latin, green evening dress ...................$95.00
   10", #40665, 2005, Sight to See Coquette Cissy, African-American, yellow beaded gown........$90.00
   10", #40666, 2005, Sight to See Coquette Cissy, yellow beaded gown..............................$90.00
   10", #40710, 2005, Like No Other Coquette Cissy, strapless evening gown .............................$85.00
   10", #40650, 2005, Well Suited Coquette Cissy, white pants outfit....................................$80.00
   10", #41635, 2006, Triple Take Coquette Cissy, blue evening gown ......................................$100.00
   10", #40025, 2006, Signature Style Coquette Cissy Trunk Set, three outfits with trunk .........$220.00
   10", #41250, 2006, Rose Shimmer, pink gown, silver accents .................................................$100.00
   10", #41655, 2006, Classic with a Twist Coquette Jacqui, blue dress and coat........................$95.00
   10", #41620, 2006, Crowd Pleaser Coquette Cissy, brown feather outfit .................................$95.00
   10", #41640, 2006, Club Hopping Coquette Cecee, African-American, blue pants outfit .........$90.00
**Coral and Leopard Travel Ensemble** — 10", #22180, 1997...............................$110.00
**Cornelia** — Cloth and felt, 1930s..................................................................$700.00 up
   21", #2191, 1972, Portrait, dressed in pink with full cape (Jacqueline) ...............$425.00
   #2191, 1973, pink with ¾ length jacket ...........................................................$400.00
   #2296, 1974, blue with black trim....................................................................$350.00
   #2290, 1975, rose red with black trim and hat ..............................................$350.00
   #2293, 1976, pink with black trim and hat .......................................................$325.00
   #2212, 1978, blue with full cape.......................................................................$300.00
**Coroner** — 8", #38395, 2004 – 2005, Wizard of Oz series, has death certificate for
   Wicked Witch ...................................................................$80.00
**Cossack** — 8" h.p., #511, 1989 – 1991 (Wendy Ann) ......................................................$60.00
**Costume Party** — #37785, 2003 – 2004, mask, dog, black hat.................................$80.00
**Country Christmas** — 14", #1543, 1991 – 1992 only, Classic Series (Mary Ann) ..$125.00
   8", #20190, 1999 – 2000, calico dress, snowman .......................................$60.00
**Country Club** — 8", #37980, Latin, 2004 – 2005, blue flower dress, large straw hat..$90.00
**Country Cousins** — 10" cloth, 1940s ..................................................................$575.00
   26" cloth, 1940s ..................................................................$650.00
   30" cloth, 1940s ..................................................................$750.00
   16½", 1958, mint (Mary-Bel) .....................................................$375.00
**Country Fair** — (see Wendy Loves)
**Count Your Blessings Angel** — 10", #36575, 2004 – 2005, pink costume ...........$125.00
**Courtney and Friends** — (see Madame Alexander Doll Company under Special Events/Exclusives)
**Courtyard** — 8", #38840, 2004, pink elaborate gown, limited to 1,000..................$140.00
**Cousin Grace** — 8" h.p., BKW, #432, 1957 only (Wendy Ann) .......................................$1,900.00 up
**Cousin Karen** — 8" h.p., BKW, #620, 1956 only (Wendy Ann) .......................................$1,800.00 up
**Cousin Marie & Mary** — 8" h.p. (Marie, #465; Mary, #462), 1963 only (Wendy Ann), each.. $1,000.00 up
**Cowardly Lion** — 8", #431, 1993, Storybook Series, #140431, 1994 – 1996..................$75.00
   #13220, #13211, 1997, 2003 – 2006 (Wizard of Oz), tan lion costume.......................$70.00
   5", #28695, 2001 – 2002, porcelain..................................................................$85.00
   5", #36350, 2005, petitie ..................................................................$25.00
   9", #39795, 2005 – 2006, lion outfit .............................................................$35.00
**Cowboy** — 8" h.p., BK, #732, 1967 – 1969, Americana Series (Wendy Ann)..............$350.00
   8", 1987 (see M.A.D.C. under Special Events/Exclusives)
**Cowgirl** — 8" h.p., BK, #724, 1967 – 1970, Americana/Storybook Series (Wendy Ann) ...........$350.00

Cornelia, 21", #2293, 1976 (Jacqueline).

Crockett, Davy, 8", SLW, 1955.

**Congratulations** — 8" h.p., #21180, 1998 (Maggie), pink dress, balloons.....................................$55.00
    10", #1132, 1990 – 1991, Portrette, white/red outfit (Cissette) ....................................................$75.00
**Crayola, Americana** — 8", #17840 – 17873, felt outfits, with Crayola crayons....................$45.00 ea.
**Crayola Meagan** — 14", #25470, 2000, brown dress, with Crayola crayons..............................$75.00
**Crete** — 8" straight legs, #529, 1987 only.....................................................................................$75.00
**Croatia** — 8" h.p., #110543, 1994 (Wendy Ann)..........................................................................$65.00
**Crockett, Davy, Boy or Girl** — 8" h.p., 1955 only  (Boy – #446; Girl – #443)
    (Wendy Ann) .............................................................................................................$700.00 up, ea.
**Croquet Match** — 8", #39725, 2005, white dress, green sweater, croquet set ...........................$85.00
**Cruella DeVille** — 10", #38370, 2004 – 2005, with three 2" puppies.....................................$150.00
**Cry Dolly** — 14" – 16" vinyl, 1953, 12-piece layette .................................................................$250.00
    14", 16", 19", in swimsuit..................................................................................$100.00 – 185.00
    16" – 19" all vinyl, dress or rompers.................................................................$125.00 – 250.00
**Cuba** — 8", #11548, 1995 only, has round brown face .................................................................$65.00
    8", #38600, 2004 – 2005, includes maracas.........................................................................$85.00
**Cuddly** — 10½" cloth, 1942 – 1944 ............................................................................................$375.00
    17" cloth, 1942 – 1944...........................................................................................................$400.00
**Cupid** — 8", #13860, 1998 – 1999 (Maggie), white costume, bow, arrow ...............................$70.00
**Curly Locks** — 8" h.p., #472, 1955 only (Wendy Ann) ..........................................................$950.00 up
    8" straight leg, #421, 1987 – 1988, Storybook Series, 1997 (Wendy Ann) ..............................$65.00
    8", #28315, 2001 – 2002, print dress with flowers.................................................................$80.00
**Cute Little Baby** — 14", 1994 – 1995, doll only, $85.00.  With layette and basket................$200.00
**Cutie Patootie** — 18", #28320, 2001, cloth, Mary Engelbreit, pink dress.............................$45.00
**Cynthia** — 15" h.p., 1952 only (black "Margaret")..................................................................$850.00 up
    18", 1952 only ...................................................................................................................$900.00 up
    23", 1952 only ...............................................................................................................$1,200.00 up
**Cyrano** — 8" h.p., #140505, 1994 only, Storyland Series (Pinocchio) ......................................$65.00
**Czarina Alexandra** — 8", #12620, 1999, blue satin and gold.....................................................$75.00
**Czechoslovakia** — 7" compo., 1935 – 1937 (Tiny Betty) .........................................................$325.00
    8" h.p., BK, #764, 1972 (Wendy Ann) ................................................................................$90.00
        Straight legs, #0764, #564, 1973 – 1975, marked "Alex" .............................................$65.00
        Straight legs, #536, 1976 – 1987, marked "Alexander".................................................$55.00
    8", #536, 1985 – 1987 .............................................................................................................$55.00
    8", #521, reintroduced 1992 – 1993 only (Wendy Ann) .........................................................$55.00
**Daddy's Little Princess** — 8", #38920, 2004 – 2005, pink dress, tiara..................................$85.00
**Daddy's My Hero** — 8", #36765, 2003 – 2004, blue pleated dress, police hat ...........................$80.00
**Daffy Down Dilly** — 8" straight legs, #429, 1986 only, Storybook Series
    (Wendy Ann or Maggie) ...........................................................................................................$60.00
**Dahl, Arlene (Pink Champagne)** — 18" h.p., 1950 – 1951, red wig, lavender gown
    (Maggie), mint ...........................................................................................................$7,000.00 up
**Daisy** — 10", #1110, 1987 – 1989, Portrette Series, white lace over yellow (Cissette) .................$65.00
**Daisy Fairy** — 8", #36890, 2003 – 2004, long pink dress, yellow petal trim ............................$90.00
**Daisy Munchkin** — 8", #28770, 2001, white outfit with daisies.................................................$75.00
**Daisy Resort Cissette Ensemble** — 10", #22380, 1998, silk, linen outfit, chair ....................$150.00
**Dance of the Flowers** — 8", #25225, 2000 – 2001, blue embroidered tutu ...........................$60.00
**Dancing Clara** — 8", #34305, 2002, pink dress, holding nutcracker...........................................$80.00
**Dancing Princess Blue** — 10", #32050, 2000, blue tulle gown .............................................$100.00
**Dancing Princess Gold** — 10", #32055, 2000, gold tulle gown..............................................$100.00
**Dancing Princess Magenta** — 10", #32045, 2000, tulle and lace gown .................................$100.00
**Dancing Queen Total Moves Wendy** — 8", #38265, 2004.......................................................$95.00
**Danger's Bath** — 8", #38490, 2004 – 2005, swimsuit with dog, tub, etc. ..................................$95.00
**Danger's First Easter** — 8", #45430, lavender dress, dog.........................................................$80.00
**Danish** — 7" compo., 1937 – 1941 (Tiny Betty).........................................................................$325.00
    9" compo., 1938 – 1940 (Little Betty) ..................................................................................$350.00

**Dare, Virginia** — 9" compo., 1940 – 1941 (Little Betty)................................................$450.00

**Darlene** — 18" cloth/vinyl, 1991 – 1992 ................................................................$85.00

**Darling Little Dancer** — 8", #30335, 1999, pink tulle, limited to 2,500.....................$90.00

**David and Diana** — (see FAO Schwarz under Special Events/Exclusives)

**David Copperfield** — 7" compo., 1936 – 1938 (Tiny Betty).......................................$375.00

    14" compo., 1938 only (Wendy Ann)................................................................$750.00

    16" cloth, early 1930s, Dickens character.................................................... $850.00 up

**David Quack-a-Field or Twistail** — cloth/felt, 1930s ........................................ $700.00 up

**David, the Little Rabbi** — (see Celia's Dolls under Special Events/Exclusives)

**Day of Week Dolls** — 7", 1935 – 1940 (Tiny Betty).........................................$350.00 ea.

    9" – 11" compo., 1936 – 1938 (Little Betty).................................................$375.00 ea.

    13" compo., 1939 (Wendy Ann)....................................................................$450.00

**Day to Remember** — 10", 2001, bride.................................................................$115.00

**Dazzling Winter Skater** — 8", #45425, 2006, blue and white costume ....................$85.00

**Dear America Series** — 18" re-creations from *Dear America* book series

    Abigail Jane Stewart, 1999 – 2000, 18", blue print dress....................................$75.00

    Catherine Carey Logan, 1999 – 2000, 18", Pilgrim costume ..............................$75.00

    Margaret Ann Brady, 1999 – 2000, 18", pink dress............................................$75.00

    Remember Patience Whipple, 1999 – 2000, 18", red vest, skirt............................$75.00

    Clotee, a Slave Girl, 2000, #25665, African-American, brown outfit.........................$85.00

    Emma Simpson, a Southern Belle, 2000, #25660, long beige dress .........................$75.00

    Sara Nita, a Navajo Girl, 2000, #25655, black Indian outfit ...............................$75.00

    Zipporah Feldman, a Jewish Immigrant, 2000, #25650................................................$75.00

**Dearest** — 12" vinyl baby, 1962 – 1964 ......................................................$125.00 – 175.00

**Deborah Bride** — 16", #25595, 2000, remake of 1949 – 1951 costume ....................$185.00

**Debra (Deborah)** — 21", 1949 – 1951, Portrette, ballerina with extra make-up (Margaret) . $7,000.00 up

    21", 1949 – 1951, bride with five-piece layered bustle in back ........................ $7,500.00 up

**Debutante** — 18" h.p., 1953 only (Maggie) .............................................. $1,250.00 up

**December** — 14", #1528, 1989 only, Classic Series (Mary Ann)....................................$85.00

**Deck the Halls** — 8", #35990, 2003 – 2004, red print dress with garland ...................$85.00

**Decorating the Tree** — 8", #41145, 2006, green dress, ornament ...........................$70.00

**DeFoe, Dr. Allen** — 14" – 15" compo., 1937 – 1939.................................. $1,600.00 up

**Degas** — 21" compo., 1945 – 1946, Portrait (Wendy Ann) ............................... $2,300.00 up

**Degas Ballerina (The Star)** — 10", #13910, 1998 – 1999 (Cissette), white tutu.....................$85.00

    10", #25305, 2000 – 2001, long pink tutu with flowers ......................................$80.00

**Degas Ballerina Wendy Ann Felt** — 12", #42015, 2006, limited to 400 ...............................$300.00

**Degas "Dance Lesson"** — 14", #241598, 1994..........................................................$80.00

**Degas Girl** — 14", #1475 (#1575 from 1974), 1967 – 1987 (20-year production), Portrait

    Children and Fine Arts Series (Mary Ann) ..................................................$60.00

**Degas' Rehearsal Shadow Box** — 10", 2001, #28410, white costume,

    gold shadow box ................................................................ $150.00

**Delicious Wishes** — 8", #41970, 2006, plum and plaid trimmed dress$80.00

**Delightful Afternoon** — 10", #30410, 2001, long pink gown....... $120.00

**Delilah** — 8" h.p., #14583, 1995 only, Bible Character Dolls Series .. $100.00

**Denmark** — 10" h.p., 1962 – 1963 (Cissette) ................................. $700.00

    8" h.p., BK, #769, 1970 – 1972 (Wendy Ann) ........................... $100.00

    8" h.p., straight legs, #0769 – 569, 1973 – 1975, marked "Alex"

        (Wendy) .................................................................... $65.00

    8" h.p., straight legs, #546, 1976 – 1989, marked "Alexander" (1985 –1987

        white face) (Wendy) ..................................................... $55.00

    8" reintroduced, #519, 1991 only (Wendy Ann) ........................... $55.00

**Desert Storm** — (see Welcome Home)

**Dewdrop Fairy** — 8", #28495, 2001 – 2002, blue tulle costume...... $80.00

**Diamond Beauty** — 21", 1998, black gown...................................................$900.00

Dionne Quints, 8", with Dr. Dafoe and Nurse. Composition dolls, 1930s.

**Diamond Dance** — 8", #26030, 2000, long pink gown, rhinestones ...........................................$100.00

**Diamond Lil** — 10" (see M.A.D.C. under Special Events/Exclusives)

**Diana** — 14", 1993 – 1994, Anne of Green Gables Series, trunk and wardrobe .......................$200.00

    Tea dress, came with tea set, 1993 only ........................................................................$125.00

    Sunday Social, 8", #260417, 1994 – 1995 (Wendy Ann) .............................................$125.00

    Sunday Social, 14", #261503, 1994 ..............................................................................$100.00

**Dickinson, Emily** — 14", #1587, 1989 only, Classic Series (Mary Ann) ...................................$90.00

**Dicksie & Ducksie** — cloth/felt, 1930s................................................................... $700.00 up

**Dietrich, Marlene Shanghai Express** — 16", #33485, 2002, long red coat dress,

    limited to 1,500.................................................................................................................$150.00

**Dilly Dally Sally** — 7" compo., 1937 – 1942 (Tiny Betty) .........................................................$325.00

    9" compo., 1938 – 1939 (Little Betty) ...........................................................................$350.00

**Ding Dong Bell** — 7" compo., 1937 – 1942 (Tiny Betty) ...........................................................$350.00

**Dinner at Eight** — 10", #1127, 1989 – 1991, Portrette, black/white dress (Cissette) .................$60.00

**Dinosaur** — 8" h.p., #343, 1993 – 1994, Americana Series ........................................................$70.00

**Dion, Celine** — 10", 1999 (Cissette), long gown, heart necklace....................................................$110.00

**Dionne Furniture** — (no dolls)

    Scooter, holds five ......................................................................................... $350.00 up

    Basket case, holds five ....................................................................................$250.00

    Divided high chair, holds five............................................................................ $350.00 up

    Table and chairs, five-piece set.......................................................................$450.00

    Ferris wheel, holds five..................................................................................... $500.00 up

    Bath/shower ..................................................................................................... $250.00 up

    Wagon, holds five............................................................................................. $425.00 up

    Playpen, holds five ........................................................................................... $300.00 up

    Crib, holds five................................................................................................. $350.00 up

    Tricycle ............................................................................................................ $175.00 up

    Merry-go-round, holds five............................................................................... $400.00 up

    High chair for one............................................................................................$150.00

**Dionne Quints** — Original mint or very slight craze. Each has own color:

        Yvonne – pink, Annette – yellow, Cecile – green, Emilie – lavender, Marie – blue

    20" compo. toddlers, 1938 – 1939................................................... $700.00 ea., $4,200.00 set

    19" compo. toddlers, 1936 – 1938................................................... $700.00 ea., $4,200.00 set

    16" – 17" compo. toddlers, 1937 – 1939 ....................................... $650.00 ea., $3,600.00 set

    11" compo. toddlers, 1937 – 1938, wigs and sleep eyes .............. $400.00 ea., $2,200.00 set

    11" compo. toddlers, 1937 – 1938, molded hair and sleep eyes ................... $400.00 ea., $2,200.00 set

    11" compo. babies, 1936, wigs and sleep eyes ............................................. $400.00 ea., $2,200.00 set

    11" compo. babies, 1936, molded hair and sleep eyes ................................. $400.00 ea., $2,200.00 set

    8" compo. toddlers, 1935 – 1939, molded hair or wigs and painted eyes .... $300.00 ea., $1,500.00 set

    8" compo. babies, 1935 – 1939, molded hair or wigs and painted eyes....... $300.00 ea., $1,500.00 set

    14" cloth/compo., 1938................................................................... $475.00 ea., $3,100.00 set

    17" cloth/compo., 1938................................................................... $575.00 ea., $3,600.00 set

    22" cloth/compo., 1936 – 1937....................................................... $750.00 up

    24" all cloth, 1935 – 1936, must be mint ..........................................................$1,200.00 ea.

    16" all cloth, 1935 – 1936, must be mint ........................................................ $900.00 up

    8" h.p., 1998, 75th Anniversary Set with carousel, #12230 .......................................$400.00

    8" Yvonne, Marie, Annette, Cecile, Emilie, 1998.................................................$70.00 ea.

    Nursery (cardboard) with Dr. Dafoe, nurse, 8" quints, and furniture

        (all composition dolls) .............................................................................$7,000.00

**Disney** — (see Special Events/Exclusives)

**Dogs** — (see Poodles)

**Doll Finders** — (see Special Events/Exclusives)

**Doll Hospital Nurse** — 8" #33575, 2002, red dress and nurse's hat with 2½" doll ....................$80.00

**Dolls 'n Bearland** — (see Special Events/Exclusives)

**Dolls of the Month** — 7" – 8" compo., 1937 – 1939, Birthday Dolls (Tiny Betty) ...................$350.00
**Dolly** — 8", #436, 1988 – 1989, Storybook Series (Wendy Ann), 1997......................................$65.00
**Dolly Dears** — (see Special Events/Exclusives)
**Dolly Dryper** — 11" vinyl, 1952 only, seven-piece layette.................................................$300.00
**Dolly Levi (Matchmaker)** — 10" Portrette, 1994 only ...................................................$75.00
**Dominican Republic** — 8" straight leg, #544, 1986 – 1988 (1985 – 1986 white face)................$55.00
**Dormouse** — 8", #13090, 1998 – 2000, mouse in sugar bowl with spoon ......................................$90.00
**Dorothy** — 14", #1532, 1990 – 1993, Wizard of Oz, all blue/white checked dress and
    solid blue pinafore (Mary Ann) .................................................................$100.00
    8" h.p., #464, 1991 – 1993, #140464, 1994 – 1995, blue/white checked dress, white bodice
      (Wendy Ann), Wizard of Oz...............................................................$100.00
    8" h.p., emerald green dress, mid-year special (see
      Madame Alexander Doll Co. under Special Events/Exclusives)
    8" h.p., #13200, 1997 – 1999, blue checked dress, basket with Toto, #13201, 2000 – 2001.......$80.00
    8", #13202, 2003 – 2006, ruby slippers, Toto in basket, blue checked dress ...............................$60.00
    8", #38715, 2004, limited to 1,000, blue checked silk dress ...........................................$95.00
    14" plastic/vinyl, #87007, 1996 ...............................................................$125.00
    15" cloth, #25545, 2000 – 2001, blue checked dress, with Toto.................................$50.00
    5" porcelain, #27065, 2000 – 2004, blue checked dress, with Toto................................$75.00
    10", #36775, 2003 – 2004, blue checked dress with 5" Lullaby, Flower Bonnet and
      Mayor Munchkin, Toto ...............................................................$180.00
    21", #36355, Dorothy Cissy, flat chested torso, Toto in basket ...............................$300.00
    9", #39975, 2005 – 2006, blue checked dress, red shoes .....................................$35.00
    5", #36335, 2005, petite, checked dress, Toto in basket ....................................$25.00
    8", #41255, 2006, Dorothy Wendy-Kin Wood with Toto ........................................$250.00
    8", #42420, 2006, Off to Oz, with lunchbox and Toto ........................................$105.00
**Dottie Dumbunnie** — cloth/felt, 1930s.........................................................$800.00 up
**Dream Dance** — 10", #26180, 2000 (Cissette), blue, short party dress ..............................$80.00
    10", #26175, 2000 (Cissette), black bodice, long tulle gown..................................$80.00
**Dressed for Opera** — 18" h.p., 1953 only (Margaret)...............................................$1,800.00 up
**Dressed Like Daddy** — 8", #17002, 1996, white or black..........................................$75.00
**Dressed Like Mommy** — 8", #17001, 1996 – 1998, white or black...................................$75.00
**Drucilla** — (see M.A.D.C. under Special Events/Exclusives)
**Drum Majorette** — (see Majorette)
**Duchess Eliza, The** — 10", #20114, 1996 Classics .................................................$90.00
**Duchess, The** — 8", #14613, 1996, Alice in Wonderland Series .....................................$100.00
    8", #39745, 2005, long elaborate red dress....................................................$90.00
**Dude Ranch** — 8" h.p., #449, 1955 only (Wendy Ann)..............................................$750.00 up
**Dudley Do-Right and Nell** — 8", #15140, 1999, Dudley in Mounty outfit (Maggie), Nell,
    (Wendy) includes rope, train track, and backdrop................................................$150.00
**Dumplin' Baby** — 20" – 23½", 1957 – 1958...................................................$175.00
**Dutch** — 7" compo., 1935 – 1939 (Tiny Betty) ..................................................$300.00
    9" compo. boy or girl, 1936 – 1941..........................................................$325.00
    8" h.p., BKW, #777, 1964, boy* (Wendy) ......................................................$350.00
      BK, #777, #0777, 1965 – 1972............................................................$100.00
    8" h.p., straight leg, #777, *0777, 1972 – 1973, marked "Alex"..............................$75.00
    8" h.p., BKW, #391 – 791, 1961 – 1964, girl*...............................................$125.00
    8" h.p., BK, #791, 1965 – 1972..............................................................$100.00
    8" BKW, #791, 1964 only (Maggie)...........................................................$150.00
**Dutch Lullaby** — 8", #499, 1993, #140499, 1994, Wynkin, Blynkin & Nod, in wooden shoe ..$150.00
**Earhart, Amelia** — 8", #40415, 2005, comes with bear with goggles...............................$80.00
**Easter** — 8" h.p., #21020, 1998, hat with bunny ears, floral dress ...............................$65.00
**Easter Bonnet** — 14", #1562, 1992 (Louisa/Jennifer) ..............................................$85.00
    8" h.p., #10383 – 10385, 1995 – 1996, three hair colors, Special Occasions Series...............$60.00

*Both became Netherlands in 1974.

8" h.p., #10401, 1996, African-American ..................................................................................$60.00

**Easter Bunny** — 8" (see Child at Heart Shop under Special Events/Exclusives)

8", #26675, 2001, blue dress, hat, basket with bunny ...............................................$100.00

**Easter Doll** — 8" h.p., 1968 only, special for West Coast, in yellow dress (Wendy Ann),
limited to 300....................................................................................... $1,400.00 up

7½" SLNW, #361, 1953, organdy dress, doll carries basket with chicken.........................$925.00 up

14" plastic/vinyl, 1968 only (Mary Ann), limited to 300.................................................... $600.00 up

**Easter Egg Hunt** — 8", #25020, 2000 – 2001, white dress, straw hat, basket.............................$75.00

**Easter Hop** — 8", #37965, 2004 – 2005, pink checked dress, bunny..........................................$70.00

**Easter Morning** — 8", #34090, 2002, pink smocked dress, bunny purse ...................................$70.00

**Easter of Yesterday** — 1995 (see C.U. under Special Events/Exclusives)

**Easter Splendor** — 8", #35445, 2003 – 2004, pink hat, white dress, basket, eggs, Bible.............$80.00

**Easter Sunday** — 8" h.p., #340 or 340-1, 1993 only, Americana Series, black or white doll .....$65.00

8", #21510 (white), #21513 (black), 1998 – 2000, yellow print dress, straw hat, basket...........$75.00

**Ebony and Ivory Houndstooth Suit** — 10", #22190, 1997 – 1998 .....................................$150.00

**Ecuador** — 8" h.p., BK and BKW, #878, 1963 – 1966 (Wendy Ann)............................................$350.00

**Edith and the Duckling** — 8", #31800, with duck and Mr. Bear ..............................................$85.00

**Edith, the Lonely Doll** — 16" plastic/vinyl, 1958 – 1959 (Mary-Bel) ...................................$325.00

22", 1958 – 1959 .................................................................................................................$400.00

8" h.p., #850, 1958 only (Wendy Ann) ..................................................................... $700.00 up

8", #34025, 2003 – 2004, pink checked dress, 3" Mr. Bear ........................................................$85.00

8", #36930, 2004, wood doll, 3" Mr. Bear, limited to 750 ........................................................$250.00

8", #37205, 2004, Holiday Trunk Set, four outfits, Mr. Bear.................................................$220.00

**Edith with Golden Hair** — 18" cloth, 1940s ........................................................................$675.00

**Edwardian** — 18" h.p., #2001A, 1953 only, pink embossed cotton long gown,
Glamour Girl Series (Margaret) ...................................................................... $2,200.00 up

8" h.p., #0200, 1953 –1954 (Wendy Ann)..................................................................... $1,000.00 up

**80th Anniversary Cissette** — 10", #34985, 2003, pink dress ................................................$125.00

**80th Anniversary Cissy** — 21" #34980, 2003, black crochet dress .........................................$475.00

**80th Anniversary Wendy** — 8", #34975, 2002, pink dress .......................................................$75.00

**Eisenhower, Mamie** — 14", 1989 – 1990, sixth set Presidents' Ladies/First Ladies Series
(Mary Ann) ....................................................................................................................$100.00

**Egypt** — 8" straight leg, #543, 1986 – 1989 (round brown face).................................................$60.00

**Egyptian** — 7" – 8" compo., 1936 – 1940 (Tiny Betty)...............................................................$350.00

9" compo., 1936 – 1940 (Little Betty) ..................................................................................$375.00

**Egypt with Sarcophagus** — 8", #24110, 1998 – 2000, pharaoh costume.................................$100.00

**Elaine** — 18" h.p., 1954 only, Me and My Shadow Series, blue organdy dress (Cissy) ..... $1,800.00 up

8" h.p., #0035E, 1954 only, matches 18" (Wendy Ann) .................................................. $950.00 up

**Elegant Emerald** — 8", #32085, 2000 – 2002, long green ball gown ........................................$90.00

**Elegant Simplicity Coquette Jacqui** — blue sweater, pink print dress.................................$85.00

**Elise** — 16½" h.p./vinyl arms (18", 1963 only), 1957 – 1964, jointed ankles and knees, face color

In street clothes or blouse, slacks, and sash ................................................. $475.00 up

In ball gown, formal, or Portrait ...................................................................... $750.00 up

In riding habit, 1963 (Mary-Bel head) .......................................................................$450.00

Ballerina, 1966 – 1991, rare yellow tutu, red hair.................................................$900.00

With Mary-Bel head, 1962 only ...................................................................................$450.00

18", 1963 only, with bouffant hairstyle ......................................................................$450.00

17" h.p./vinyl, 1961 – 1962, one-piece arms and legs, jointed ankles and knees......................$350.00

18" h.p./vinyl, 1963 – 1964, jointed ankles and knees............................................................$375.00

In riding habit .............................................................................................................$375.00

17" plastic/vinyl, 1966 only, street dress ...................................................................$375.00

17", 1966 – 1972, in trunk/trousseau ............................................................................ $650.00 up

17", 1972 – 1973, Portrait ............................................................................................$200.00

17", 1966, 1976 – 1977, in formal .................................................................................$150.00

Elise, 17", 1966 – 1991,
plastic/vinyl.

17", 1966 – 1987, Bride ..................................................................................... $125.00 up
17", 1966 – 1991, Ballerina ............................................................................... $100.00 up
17", 1966 – 1989, in any discontinued costume ................................................ $100.00 up
16", 1997, #22060, Firebird, red and gold tutu .................................................. $125.00
16", 1997, #22050, Giselle, aqua tutu, rose tiara ............................................... $125.00
16", 1997, #22040, Swan Lake, white tulle tutu ................................................. $125.00

**Elise/Leslie** — 14", #1560, 1988 only (Mary Ann) ......................................... $80.00
**Eliza** — 14", #1544, 1991 only, Classic Series (Louisa) ................................... $85.00
**Elizabethan Bride** — 10", #25005, 2000, Cissette ........................................ $150.00
**Elizabethan Pincushion** — 2000 – 2001, pink #26480, gold #25645, 8", Wendy,
   brocade as a pincushion ................................................................................ $90.00
**Eliza the Flower Girl** — 10", #20113, 1996 Classics .................................... $100.00
**Eloise** — 8", #80680, 2000 – 2002, vinyl, Eloise lace, white blouse, navy pleated skirt ................ $40.00
   8", #33405, 2002, vinyl, Eloise in Paris, gray checked coat ......................................... $45.00
   8", #27701, 2001 – 2002, Eloise at Christmas time ............................................... $45.00
   18", #80690, 2000 – 2003, cloth, Eloise face, same costume as 8" doll ......................... $45.00
   36", Just Like Me, #30936, 2001, cloth with rag doll ............................................. $200.00
   8", Eloise Tea Party, #30810, 2001 – 2002, vinyl, white dress .................................. $45.00
   8", Eloise Loves to Dance, #30815, 2001, ballet .................................................. $45.00
   12", Eloise Loves to Dance, #30935, 2001, cloth ................................................. $40.00
   12", #27225, 2000 – 2003, poseable cloth ......................................................... $30.00
   8", #33410, 2002, Eloise in Moscow, gold coat, black hat ....................................... $45.00
   8", #31670, Tea Party Trunk Set, trunk, tea set, clothes ........................................ $150.00
   12", #31855, 2002 – 2003, Eloise in Paris, blue coat, travel bag, passport ..................... $75.00
   8", #27710, 2000 – 2003, overnight kit, sleeping bag, clothes ................................. $100.00
**El Salvador** — 8", #40635, 2005, with basket of fruit .................................... $85.00
**Emerald City and Wizard Chamber** — folding playscape, #25945, 15" tall .......... $325.00
**Emerald City Guard** — 8", #31395, 2001 – 2002, black costume with sequin hat ...... $90.00
**Emerald Isle** — 8", #42800, 2006, green dress, 5" Wendy ............................... $90.00
**Emerald Lass** — 8", #27870, 2001, green dress ........................................... $70.00
**Emily** — cloth/felt, 1930s ............................................................................. $600.00
   14", #34350, 2002 – 2003, black and white dress ................................................. $90.00
   5", #27420, 2003, petite, pink dress ............................................................. $20.00
**Emily Elizabeth** — 8", #26370, 2000 – 2002 (Maggie), with cloth 16" Clifford dog ...... $90.00
   5" petite Emily Elizabeth and 10" plush red Clifford dog ........................................ $45.00
**Emma** — 10", #25335, 2000 (Cissette) long blue gown, straw hat ........................ $125.00
**Emperor and Nightingale** — 8", #33700, 2002, with birdcage ........................ $90.00
**Empire Bride** — 10" (Cissette), white lace gown (1999) .................................. $125.00
**Empress Elizabeth of Austria** — 10" (see My Doll House under Special Events/Exclusives)
**Enchanted Doll House** — (see Special Events/Exclusives)
**Enchanted Evening** — 21" Portrait, 1991 – 1992 only, different necklace than shown in
   catalog (Cissy) .......................................................................................... $325.00
**Endora** — 10", #40125, green pant suit, 2005 ................................................ $100.00
**England** — 8", #24040, 1997 – 1999, Beefeater guard outfit .............................. $70.00
   8", #28560, 2001, Queen costume .................................................................. $70.00
**English Guard** — 8" h.p., BK, #764, 1966 – 1968, Portrait Children Series (Wendy Ann) ...... $350.00
   8", #515, reintroduced 1989 – 1991, marked "Alexander" (Wendy Ann) ....................... $60.00
**Entertaining the Troops** — 8", #17550, 1999, red outfit, microphone .................. $70.00
**Equestrian Wendy** — 8", #35575, 2003 – 2005, red jacket, crop, plush horse ........... $95.00
**Eskimo** — 8" h.p., BK, #723, 1967 – 1969, Americana Series (Wendy Ann) .............. $375.00
   9" compo., 1936 – 1939 (Little Betty) ............................................................. $350.00
   With Maggie Mixup face ............................................................................. $375.00
**Esmeralda** — 9", #39960, 2005 – 2006, vinyl, long red dress ............................. $35.00
   10", #40350, 2005, long red dress ................................................................ $100.00

Elise, 16½", 1958, #1718.
Nylon dress trimmed in lace
and tiny buttons. Straw hat
with tulle and flowers.

Fashions of the Century, 18",
1954 – 1955 (Margaret). All
original including necklace.
Tagged dress and wrist tag.

**Estonia** — 8" straight legs, #545, 1986 – 1987 only (Wendy Ann)..................................................$60.00

**Estrella** — 18" h.p. (Maggie), lilac gown, 1953 ................................................ $1,200.00 up

**Ethiopia** — 8", #42535, 2006, white dress, coffee pot ..........................................$80.00

**Eva Lovelace** — 7" compo., 1935 only (Tiny Betty) ...............................................$375.00

 Cloth, 1935 only ..................................................................................................$600.00

**Evangeline** — 18" cloth, 1930s .......................................................................$650.00 up

**Eva Peron** — 10", #22030, 1997, long white lace dress (Cissette)........................$100.00

**Evening Cissette** — 10", #38745, 2004, white dress, lavender trim .....................$125.00

**Evening of Romance** — 10", #27010, 2000 (Cissette), black lace gown ................$125.00

**Evening Star** — 15" porcelain, black lace over pink satin (1999 – 2000)..............$125.00

**Evil Queen** — 10", #42630, 2006, blue outfit, magic mirror ..............................$120.00

**Evil Sorceress** — 8", #13610, 1997, long black velvet dress ...............................$70.00

**Fabulous Bloom** — 8", #40850, 2005, red checked dress, curly hair ...................$100.00

**Fairie-ality Trunk Set** — 8", #31825, log trunk, three outfits, accessories, 2003 – 2005.........$240.00

**Fairy Godmother** — 14", #1550, #1551, #1568, 1983 – 1992, Classic Series
  (Mary Ann, Louisa)......................................................................................$90.00

 Fairy Godmother outfit, 1983, M.A.D.C. (see Special Events/Exclusives)

 10" Portrette, #1156, 1993 only, blue/gold gown (Cissette)..............................$90.00

 10", #14549, 1995 only, purple gown, white wig (Cissette) ..............................$80.00

 8", #13430, 1997 – 1999, dark blue hooded cloak ..........................................$75.00

 8", #25920, 2000 – 2001 (Maggie), dark blue over light blue gown.....................$80.00

**Fairy of Beauty** — 8", #13620, 1997 – 2003, #40255, 2006, pink tulle gown, wand
 with hearts, pointed hat ....................................................................................$80.00

**Fairy of Song** — 8", #13630, 1997 – 2003, #40250, 2006, green tulle gown, wand
 with music notes.................................................................................................$80.00

**Fairy of Virtue** — 8", #13640, 1997 – 2003, #40260, 2006, blue tulle gown, wand
 with stars, pointed hat .......................................................................................$80.00

**Fairy Princess** — 7" – 8" compo., 1940 – 1943 (Tiny Betty) ..............................$375.00

 9" compo., 1939 – 1941 (Little Betty) .............................................................$400.00

 11" compo., 1939 only (Wendy Ann)................................................................$425.00

 15" – 18" compo., 1939 – 1942 (Wendy Ann) ................................................$650.00

 21" – 22" compo., 1939, 1944 – 1946 (Wendy Ann).......................................$900.00

**Fairy Queen** — 14½" compo., 1940 – 1946 (Wendy Ann).................................$700.00

 18" compo., 1940 – 1946 (Wendy Ann)...........................................................$800.00

 14½" h.p., 1948 – 1950 (Margaret) ................................................................$800.00

 18" h.p., 1949 – 1950 (Margaret) ...................................................................$950.00

**Fairy Tales** — Dumas, 9" compo., 1937 – 1941 (Little Betty)...........................$375.00

**Faith** — 8" h.p., #486, 1961 only, Americana Series, plaid jumper/organdy blouse (Wendy Ann).. $1,800.00 up

 8" h.p. (see Collectors United under Special Events/Exclusives)

**Fall Angel** — 8", #28360, 2001 – 2002, rust gown with leaves.............................$75.00

**Falling Snowflakes with Lenox Ornament** — 8", #40050, 2005 – 2006, pale pink dress......$95.00

**Fannie Elizabeth** — (see Belk & Leggett under Special Events/Exclusives)

**Fantasy** — (see Doll Finders under Special Events/Exclusives)

**FAO Schwarz** — (see Special Events/Exclusives)

**Farmer in the Dell** — 8", #37990, with dog, cat, mouse, and cheese, 2004 – 2005 ....................$85.00

**Farmer's Daughter** — (see Enchanted Doll House under Special Events/Exclusives)

**Fashions of the Century** — 14" – 18" h.p., 1954 – 1955 (Margaret, Maggie) ................ $2,500.00 up

**Father Christmas** — 8" h.p., #100351, Americana Series .........................................$75.00

**Father of the Bride** — 10", #24623, 1996, white satin wedding gown ........................$90.00

**Father of Vatican City, The** — 8", #24190, 1999, gold silk robe ...............................$75.00

**50's Kitsch Maggie** — 8", #42035, 2006, with veggie people...................................$95.00

**50th Birthday Wendy** — 8", #34710, 2002, blue dress.........................................$80.00

**50 Years of Friendship** — 8", #37950, 2003, two dolls, pink print...........................$140.00

 8", blue print, magnetic kiss..................................................................................$140.00

Fashions of the Century, 18",
1954 – 1955 (Margaret). All
original with lace gloves,
wrist tag, earrings, and purse.

**Figure Eight Total Moves Wendy** — 8", #39135, 2004, blue ice skating costume...$85.00

**Figurines** — 1999, 6", polyresin replica of Alexander dolls ......................$20.00 – 30.00

**Fiji** — 8", #38605, 2004, with plush shark ...............................................................$80.00

**Fillmore, Abigail** — 1982 – 1984, third set Presidents' Ladies/First Ladies Series
(Louisa) ..............................................................................................................$100.00

**Fill My Heart** — 8", #28745, 2002 – 2003, pink lace-trimmed dress, large hat .....$80.00
8", #28746, 2002 – 2003, African-American ................................................................$90.00

**Fill My Stocking** — 8", #36000, 2003, cream dress, gold checked apron,
Lenox stocking ornament ................................................................................$90.00

**Findlay, Jane** — 1979 – 1981, first set Presidents' Ladies/First Ladies Series
(Mary Ann) .......................................................................................................$100.00

**Finland** — 8" h.p., BK, #767, 1968 – 1972 (Wendy Ann) ....................................$100.00
8" h.p., straight legs, #0767 – 567, 1973 – 1975, marked "Alex" ................................$60.00
8" h.p., straight legs, #567, 1976 – 1987, marked "Alexander"...................................$55.00
8", #42515, 2006, with shield, helmet, and sword........................................................$85.00

**Finnish** — 7" compo., 1935 – 1937 (Tiny Betty) ...................................................$325.00

**Firefighter Wendy** — 8", #31270, 1998 – 1999, yellow coat, red hat, and dog.........$85.00

**Fireplace Stocking Holder** — #91005, 6¼", red fireplace........................................$40.00

**First Bloom** — 8", #39245, 2005, lavender dress, straw hat ....................................$80.00

**First Communion** — 8" h.p., #395, 1957 only (Wendy Ann)...............................$675.00
8" h.p., reintroduced 1994, #100347, Americana Series ...........................................$65.00
8", #10347 – 10349, 1995, three hair colors, Special Occasions Series .....................$65.00
8", #17012 – 17015, 1996, black, three hair colors (Wendy Ann) #21100, 1997 – 1998 ...........$65.00
8", #21530 (white), #21534 (black), white dress, veil, Bible, 1999 – 2000 ................$65.00
8", #30656, 2001 – 2003, Latin American, lacy white dress, veil.................................$65.00
8", #30655, 2001 – 2003, Caucasian, white dress, veil, gold necklace with cross .....................$70.00
8", #30658, 2002 – 2003, African-American (#30657, brunette) ...............................$70.00
14", #1545, 1991 – 1992 only, Classic Series (Louisa) .............................................$100.00

**First Dance** — 10", #36175, 2003, long black dress, red gloves...............................$125.00

**First Dance Pair** — 8", 1996 .....................................................................................$125.00

**First Day at School** — 8", #32995, 2002 – 2003 (Maggie), sweater, plaid skirt, book ...$65.00

**First Ladies** — (see Presidents' Ladies and individual names)

**First Modern Doll Club** — (see Special Events/Exclusives)

**First Recital** — 8", #17024 (white), #17037 (black), lacy dress........................................$60.00

**Fischer Quints** — 7" h.p./vinyl, 1964 only, one boy and four girls (Little Genius) . $600.00 set

**Five Little Peppers** — 13" and 16" compo., 1936 only....................................$750.00 ea.

**Flapper** — 10" Portrette, 1988 – 1991 (Cissette), red dress................................$60.00
10", #1118, 1988, black dress (all white dress in 1991) (see M.A.D.C. under
Special Events/Exclusives)
8", #14105, 1995, three-tiered rose colored dress with matching headband,
Nostalgia Series ..........................................................................................$60.00

**Flies a Kite** — 8", #33030, 2002 – 2003, red, white, and blue dress, patriotic outfit, with kite...$75.00

**Floral Romance Bridesmaid** — 10", #42505, 2006, long pink dress ...........................$110.00

**Floral Whimsey Wendy-Kin Wood** — 8", #42010, 2006, wood doll, pink dress.......$250.00

**Flora McFlimsey** — (with and without "e")
9" compo., 1938 – 1941 (Little Betty) ..................................................................$425.00
22" compo., 1938 – 1944 (Princess Elizabeth) .....................................................$800.00 up
15" – 16" compo., 1938 – 1944 (Princess Elizabeth) .............................................$650.00 up
16" – 17" compo., 1936 – 1937 (Wendy Ann)......................................................$600.00
14" compo., 1938 – 1944 (Princess Elizabeth) .....................................................$500.00 up
12" compo., 1944 only, holds 5" "Nancy Ann" doll, tagged "Margie Ann" (Wendy Ann).............$950.00 up
15" Miss Flora McFlimsey, vinyl head (must have good color), 1953 only (Cissy) ...........$750.00 up
14", #25502, 1995, tiers of pink, white, and black, Buttons & Bows Series (Mary Ann) ........$100.00

**Flower Child** — 8", #17790, 1999 (Maggie) ...............................................................$60.00

Fischer Quints, 8", 1964 only (Little Genius). Hard plastic heads, vinyl bodies.

Flower Girl, 18", #1835, 1954 (Cissy).

**Flower for the Bride** — 8", #36880, 2003 – 2004, pale pink short dress, with lace ....................$80.00

**Flower Girl** — 16" – 18" compo., 1939, 1944 – 1947 (Princess Elizabeth) ..............................$650.00

    20" – 24" compo., 1939, 1944 – 1947 (Princess Elizabeth) ........................................$650.00 – 850.00

    15" – 18" h.p., 1954 only (Cissy) ....................................................................$500.00 – 950.00

    15" h.p., 1954 only (Margaret) ...................................................................................$800.00 up

    8" h.p., #602, 1956 (Wendy Ann) ..............................................................................$950.00 up

    8" h.p., #445, 1959 (Wendy), blue nylon pleated dress......................................................$675.00 up

    8" h.p., #334, 1992 – 1993, Americana Series, white doll (Wendy Ann) ...................................$70.00

    8", #334-1, 1992 only, black doll................................................................................$70.00

    10", #1122, 1988 – 1990, Portrette, pink dotted Swiss dress (Cissette) ....................................$80.00

    8", #22620, 1999, mauve satin, rose crown, limited to 2,700 ..............................................$80.00

**Flowery Goodness** — 8", #42185, 2006, with Chaos bear, watering can ..................................$100.00

**Follow Your Dreams Angel** — 8", #38580, 2004, white and gold ........................................$90.00

**Forget-Me-Not** — 8", #28465, 2001 – 2002, yellow and pink dress with flowers, hat ................$75.00

    8", #37890, 2004, blue dress, holding flowers.................................................................$85.00

**Forrest** — 8" h.p., #10750, 1998, Tyrolean outfit ....................................................$60.00

**40's Sweet 'N Petite** — 8", #42025, 2006, with sheep ..................................................$70.00

**For Your One and Only** — 8", #42155, 2006, plush bear with hearts ...................................$85.00

**Four-leaf Clover Fairy** — 8", #35930, 2003 – 2004, green costume ....................................$85.00

**Four of Us, The** — 8", #37215, 2003 – 2004, pink dress, green sweater, bear, dog, and cat......$125.00

**France** — 7" compo., 1936 – 1943 (Tiny Betty) ........................................................$325.00

    9" compo., 1937 – 1941 (Little Betty) .........................................................................$350.00

    8" h.p., BKW, #390, #790, 1961 – 1965 (Wendy Ann) ....................................................$125.00

    8" h.p., BK, #790, 1965 – 1972 ................................................................................$90.00

    8" h.p., straight leg, #0790, #590, 1973 – 1975, marked "Alex"..............................................$65.00

    8" straight leg, #590, #552 (1985 – 1987), #517, #582 (1976 – 1993), marked "Alexander" ..............$60.00

    8" h.p., reissued 1994 – 1995, #110538 (Wendy) ............................................................$60.00

    8" h.p., #11557, 1996 International, Cancan costume (#24020 – 1998) ...................................$60.00

**French Aristocrat** — 10" Portrette, #1143, 1991 – 1992 only, bright pink/white (Cissette)............$175.00

**French Blue Godey** — 10", #33565, 2002, long blue dress, striped top, limited to 750 ............$100.00

**French Court Girl** — 8", #40790, 2005, powdered wig, pink vintage outfit with dress form ..............$160.00

**French Flower Girl** — 8" h.p., #610, 1956 only (Wendy Ann) ..........................................$800.00 up

**French Kitty** — 10", #40045, #40590, #39995, 2005 – 2006, Feline fashion doll..........................$25.00

    10", #42665, #42605, #42655, 2006 ..........................................................................$25.00

**French White Godey** — 10", #33560, 2002, white dress, pink trim, limited to 750.................$100.00

**Friar Tuck** — 8" h.p., #493, 1989 – 1991, Storybook Series (Maggie Mixup) ..........................$60.00

**Friday's Child** — 8", #27790, 2001, lavender dress ....................................................$80.00

**Friedrich** — (see Sound of Music)

**Fright Night Fun Wendy** — 8", #42270, 2006, black pants, orange sweater ...........................$70.00

**Frog Princess** — 8", #27755, 2001 – 2002, includes frog, pink dress, puff sleeves.....................$85.00

**Frost Fairy Boy** — 8", #25140, 2000, silver costume and crown .......................................$65.00

**Frost Fairy Girl** — 8", #25145, 2000, silver ballerina costume .......................................$65.00

**Frou-Frou** — 40" all cloth, 1951 only, ballerina with yarn hair, dressed in green or lilac .....$800.00 up

**Fun Fun Chloe** — 14", #30115, 2001, vinyl ............................................................$65.00

**Funny** — 18" cloth, 1963 – 1977........................................................................$65.00

**Funny Maggie** — 8" (Maggie), #140506, 1994 – 1995, Storyland Series, yarn hair ...................$55.00

**Gainsborough** — 20" h.p., 1957, Models Formal Gowns Series, taffeta gown,

    large picture hat (Cissy) ................................................................... $1,700.00 up

    #2184, 21" h.p., vinyl arms, 1968, blue with white lace jacket (Jacqueline) ...........................$650.00

    #2192, 21", 1972, yellow with full white lace overskirt (Jacqueline)....................................$675.00

    #2192, 21", 1973, pale blue, scallop lace overskirt (Jacqueline) ......................................$525.00

    #2211, 21", 1978, pink with full lace overdress (Jacqueline) .........................................$325.00

    10" pink gown and hat, 1957 Portrette (Cissette) ..........................................................$750.00

    10", #45201, 1995, pink with lace overlay, Madame's Portfolio Series ...................................$100.00

Funny Maggie, 8" (Maggie), #140506, 1994 – 1995. Yarn hair.

**Garbo, Greta, Grand Hotel** — 16", #33480, 2002 – 2003, wool dress, coat, limited to 1,500 .. $150.00

    16", #31555, 2003, Greta Garbo Camille, pink gown, limited to 500 ....................................$175.00

**Garden Fairy** — 8", #28500, 2001 – 2002, pink costume with roses ............................................$80.00

**Garden Fun** — 8", #42315, 2006, green dress, trunk ....................................................................$105.00

**Gardenia** — 10", #22360, 1998 (Cissette), yellow satin long gown ..............................................$100.00

**Garden Party** — 18" h.p., 1953 only (Margaret)................................................................... $1,700.00 up

    20" h.p., 1956 – 1957 (Cissy).................................................................................... $1,600.00 up

    8" h.p., #488, 1955 only (Wendy Ann) ................................................................... $1,800.00 up

**Garden Rose** — 10" (Cissette), #22530, 1999, pink tulle with roses.............................................$90.00

**Garfield, Lucretia** — 1985 – 1987, fourth set Presidents' Ladies/First Ladies Series (Louisa) ..$100.00

**Garland, Judy Meet Me in St. Louis** — 16", #32175, 2002 – 2003, white dress,

    limited to 1,500..........................................................................................................................$150.00

**Gemini** — 8", #21350, 1998, African-American, two dolls, yellow outfit.....................................$150.00

    8", #21351, 1998, white, two dolls...........................................................................................$150.00

**Genius Baby** — 21" – 30" plastic/vinyl, 1960 – 1961, has flirty eyes..........................$125.00 – 150.00

    Little, 8" h.p. head/vinyl, 1956 – 1962 (see Little Genius)

**Geppetto** — 8", #478, 1993, #140478, 1994, Storybook Series........................................................$65.00

**Geppetto and Pinocchio** — 8", 5", #32130, 2000, navy jacket, hat...............................................$90.00

**Geranium** — 9" early vinyl toddler, 1953 only, red organdy dress and bonnet ...........................$100.00

**German (Germany)** — 8" h.p., BK, #763, 1966 – 1972 (Wendy Ann) ............................................$90.00

    8" h.p., straight legs, #0763 – 563, 1973 – 1975, marked "Alex" .....................................$65.00

    10" h.p., 1962 – 1963 (Cissette)..............................................................................................$925.00

    8" straight legs, #563, #535, #506, 1976 – 1989, marked "Alexander" ............................$60.00

    8", 1990 – 1991, marked "Alexander" ..................................................................................$60.00

    8", #535, 1986 .............................................................................................................................$60.00

    8" h.p., #110542, 1994 – 1995, outfit in 1994 Neiman-Marcus trunk set (Maggie) ..................$55.00

    8", #25800, 2000 – 2001 (Maggie), blue print dress, beer stein........................................$100.00

**Get Well** — 8" h.p., #21090, 1998 – 1999, red striped outfit, vase of flowers ...............................$65.00

**Get Well Wishes** — #10363 – 10365, 1995, three hair colors,

        nurse with bear, Special Occasions Series...............................................................$60.00

**Ghost of Christmas Past** — 8", #18002, 1996, Dickens, long white gown ................................$60.00

**Ghost of Christmas Present** — 14", #18406, 1996, Dickens, sold as set only with

    8" Ignorance (boy) and 8" Want (girl)......................................................................................$250.00

**Gibson Girl** — 10" h.p., 1962, eyeshadow (Cissette) ........................................................... $800.00 up

    10", 1963, plain blouse with no stripes...................................................................... $800.00 up

    16" cloth, 1930s ........................................................................................................................$850.00

    10", #1124, 1988 – 1990, Portrette, red and black (Cissette) .........................................$65.00

    10", #17750, 1999, navy blue gown ........................................................................................$90.00

**Gidget** — 14" plastic/vinyl, #1415, #1420, #1421, 1966 only (Mary Ann)................................$250.00

**Gift from Grandma** — 8", #38195, 2004 – 2005, pink checked dress..........................................$85.00

**Gift of Beauty Fairy** — 8", #39045, 2004 – 2005, pink outfit ..................................................$85.00

**Gift of Song Fairy** — 8", #39055, 2004 – 2005, blue gown .....................................................$85.00

**Gift of Virtue Fairy** — 8", #39050, 2004 – 2005, blue gown ...................................................$85.00

**Gigi** — 14", #1597, 1986 – 1987, Classic Series (Mary Ann) ......................................................$100.00

    14", #87011, 1996, plaid dress, straw hat (Mary Ann) ...............................................$100.00

    8" h.p., #13990, 1998 – 1999, pleated plaid dress, straw hat (Maggie) .......................$65.00

**Gilbert** — 8", #260420, 1994 – 1995, Anne of Green Gables Series ............................................$85.00

**Gingerbread House** — Candy-trimmed house, #26595, 2001 – 2003.......................................$110.00

**Girl on a Swing** — 8", #28640, 2001 – 2002, white dress with swing, flower rope .....................$80.00

**Girl on Flying Trapeze** — 40" cloth, 1951 only, dressed in pink satin tutu

    (sold at FAO Schwarz).............................................................................................................$950.00

**Giselle** — 16", #22050, 1998, aqua tutu ......................................................................................$100.00

**Glamour Girl 1953** — 10" h.p., 2000, (Cissette) pink and black gown......................................$100.00

**Glamour Girls** — 18" h.p., 1953 only (Margaret, Maggie) ................................................ $1,800.00 up

**Glinda the Good Witch** — 8", #473, 1992 – 1993, Storyland Series (Wendy Ann),
   #140473, 1994 – 1995 ..............................................................................................$125.00
   14" plastic/vinyl, #141573, 1994 only..............................................................$100.00
   10", #13250, 1997 – 2001 – 2005, #42405 (2006) pink tulle and taffeta dress (Cissette),
   silver crown ..................................................................................................$150.00
   15", #25546, 2001, cloth, pink gown ...............................................................$60.00
   5", #33765, 2002, porcelain, pink dress............................................................$75.00
   9", #40920, 2005, long pink dress, silver crown ..............................................$45.00
**Glorious Angel** — 10½" h.p., #54860 (see Tree Topper)
**Godey** — 21" compo., 1945 – 1947 (Wendy Ann), white lace over pink satin ...................$2,700.00 up
   14" h.p., 1950 – 1951 (Margaret) ...................................................................$1,500.00 up
   21" h.p., 1951 only, lace ¾ top with long sleeves, pink satin two-tiered skirt (Margaret)...$1,500.00 up
   18" h.p., #2010A, 1953 only, Glamour Girl Series, red gown with gray fur stole (Maggie).$1,200.00 up
   21" h.p., vinyl straight arms, 1961 only, lavender coat and hat (Cissy) .....................$1,600.00
   21", 1962, bright orange gown, white lace ruffles on bodice ...............................$1,600.00
   21", #2153, 1965, dressed in all red, blonde hair (Jacqueline)..............................$800.00
   21" plastic/vinyl, 1966 only, red with short black jacket and hat (Coco)........................$2,300.00 up
   21" h.p., vinyl arms, #2172, 1967, dressed in pink and ecru (Jacqueline)................$600.00
      #2195, 1969, red with black trim..................................................................$600.00
      #2195, 1970, pink with short burgundy jacket.................................................$300.00
      #2161, 1971, pink, black trim, short jacket.....................................................$350.00
      #2298, 1977, ecru with red jacket and bonnet...............................................$300.00
   8" SLW, #491, 1955 only (Wendy Ann)............................................................$1,400.00 up
   10" h.p., #1172, 1968, dressed in all pink with ecru lace, bows down front (Cissette) ...........$450.00
      #1172, 1969, all yellow with bows down front.............................................$475.00
      #1183, 1970, all lace pink dress with natural straw hat ................................$425.00
**Godey Bride** — 14" h.p., 1950, lace ¾ top over satin gown with long train (Margaret) ... $1,000.00 up
   18" h.p., 1950 – 1951 (Margaret) ..................................................................$1,400.00 up
   21" porcelain, 1993 (Cissy)............................................................................$375.00
**Godey Groom/Man** — 14" h.p., 1950, has curls over ears, wearing black
   jacket and tan pants (Margaret) .....................................................................$975.00 up
   18" h.p., 1950 – 1951 (Margaret) ..................................................................$1,300.00 up
**Godey Lady** — 14" h.p., 1950, green velvet dress with pink/bright orange
   pleated ruffles, peach/white bodice (Margaret) ..............................................$1,000.00 up
   18" h.p., 1950 – 1951 (Margaret) ..................................................................$1,500.00 up
**Golden Christmas Angel** — 10", #38565, 2004, white and gold costume..............................$125.00
**Golden Girl 1920** — 10", #17740, 1999, black and gold dress...................................$100.00
**Goldfish** — 8" h.p., #344, Americana Series, 1993 – 1994.....................................$70.00
**Goldilocks** — 18" cloth, 1930s..................................................................$875.00
   7" – 8" compo., 1938 – 1942 (Tiny Betty).........................................................$325.00
   18" h.p., 1951 only (Maggie) ......................................................................$1,200.00
   14" plastic/vinyl, #1520, 1978 – 1979, Classic Series, satin dress (Mary Ann) ..........................$80.00
   14", #1520, 1980 – 1983, blue satin or cotton dress (Mary Ann) ........................$80.00
   14", #1553, 1991 only, Classic Series, long side curls tied with ribbon (Mary Ann)................$85.00
   8", #497, 1990 – 1991 only, Storyland Series (1991 dress in different plaid) (Wendy Ann) .....$70.00
   8", #140500, 1994 – 1995, Storyland Series, floral print dress, bear........................$70.00
   8", #25965, 2000 – 2003 (Wendy), blue dress, eyelet apron with bear ...................$60.00
   8", #39860, 2005 – 2006, lavender dress with three Chaos bears.............................$150.00
**Gold Rush** — 10" h.p., 1963 only (Cissette) ....................................................$1,400.00
**Golf Boy** — 8", 1998, #16402 (Maggie) green coat, checked hat, pants, golf club......................$65.00
**Golf Girl** — 8", 1998, #16412 (Wendy) ivory sweater, navy skirt, golf club.....................$65.00
**Gone Fishing** — 8", #28190, 2001, green dress, hat, fishing pole .................................$80.00
**Gone With the Wind (Scarlett)** — 14", #1490, #1590, 1969 – 1986, all white dress/green sash,
   made 17 years without a change (Mary Ann) (dress must be mint)........................$125.00

Godey Lady, 14" (Margaret),
1950 – 1951, hard plastic.
Tagged "Godey Lady."
Unique hairstyle, mint lavender gown.

**Good Fairy** — 14" h.p., 1948 – 1949 (Margaret) .................................................... $725.00 up

**Good Little Girl** — 16" cloth, 1966 only, mate to "Bad Little Girl," wears pink dress.............$185.00

**Goya** — 8" h.p., #314, 1953 only (Wendy Ann) ..................................................... $1,100.00 up

    21" h.p./vinyl arms, #2183, 1968, multi-tiered pink dress (Jacqueline).........................$550.00

    21", #2235, 1982 – 1983, maroon dress with black Spanish lace (Jacqueline) .......................$275.00

**Grace** — 14" vinyl, #34320, 2002 – 2003, African-American baby, pajamas...................................$85.00

**Graceful Garnet** — 8", #32170, 2000 – 2002, red and gold ball gown, garnet jewelry ...............$90.00

**Graduation** — 8" h.p., #399, 1957 only (Wendy Ann)............................................. $900.00 up

    12", 1957 only (Lissy) ............................................................................. $1,000.00 up

    8", #307, 1990 – 1991, Americana Series (white doll only) (Wendy Ann) ............................. $60.00

    8", #307, #307-1, 1991 – 1992, Americana Series, white or black doll ............................$65.00

    8", #10307 – 10309 (black), #10310 (white), 1995, blue robe, Special Occasions Series .........$65.00

    8", #26105 (blonde), #26106 (brunette), #26107 (African-American), 2000 – 2003,

        white robe, red dress, hat, diploma ...................................................................$80.00

    8", #38895, 2004 – 2005, blonde, white dress, blue robe, hat ....................................$85.00

    8", #38896, 2004 – 2005, brunette, white dress, blue robe, hat ..................................$85.00

    8", #38897, 2004 – 2005, African-American, white dress, blue robe, hat...........................$85.00

**Grandma Jane** — 14" plastic/vinyl, #1420, 1970 – 1972 (Mary Ann) ...........................$225.00

**Grand Ole Opry Boy** — 8", #77005, 1996 Classic .............................................$70.00

**Grand Ole Opry Girl** — 8", #77004, 1996 Classic .............................................$70.00

**Grant, Julia** — 1982 – 1984, third set Presidents' Ladies/First Ladies Series (Louisa).............$100.00

**Grave, Alice** — 18" cloth, 1930s.................................................................. $750.00 up

**Grayson, Kathryn** — 20" – 21" h.p., 1949 only (Margaret)................................... $6,000.00 up

**Great Britain** — 8" h.p., #558, 1977 – 1988 (Wendy Ann) ....................................$55.00

**Great Gatsby Pair** — 10", #15310, 1997, Classic characters .....................................$140.00

**Greece** — 8", #35970, 2003 – 2004, blue and red cultural costume, bouzaki..................$85.00

**Greece Boy** — 8" h.p., #527, 1992 – 1993 only (Wendy Ann) .................................$50.00

**Greek Boy** — 8" h.p., BK, 1965, BKW, 1966 – 1968, #769 (Wendy Ann) .................$300.00

**Greek Girl** — 8" h.p., BK, #765, 1968 – 1972 (Wendy Ann) .................................$100.00

    8" h.p., straight legs, #0765, #565, 1973 – 1975, marked "Alex" .................................$60.00

    8" h.p., straight legs, #565, #527, 1976 – 1987 (1985 – 1987), marked "Alexander".................$55.00

**Gretel** — 7" compo., 1935 – 1942 (Tiny Betty) ..................................................$325.00

    9" compo., 1938 – 1940 (Little Betty) ............................................................$350.00

    18" h.p., 1948 only (Margaret)................................................................ $1,000.00 up

    7½" – 8" h.p., SLW, #470, 1955 (Wendy Ann) .................................................. $550.00 up

    8" h.p., BK, #754, 1966 – 1972, Storybook Series (Wendy)....................................$100.00

    8" h.p., straight legs, #0754, #454, 1973 – 1975, marked "Alex" .................................$65.00

    8" h.p., straight legs, #454, 1976 – 1986, marked "Alexander"...................................$60.00

    8" h.p., #462, 1991 – 1992 only, Storyland Series, reintroduced doll (Wendy Ann).................$60.00

    8" h.p., #26600, 2001 – 2003, red stripe skirt, eyelet apron, green felt hat ...............$70.00

**Gretel Brinker** — 12", 1993 only (Lissy).......................................................$125.00

    8", #14650, 1996 ................................................................................$60.00

**Gretl** — (see Sound of Music)

**Groom** — 18" – 21" compo., 1946 – 1947, mint (Margaret) ...................................$975.00 up

    18" – 21" h.p., 1949 – 1951 (Margaret).....................................................$975.00 – 1,500.00

    14" – 16" h.p., 1949 – 1951 (Margaret)......................................................... $750.00 up

    7½" h.p., SL and SLW, #577, #464, #466, 1953 – 1955 (Wendy Ann) ............................... $550.00 up

    8" BKW, #577, 1956....................................................................................$425.00

    8" BKW, #377, 1957....................................................................................$400.00

    8" BKW, #572, 1958....................................................................................$400.00

    8" h.p., BKW, #421, #442, 1961 – 1963 (Wendy Ann) ..........................................$350.00

    8", #488, #388, reintroduced 1989 – 1991 only (Wendy Ann) ...................................$60.00

    8", #339, 1993, black pants, peach tie, white jacket ............................................$60.00

    8", #17020, 1996, black velvet tails, black pants, pink tie .......................................$65.00

8", #17023, 1996, black velvet tails, etc., black doll..................................................................$65.00

8", #21071, 1997 – 2005, velvet tailcoat, top hat,  #21073 – 21074, African-American
    (1997 – 2006) ................................................................................................................$90.00

**Groovy Girl 1970** — 8", #17800, 1999, BK, denim pants, hat ......................................$60.00

**Guardian Angel** — 10", #10602 – 1995, first in series, 100th Anniversary Special, all pink
    with white wings ..............................................................................................................$125.00

10", #10720, 1998, rose print brocade gown, feather wings ............................................$100.00

10", of Harmony, #10691, 1996 ..........................................................................................$100.00

10", of Hope, #10609, 1996..................................................................................................$100.00

10", of Love, frosted ivy, #10605, 1996...............................................................................$100.00

10", of Love, heather blue #10607, 1996.............................................................................$100.00

10", of Love, misty rose, #10603, 1996...............................................................................$100.00

10", Pink Pristine, #10700, 1997 – 2000, pink tulle dress ...............................................$100.00

10", #10720, 1999, pink print brocade gown, feather wings ...........................................$100.00

**Guatemala** — 8", #24180, 1999, red and black outfit ...................................................$60.00

**Guinevere** — 10", #1146, 1992 only, Portrette, forest green/gold.................................$100.00

8", #13570, 1999, blue dress with white brocade over dress.............................................$80.00

**Gymnastics Class** — 8", #42120, 2006, pink bodysuit, balance beam ........................$70.00

**Gypsy of the World** — 8", #28570, 2001, purple costume, tarot cards .......................$75.00

**Hairdresser** — 8", #33585, 2003 (Wizard of Oz), green dress, mini scissors, blonde with curls .$75.00

**Halloween Treats** — 8", #38590, 2004 – 2005, with bear and treat bag......................$85.00

**Halloween Witch** — 8" (see Collectors United/C. U. under Special Events/Exclusives)

**Hamlet** — 12", Romance Series (Nancy Drew)................................................................$70.00

12", 1993 only (Lissy) .........................................................................................................$100.00

**Hannah** — 10", #28310, 2002 – 2004, jeans, sweater, hat.............................................$40.00

10", #28300, 2002 – 2004, skirt, striped jacket ................................................................$40.00

10", #40615, 2005, Summertime Fun Playset, with dog ....................................................$95.00

**Hannah Pepper Trunk Set** — 10", #35450, 2003 – 2004, clothes, trunk...............$120.00

**Hans Brinker** — 12", 1993 only (Lissy)..........................................................................$100.00

8", #14649, 1996 ...................................................................................................................$60.00

**Hansel** — 7" compo., 1935 – 1942 (Tiny Betty) ..............................................................$325.00

9" compo., 1938 – 1940 (Little Betty)..................................................................................$350.00

18" h.p., 1948 only (Margaret)......................................................................................... $900.00 up

8" h.p., SLW, #470, 1955 only (Wendy Ann) ................................................................ $650.00 up

8" h.p., BK, #753, 1966 – 1972, Storybook Series (Wendy Ann) .....................................$100.00

8" h.p., straight legs, #0753, #543, 1973 – 1975, marked "Alex" ......................................$70.00

8" h.p., straight legs, #543, 1976 – 1986 (1986 white face), marked "Alexander".....................$60.00

8" h.p., #461, 1991 – 1992 only, Storyland Series, reintroduced doll (Wendy Ann)..................$60.00

8" h.p., #26605, 2001 – 2003, green costume ....................................................................$75.00

**Happy** — 20" cloth/vinyl, 1970 only.................................................................................$200.00

**Happy Birthday** — 1985 (see M.A.D.C. under Special Events/Exclusives)

8" h.p., #325, #325-1, 1992 – 1993, Americana Series, black or white doll (Wendy Ann) ........$65.00

8" h.p., #100325, 1994, white only .....................................................................................$65.00

8", #10325 – 10327, 1995, three hair colors, Special Occasions Series.............................$65.00

8", #17004 – 17010, 1996, three hair colors, black or white doll (Wendy, Maggie)..................$65.00

14" plastic/vinyl, #241596, 1994 only .................................................................................$70.00

8", #21520 (blonde),#21521 (brunette), #21523 (black), pink print dress, 1999 – 2000 ..........$65.00

8", #27240 (blonde), #27241 (brunette), #27242, African-American, 2001 – 2002....................$75.00

8", #35925 (blonde), 2003 – 2005, pink dress, slice of cake.............................................$70.00

8", #35926 (brunette), 2003 – 2005, with gift...................................................................$70.00

8", #35927, African-American, 2003 – 2005, with gift .....................................................$70.00

**Happy Birthday Billie** — 8" h.p., #345, #345-1, Americana Series, black or white boy, 1993 only..$60.00

**Happy Birthday Maggie** — 8", #21080 – white, #21083 – black, 1997 – 1998 .........................$70.00

**Happy Chanukah** — 8", #10367, 1996 Holiday, #19630, 1997 – 1999 .......................................$70.00

**Happy the Clown** — 8", #10414, 1996 Classic Circus ................................................................$60.00
**Harding, Florence** — 1988, fifth set Presidents' Ladies/First Ladies Series (Louisa) ..............$100.00
**Harlequin** — 8", #14574, 1995, Nutcracker Series........................................................................$70.00
**Harley-Davidson** — 8" h.p., #77002, 1996 (Wendy) Classic American, #17420, 1997.............$100.00
    8" h.p., #77005, 1996 (Billy), Classic American, #17410, 1997 .........................................$100.00
    10" h.p., #77102, 1996, pictured 1996 catalog .......................................not available for sale
    10", #17440, 1997, Cissette, black leather coat, boots.........................................................$175.00
    10", #17430, 1997, David, jeans, black leather jacket .........................................................$125.00
    10", #17390, 1998, Cissette, faux leather halter and skirt and backpack ........................$150.00
**Harriet the Spy** — 12", #38565, 2004 – 2005, cloth dog ...........................................................$30.00
**Harrison, Caroline** — 1985 – 1987, fourth set Presidents' Ladies/First Ladies Series
    (Louisa) ....................................................................................................................................$100.00
**Harry Potter** — 8", #38415, 2004, with broom.........................................................................$85.00
**Harvest Greetings** — 8", #40600, 2005 – 2006, with cornucopia ...........................................$80.00
**Hats Off to Wendy** — 8", #37800, 2003, white dress, pink trim .............................................$80.00
**Hawaii** — 8", #301, 1990 – 1991 only, Americana Series (Wendy Ann)...................................$60.00
**Hawaiian** — 8" h.p., BK, #722, 1966 – 1969, Americana Series (Wendy Ann).........................$350.00
    7" compo., 1936 – 1939 (Tiny Betty) ....................................................................................$325.00
    9" compo., 1937 – 1944 (Little Betty) ...................................................................................$350.00
**Hayes, Lucy** — 1985 – 1987, fourth set Presidents' Ladies/First Ladies Series (Louisa) ..........$100.00
**Heather** — 18" cloth/vinyl, 1990 only.........................................................................................$80.00
    8" h.p., #10760, 1998, Tyrolean outfit with basket ..............................................................$75.00
**Heavenly Pink Angel** — 8", #26285, 2000 – 2001, pink costume, white feather wings............$100.00
**Heavenly Star Angel Tree Topper** — 8", #42230, 2006, blue outfit.......................................$140.00
**Heidi** — 7" compo., 1938 – 1939 (Tiny Betty) ..............................................................................$325.00
    8" h.p., #460, 1991 – 1992, Storyland Series (Maggie).........................................................$70.00
    14" plastic/vinyl, #1480, #1580, #1581, 1969 – 1985 (16-year production),
        Classic Series (Mary Ann) ..............................................................................................$70.00
    14", #1581, 1986 – 1988, solid green dress, floral apron .....................................................$70.00
    14", #25503, 1995, Ribbons & Bows Series (not on order sheet).........................not available for sale
    8" h.p., #15100, 1998 – 2000, green dress, lace apron, straw hat, goat ...............................$70.00
    8", #42560, 2006, red print skirt, straw hat, goat ................................................................$75.00
**Hello Baby** — 22", 1962 only .......................................................................................................$175.00
**He Loves Me, He Loves Me Not** — 8", #37895, 2004 (Wendy) ..............................................$75.00
**Henie, Sonja** — 13" – 15" compo., 1939 – 1942 .........................................................................$675.00
    7" compo., 1939 – 1942 (Tiny Betty) ....................................................................................$450.00
    9" compo., 1940 – 1941 (Little Betty) ...................................................................................$575.00
    11" compo. (Wendy Ann)..........................................................................................................$650.00
    14" compo. ...............................................................................................................................$650.00
    14" in case/wardrobe ........................................................................................$1,800.00 up
    17" – 18" compo.......................................................................................................................$950.00
    20" – 23" compo.......................................................................................$1,200.00 – 1,600.00
    13" – 14" compo., jointed waist...............................................................................................$750.00
    15" – 18" h.p./vinyl, 1951 only, no extra joints, must have good face color (Madeline)...........$750.00
**Her First Day at School** — (see Wendy Loves Series)
**Her Lady and Child (Thumbelina)** — 21" porcelain, 8" h.p., #010, 1992 – 1994,
    limited to 2,500................................................................................................................$475.00
**Hermione Granger** — 8", #38420, 2004, with books .................................................................$80.00
    10", #38640, 2004, vinyl .........................................................................................................$35.00
**Hershey's Kisses Doll** — 8", #17880, 2000, pink and silver costume .........................................$65.00
**Her Sunday Best** — (see Wendy Loves Series)
**Hey Diddle Diddle** — 8", #42455, 2006, print dress, dish and spoon.........................................$75.00
**Hiawatha** — 8" h.p., #720, 1967 – 1969, Americana Series (Wendy Ann) .................................$375.00
    7" compo. (Tiny Betty) .............................................................................................................$325.00

Hickory Dickory Dock, 8",
#11650, 1998 – 1999, clock
costume.

Hulda, 18", 1949 (Margaret),
black doll. Altered features,
full lips, thicker eyebrows,
very large eyes, and lamb's
wool wig.

18" cloth, early 1930s ...................................................................................$800.00
**Hickory Dickory Dock** — 8", #11650, 1998 – 1999, clock costume ...........................$70.00
   8", #42450, 2006, blue print dress, clock..............................................$85.00
**Highland Fling** — 8" h.p., #484, 1955 only (Wendy Ann) .................................$750.00
**Hocus Pocus Wonder** — 8", #42125, 2006, wand and rabbit................................$85.00
**Holiday Ballerina** — 8", #28525, 2001, long white dress with gold and red trim.......$70.00
**Holiday Jubilee** — 8", #40360, 2005 – 2006, red dress, gift box........................$85.00
**Holiday on Ice** — 8" h.p., #319, 1992 – 1993 only, red with white fur hat and muff,
   some tagged "Christmas on Ice"......................................................$125.00
**Holiday Snowflake Skater** — 8", #28520, 2001 – 2002 (Maggie), red skating outfit .............$80.00
**Holland** — 7" compo., 1936 – 1943 (Tiny Betty) ........................................$325.00
   8", #33490, 2002, blue print pinafore, with spoon.....................................$100.00
**Holly** — 10", #1135, 1990 – 1991, Portrette, white/red roses Cissette .................$90.00
**Holly Hobbie** — 8", #45505, 2006, calico dress, bonnet................................$85.00
**Hollywood Glamour 1930** — 10", #17760, 1999, blue taffeta dress .......................$100.00
**Hollywood Trunk Set** — 8", #15340, 1997............................................$225.00
**Homecoming** — 8", 1993 (see M.A.D.C. under Special Events/Exclusives)
**Homecoming Lissy** — 12", #42045, 2006, navy blue dress, hat..........................$100.00
**Home for Holidays** — 14", #24606, 1995, Christmas Series .............................$85.00
**Homefront Pals** — 8", pair, #34335, 2002, boy, denim, girl, star dress................$150.00
**Honeybea** — 12" vinyl, 1963 only .....................................................$175.00
**Honeybun** — 18" – 19", 1951 – 1952 only...............................................$225.00
   23" – 26".............................................................................$300.00
**Honeyette Baby** — 16" compo./cloth, 1941 – 1942.......................................$225.00
   7" compo., 1934 – 1937, little girl dress (Tiny Betty)................................$275.00
**Honeymoon in New Orleans** — (see Scarlett O'Hara)
**Honeymoon Sweet Dreams** — (see Bride or Groom)
**Hooray for M.A.!** — 8", #42115, 2006, pink cheerleader ..............................$75.00
**Hoover, Lou** — 14", 1989 – 1990, sixth set Presidents' Ladies/First Ladies Series (Mary Ann)...$100.00
**Hope** — 8" (see Collectors United under Special Events/Exclusives)
**Horse Around** —8", #40760, 2005, with stick horse....................................$75.00
**Hot Cross Buns** — 8", #33055, 2002, pink dress, buns on tray ........................$65.00
**House That Wendy Built, The** — 8", #42160, 2006, house, tools .......................$115.00
**How Does Your Garden Grow** — 8", #34085, 2002, with watering can.....................$65.00
**Howdy Doody Time, It's** — 8", #15230, 1999 – 2000, marionette.......................$100.00
**How Much Is That Doggie in the Window** — 8", #38780, 2004 – 2005, with
   store front and dog...................................................................$95.00
**Huckleberry Finn** — 8" h.p., #490, 1989 – 1991 only, Storybook Series (Wendy Ann)............$65.00
**Huggums, Big** — 25", 1963 – 1979, boy or girl......................................$100.00
**Huggums, Little** — 14", 1986 only, molded hair .....................................$50.00
   12", 1963 – 1995, molded hair, available in 7 – 10 outfits (first black version
     available in 1995) ...........................................................$50.00
   12", 1963 – 1982, 1988, rooted hair..................................................$50.00
   1991, special outfits (see Imaginarium Shop under Special Events/Exclusives)
   1996 – 2003, variety of outfits .............................................$40.00 – 65.00
   12", #29700, 1998, 75th Anniversary Huggums, white dress with flowers........$40.00 – 65.00
   12", 2006, Christening #38900, Mint Julep #40375, Piglet #42745 .............$50.00 – 70.00
**Huggums, Lively** — 25", 1963 only, knob makes limbs and head move....................$150.00
**Huggums Man in the Moon Mobile** — #14700, 8" boy, star costume, cloth moon, star mobiles...$70.00
**Hug Me Pets** — #76001 – 76007, plush animal bodies, Huggums face ....................$45.00
**Hula Hoop Total Moves Wendy** — 8", #40440, 2005 – 2006, blue outfit, hoop.............$80.00
**Hulda** — 18" h.p., 1949 only, lamb's wool wig, black doll (Margaret)................$1,900.00 up
   14" h.p., 1948 – 1949, lamb's wool wig, black doll .............................$1,300.00 up
**Humpty Dumpty** — 8", #13060, 1997 – 1998, plaid tailcoat, brick wall .................$70.00

**Kelly Pink Butterfly** — 20", #29920, 1999, pink dress and pinafore .........................................$90.00
**Kelly Pink Dot Tulle** — 18", #29230, 1997, vinyl ................................................................$85.00
**Kelly Pink Snowflake** — 18", #29110, 1997, vinyl ............................................................$85.00
**Kelly's Little Sister, Katie** — 12", #29940, 1999, pink plaid dress .....................................$55.00
**Kelly Teacher's Pet** — 15", #29760, 1999, plaid dress and hat ...........................................$70.00
**Kelly Teatime** — 15", #29300, 1998, blue dress, straw hat ................................................$70.00
**Kelly Tree Trimming** — 18", #29240, 1997, vinyl .............................................................$110.00
**Kelly White Floral Party** — 15" vinyl, #29390, 1998 – 1999 ..............................................$85.00
**Kennedy, Jacqueline** — 14", 1989 – 1990, sixth set Presidents' Ladies/First
    Ladies Series (Mary Ann) ...............................................................................$175.00
**Kenya** — 8", 1994, outfit tagged, in Neiman-Marcus trunk set .............................................$70.00
    8", issued 1995 only, same outfit but sold as Nigeria...........................no price available
**Kick It** — 8", #38890, 2004 – 2006, with soccer ball.............................................................$50.00
**Kikki** — 9", #39965, 2005, vinyl, jeans, red bag.....................................................................$30.00
**King** — 21" compo., 1942 – 1946 , extra make-up, red chest ribbon, gold-trimmed cape
    (Wendy Ann) .............................................................................................$2,700.00 up
**King of Hearts** — 8", #14611, 1996, Alice in Wonderland Series .........................................$60.00
**Kitten** — 14" – 18" cloth/vinyl, 1962 – 1963 ...............................................$50.00 – 95.00
    24", 1961 only, has rooted hair .........................................................................$95.00
    20" nurser, 1968 only, has cryer box, doesn't wet.............................................$100.00
    20", 1985 – 1986 only, dressed in pink ..............................................................$90.00
    8", 1998, #29310 Powder Pink or #29423 Sunny ............................................$60.00
**Kitten Kries** — 20" cloth/vinyl, 1967 only .........................................................................$100.00
**Kitten, Littlest** — (see Littlest Kitten)
**Kitten, Lively** — (see Lively Kitten)
**Kitty Baby** — 21" compo., 1941 – 1942 .............................................................................$175.00
**Klondike Kate** — 10" h.p., 1963 only, Portrette (Cissette) ...........................$1,500.00 up
**Knave** — 8", #13040, 1997 – 1998, brocade suit, large playing card, 5 of spades ........$70.00
**Knight** — 8", #25915 (Wendy), 2000 – 2001, Alice in Wonderland Series...................$75.00
**Kong, the 8th Wonder of the World** — 10" doll, 20" gorilla ........................................$150.00
**Korea** — 8" h.p., BK, #772, 1968 – 1970 (Wendy).........................................................$200.00
    BKW and BK, #772 (Maggie Mixup) .............................................................$225.00
    #522, reintroduced 1988 – 1989 (Maggie Mixup) ............................................$60.00
**Kukla** — 8", #11101, 1995 only, International Folk Tales (Russia) (Wendy)...................$60.00
**Kwanzaa Celebration** — 10" h.p., #10368, 1996 Holiday ..............................................$90.00
**Lady and Her Child** — 21" porcelain, 8" h.p., 1993 .............................................$475.00 set
**Lady Bird** — 8", #438, 1988 – 1989, Storybook Series (Maggie)......................................$55.00
**Ladybug** — 8", #27725, 2001 – 2002, red checked dress, green jacket and hat.............$70.00
**Ladybug, Ladybug** — 8", #40100, 2005, red dress ...........................................................$70.00
**Lady Godiva** — 10", #40835, 2005, brown over dress.....................................................$110.00
**Lady Hamilton** — 20" h.p./vinyl arms, 1957 only, Models Formal Gowns Series,
    picture hat, blue gown with shoulder shawl effect (Cissy)......................$1,300.00 up
    11" h.p., 1957, pink silk gown, picture hat with roses (Cissette) ......................$750.00 up
    21", #2182, 1968, beige lace over pink gown (Jacqueline)...............................$475.00
    12" vinyl, #1338, 1984 – 1986, Portraits of History (Nancy Drew)..................$70.00
**Lady in Red** — 20", #2285, 1958 only, red taffeta (Cissy)......................................$2,900.00 up
    10", #1134, 1990, Portrette (Cissette) ...............................................................$85.00
**Lady in Waiting** — 8" h.p., #487, 1955 only (Wendy Ann).................................$1,700.00 up
**Lady Jane Grey** — 10", #40840, 2005, green court gown.................................................$120.00
**Lady Lee** — 8", #442, 1988 only, Storybook Series............................................................$60.00
**Lady Lovelace** — cloth/felt, 1930s...................................................................................$650.00
**Lady Valentine** — 8", #140503, 1994 only (Wendy Ann)...................................................$65.00
**Lady Windemere** — 21" compo., 1945 – 1946, extra make-up, Portrait Series ............$2,500.00 up
**Lady with the Alligator Purse** — 8", #39830, 2005, red plaid dress.............................$80.00

Lady Windemere, 21", late 30s, early 40s. Composition and all original. A very rare doll.

Close-up of Portrait Lady Windemere.

Laurie, 12", 1967, #1226 (Lissy). Made one year only.

Leslie, 17", #1650, 1968 (Black Polly). Tulle gown, all original.

**Lancelot** — 8", #79529, 1995, 100th Anniversary (copy of 1995 Disney auction doll) ...............$100.00
    8", #13550, 1999, blue and black outfit with sword ..........................................................$75.00
**Lane, Harriet** — 1982 – 1984, third set Presidents' Ladies/First Ladies Series (Mary Ann)....$100.00
**Laos** — 8" straight legs, #525, 1987 – 1988 ...................................................................$55.00
**La Petite Mademoiselle** — 8", #37210, 2003 –2004, toile dress, bear in wagon..............$90.00
**Lapland** — 8" h.p., #537, 1993 ......................................................................................$60.00
**Lassie** — 8", #11102, 1995 only, International Folk Tales (Norway)..............................$60.00
**Latvia** — 8" straight legs, #527, 1987 only ...................................................................$65.00
**Laughing Allegra** — cloth, 1932 ..................................................................................$650.00
**Laura Ingalls Wilder** — 8", #14110, 1998 – 1999, patchwork print outfit .....................$85.00
**Laurie, Little Men** — 8" h.p., BK, #781, #755, 1966 – 1972 (Wendy Ann) ...........$150.00
    Straight legs, #0755, #416, 1973 – 1975, marked "Alex" .........................................$75.00
    Checked pants, marked "Alexander" ....................................................................$70.00
    Straight legs, #416, #410, 1976 – 1992 .................................................................$70.00
    8", #14620, 1996, waistcoat, houndstooth trousers ............................................$60.00
    12" all h.p., 1966 only (Lissy) ..............................................................................$600.00
    12" plastic/vinyl, 1967 – 1988 (Nancy Drew) ......................................................$70.00
**Laurie, Piper** — 14" h.p., 1950 only (Margaret) ...................................................$2,400.00 up
    21" h.p., 1950 only (Margaret) ......................................................................$2,900.00 up
**Lavender Bouquet** — 8", #30895, 2001 – 2002, white, long black gown with lavender flowers............$80.00
**Lavender Sachet** — 8", #33645, 2004 – 2005, lavender dress ....................................$90.00
**Laverne and Shirley Set** — 10", #25755, 2000, with Boo Boo Kitty .......................$175.00
**Lazy Mary** — 7" compo., 1936 – 1938 (Tiny Betty) ..................................................$275.00
**Leaf Fairy** — 8", #28505, 2001 – 2002, rust costume with leaves ...............................$75.00
**Lemonade Girl** — 8", #14130, 1998 – 1999 (Maggie), doll with stand, etc .................$80.00
**Lena (Riverboat Queen)** — (see M.A.D.C. under Special Events/Exclusives)
**Lennox, Mary** — 14" Classic Series, 1993 – 1994 ........................................................$75.00
**Leo** — 8", #21370, 1998, golden lion costume ...........................................................$90.00
**Leopard with Shopping Bag** — 10", Cissette, 1997 – 1998 ...................................$100.00
**Le Petit Boudoir** — 1993 (see Collectors United under Special Events/Exclusives)
**Leslie (black Polly)** — 17" vinyl, 1965 – 1971, in dress........................................$275.00
    1966 – 1971, as bride .........................................................................................$300.00
    1965 – 1971, in formal or ball gown......................................................................$375.00
    In trunk with wardrobe......................................................................................$650.00 up
    1966 – 1971, as ballerina ....................................................................................$400.00
**Let's Ride Total Moves Wendy** — 8", #40435, with scooter ....................................$75.00
**Letty Bridesmaid** — 7" – 8" compo., 1938 – 1940 (Tiny Betty) ................................$350.00
**Lewis, Shari** — 14", 1958 – 1959 .................................................................................$675.00
    21", 1958 – 1959 ..................................................................................................$850.00
**Liberace with Candelabra** — 8", #22080, 1997, velvet cape ..................................$100.00
**Liberty Angel** — 10", #34300, 2002, white gown, feather wings with jewels ............$125.00
**Libra** — 8", #21390, 1998, balanced scale headpiece, purple costume .......................$80.00
**Liesl** — (see Sound of Music)
**Lila Bridesmaid** — 7" – 8" compo., 1938 – 1940 (Tiny Betty) ..................................$325.00
**Lilac Fairy** — 21", 1993, Portrait Ballerina........................................................$300.00
**Lilac Rococo Lady** — 5", #27020, porcelain, 2000, embroidered gown ....................$65.00
**'Lil Christmas Candy** — 8" h.p., #100348, 1994 only, Americana Series................$65.00
**'Lil Christmas Cookie** — 8", #341, 1993 – 1994, Americana Series .........................$65.00
**'Lil Clara and the Nutcracker** — 8", #140480, 1994, Storyland Series ...................$65.00
**Lilibet** — 16" compo., 1938 (Princess Elizabeth)........................................................$750.00 up
**'Lil Miss Genius** — 7", #702 and #400702 vinyl, painted eyes, 1993 – 1995, pink lacy dress .....$40.00
**'Lil Sir Genius** — 7", #701 and #400701 vinyl, painted eyes, 1993, blue jumpsuit.......................$40.00
**Lily** — 10", #1114, 1987 – 1988, red/black (Cissette).................................................$65.00
**Lily of the Valley** — 10", satin gown with lilies of the valley.....................................$110.00

**Lily of the Valley Fairy** — 8", #36885, 2003 – 2004, lace and tulle gown ...................................$90.00
**Lincoln, Mary Todd** — 1982 – 1984, third set Presidents' Ladies/First Ladies
    Series (Louisa) .............................................................................................................$150.00
**Lind, Jenny** — 21" h.p./vinyl arms, #2191, 1969, dressed in all pink, no trim (Jacqueline) ..$1,400.00
    21", #2181, 1970, all pink with lace trim ...........................................................................$1,500.00
    10", #1171, 1969, Portrette, all pink, no trim (Cissette) ...........................................$575.00
    10", #1184, 1970, Portrette, pink with lace trim (Cissette)......................................$650.00
    14" plastic/vinyl, #1491, 1970 only, Portrait Children Series (Mary Ann), pink, lace trim.....$350.00
    10", #27375, 2000, long white gown.............................................................................$100.00
**Lind, Jenny and Listening Cat** — 14", #1470, 1969 – 1971, Portrait Children Series,
    blue dot dress apron and holds plush kitten (must have kitten) (Mary Ann)........................$325.00
**Linus** — 10", #26435, 2001 – 2002, Peanuts Gang, red stripe shirt, blue blanket .........................$30.00
    10", #35895, 2003 – 2004, Trick or Treat, blanket, sign, pumpkin ...............................$45.00
**Lion Tamer** — 8", #306, 1990, Americana Series (Wendy Ann) .............................................$60.00
**Lissy** — 11½" – 12" h.p., 1956 – 1958, jointed knees and elbows
    1956 – 1958, as ballerina ...........................................................................................$475.00
    1956 – 1958, as bride .........................................................................................$475.00 up
    1956 – 1957, as bridesmaid......................................................................................$700.00 up
    1958, dressed in formal.............................................................................................$800.00 up
    1956 – 1958, in street dresses .................................................................................$400.00 up
    1956, in window box with wardrobe ......................................................................$1,600.00
    21", one-piece arm, pink tulle pleated skirt (Cissy) .........................................$1,450.00
    21", #2051, 1966, pink with tiara (Coco) ........................................................$2,200.00
    12" h.p., 1957, jointed elbows and knees, in window box with wardrobe (Lissy) ....$1,500.00 up
    12" h.p., one-piece arms and legs in window box/wardrobe, 1959 – 1966 (Lissy)...$1,000.00 up
    12", Spring Parade, #42050, 2006, blue coat, straw hat.......................................$100.00
    12", Homecoming Lissy, #42045, 2006, blue dress and hat ...............................$100.00
    Classics (see individuals, examples: McGuffey Ana, Scarlett, Cinderella)
**Lithuania** — 8" h.p., #110544, 1994 only (Maggie)...........................................................$55.00
**Little Angel** — 9" latex/vinyl, 1950 – 1957 ..........................................................................$200.00

Shari Lewis, 21", 1958 – 1959, all original.

# *Dating Lissy Dolls*

12" Lissy and Lissy face dolls are all hard plastic with glued-on wigs. Lissy is not marked anywhere on the body. Only the clothes were tagged.

**1956 – 1958:** Lissy had jointed elbows and knees which allowed her to sit. Her feet were slightly arched to wear sandals with hose or white socks. The 1957 – 1958 Lissy Little Women wore black sandals.

**1959 – 1967:** The Lissy face dolls had the Lissy face but have non-jointed arms and legs. The feet were flat.

**1959 – 1967:** Lissy face Little Women were made.

1959: Kelly (Lissy face) was produced in 1959 only, in a variety of outfits.

**1962:** Pamela (Lissy face) had three interchangeable outfits with extra clothing in a gift set. Pamela had a Velcro strip to attach the wigs. Pamelas were made for several years as store specials. Pamela was also made with the later Nancy Drew vinyl head.

**1962:** Lissy face Katie and Tommy were made for FAO Schwarz's 100th Anniversary.

**1963:** McGuffey Ana, Southern Belle, and Scarlett O'Hara were made using the Lissy face doll.

**1965:** Brigitta of the large set of the Sound of Music was made using the Lissy face doll in an Alpine outfit and the rare sailor costume.

**1966:** Lissy face Cinderella was available in "Poor" outfit or in blue satin ball gown. A gift set featured the doll and both outfits.

**1967:** Only year Laurie of Little Women was made using the Lissy face.

**1993:** Nine Lissy face dolls were made for the regular line: Amy, Beth, Jo, Meg, Ballerina, Greta Brinker, Hans Brinker, Hamlet, and Ophelia.

**1993:** Special for Horchow. Pamela Plays Dress Up was a Lissy face doll with wigs, clothes, and a trunk. Lissy face Alice in Wonderland with Jabberwocky was made for Disney, and the Columbian Sailor was made for the U.F.D.C. Luncheon.

Lissy, 12", 1956, #1226. Polished cotton dress with taffeta pinafore and hat.

Little Colonel, 8½", composition, 1935, closed mouth (Betty). Original wrist tag, tagged dress, and straw bonnet. Blue Ribbon winner.

Little Genius, 8", 1957, #205, vinyl body, hard plastic head.

**Little Audrey** — Vinyl, 1954 only ....................................................................................$475.00 up

**Little Betty** — 9" – 11" compo., 1935 – 1943, must be mint.........................................$250.00 – 375.00

**Little Bitsey** — 9" all vinyl nurser, 1967 – 1968 (Sweet Tears)....................................$150.00

**Little Boop Beep** — 10", #28970, 2001 (Betty Boop), pink dress ...............................$110.00

**Little Bo Peep** — (see Bo Peep, Little)

**Little Boy Blue** — 7" compo., 1937 – 1939 (Tiny Betty).............................................$325.00

**Little Butch** — 9" all vinyl nurser, 1967 – 1968 (Sweet Tears) ...................................$150.00

**Little Cherub** — 11" compo., 1945 – 1946 ...............................................................$275.00

    7" all vinyl, 1960 only..........................................................................................$225.00

**Little Christmas Princess** — 8", #10369, 1996 Holiday............................................$70.00

**Little Colonel** — 8½" – 9" compo. (rare size), 1935, closed mouth (Betty) ...............$650.00

    11" – 13" compo. (rare size), closed mouth (Betty)...............................$550.00 – 750.00

    17" compo., closed mouth (Betty) ............................................................$750.00 up

    14", open mouth (Betty) ..........................................................................$650.00 up

    17" – 23", open mouth .........................................................................$700.00 – 950.00

    26" – 27", open mouth ..............................................................................$1,300.00 up

**Little Countess** — 8", #28890, 2001, white lacy dress ...............................................$100.00

**Little Devil** — 8" h.p., Americana Series, 1992 – 1993 only........................................$65.00

**Little Dorrit** — 16" cloth, early 1930s, Dickens character...........................................$700.00

**Little Edwardian** — 8" h.p., SL, SLW, #0200, 1953 – 1955, long dotted navy gown...........$1,000.00 up

**Little Emily** — 16" cloth, early 1930s, Dickens character ...........................................$650.00

**Little Emperor** — (see U.F.D.C. under Special Events/Exclusives)

**Little Gardenia Bridesmaid** — 8", 2001, white dress ...............................................$100.00

**Little Genius** — 12" – 14" compo./cloth, 1935 – 1940, 1942 – 1946 ............................$250.00

    16" – 20" compo./cloth, 1935 – 1937, 1942 – 1946 ....................................$250.00

    24" – 25", 1936 – 1940..............................................................................$275.00

    8" h.p./vinyl, 1956 – 1962, nude (clean condition), good face color....................$100.00

        In cotton play dress ...........................................................................$200.00

        In dressy, lacy outfit with bonnet and/or coat......................................$350.00

        In christening outfit ...........................................................................$375.00

        Sewing or Gift Set, 1950s..................................................................... $850.00 up

    7" vinyl, 1993 – 1995, reintroduced doll with painted eyes ..................................$40.00

        #701 and #400701, 1993 – 1995, dressed in blue jumpsuit ('Lil Sir Genius).....................$40.00

        #702 and #400702, 1993 – 1995, dressed in pink lacy dress ('Lil Miss Genius) ................$40.00

        1993, extra packaged outfits...................................................................$25.00 ea.

    Christening Baby, #400703, 1994 – 1995 .............................................................$45.00

    Super Genius, #400704, 1994 – 1995, dressed in Superman style outfit .................$40.00

    Birthday Party, #400705, 1994 only.....................................................................$45.00

    Genius Elf, #400706, 1994 – 1995, dressed in Christmas outfit ............................$45.00

**Little Genius Toddler** — 8" h.p., 1954 – 1955 (Wendy Ann), caracul hair.........................$275.00 up

**Little Girl with a Curl** — 8", #28965, 2001, pink dress .............................................$75.00

**Little Godey** — 8" h.p., #491, 1953 – 1955 (Wendy Ann) .........................................$1,400.00 up

**Little Granny** — 14" plastic/vinyl, #1431, 1966 only, floral gown (Mary Ann) .........$200.00

    14", #1430, 1966 only, pinstriped gown (also variations) (Mary Ann)....................$225.00

**Little Huggums** — (see Huggums, Little)

**Little Irish Dancer** — 8", #32125, 2000 – 2004, navy decorated dress, bend knees ..................$85.00

**Little Irish Lass** — 8", #42260, 2006, green dress, shillelagh.......................................$75.00

**Little Jack Horner** — 7" compo., 1937 – 1943 (Tiny Betty).......................................$300.00

**Little Jumping Joan** — 8", #487, 1989 – 1990, Storybook Series (Maggie Mixup) .................$55.00

**Little Lady Doll** — 8" h.p., #1050, 1960 only, Gift Set in mint condition (Maggie Mixup)... $850.00 up

    8" doll only, must have correct hairdo and excellent face color............................$300.00

    21" h.p., 1949, has braids and colonial gown, extra make-up, Portrait Series (Wendy Ann) ..$2,400.00

**Little Lord Fauntleroy** — cloth, 1930s.................................................................$750.00

    13" compo., 1936 – 1937 (Wendy Ann)................................................................ $650.00 up

**Little Love Angel** — 8", #28350, 2001 – 2002, pink costume with wings.........................$100.00
    10", #28355, 2001, lavender dress, feather wings ......................................$100.00
**Little Lucy Locket** — 8", #40445, 2005, blue dress, black hat...........................$75.00
**Little Madeline** — 8" h.p., 1953 – 1954 (Wendy Ann) ...................................$750.00 up
**Little Maid** — 8" straight legs, #423, 1987 – 1988, Storybook Series (Wendy Ann)..........$55.00
**Little Men** — 15" h.p., 1950 – 1952 (Margaret and Maggie) ...............................$850.00 up, ea.
**Little Men** — Set with Tommy, Nat, and Stuffy, must be in excellent condition ..... $2,600.00 set
**Little Mermaid** — 10", #1145, 1992 – 1993, Portrette, green/blue outfit (Cissette).........$100.00
    8", #14531, 1995, Hans Christian Andersen Series, long black hair ................................$60.00
    8", #42550, 2006, mermaid body, shell, and pillow...........................................$90.00
**Little Minister** — 8" h.p., #411, 1957 only (Wendy Ann) ......................................$3,200.00 up
**Little Miss** — 8" h.p., #489, 1989 – 1991 only, Storybook Series (Maggie Mixup)............$60.00
**Little Miss Godey** — (see M.A.D.C. under Special Events/Exclusives)
**Little Miss Magnin** — (see I. Magnin under Special Events/Exclusives)
**Little Miss Sunshine** — 8", #35065, 2003 – 2004 (Maggie), yellow print dress ..............$50.00
**Little Nannie Etticoat** — #428, 1986 – 1988, straight legs, Storybook Series.................$55.00
**Little Nell** — 16" cloth, early 1930s, Dickens character .........................................$650.00 up
    14" compo., 1938 – 1940 (Wendy Ann) .................................................................$700.00
**Little Orphan Annie** — 8", #13740, 1999 – 2002, red dress, comes with dog Sandy ...............$70.00
**Little Pearl Bridesmaid** — 8", 2001, white dress, rose crown...................................$85.00
**Little Princess** — 14", #26415, 1995 only, has trunk and wardrobe (Louisa) ...........$200.00
**Little Princess, A** — 8", #14120, 1998 – 1999, pink taffeta, with doll ...........................$80.00
**Little Shaver** — 10" cloth, 1940 – 1944..............................................................$475.00 up
    7" cloth, 1940 – 1944 .........................................................................$550.00
    15" cloth, 1940 – 1944 ........................................................................$650.00
    22" cloth, 1940 – 1944 ........................................................................ $700.00 up
    12" cloth, 1941 – 1943 (see Baby Shaver)
    12" plastic/vinyl, 1963 – 1965, has painted eyes ........................................$225.00
    10", #26820, 2000, cloth, gray/cream, remake of 1940s .........................$55.00
    10", #26825, 2000 – 2001, cloth, pink/cream, remake of 1940s .................$55.00
    6", #26830, 2000 – 2001, cloth, gray/cream, remake of 1940s ..................$55.00
**Little Southern Boy/Girl** — 10" latex/vinyl, 1950 – 1951 ........................................$195.00 ea.
**Little Southern Girl** — 8" h.p., #305, 1953 only (Wendy Ann)..........................$950.00 up

Little Genius, 8", #265, 1957, flannel coat and hat with velvet trim (see page 56).

Little Shaver, 12", 1963 – 1965, plastic/vinyl, painted eyes.

Little Shaver, 7", cloth, 1940 – 1944. Mint and all original.

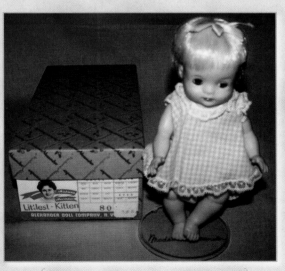

Littlest Kitten, 8", 1963, plastic/vinyl.

Little Women, Meg, 8", BKW, 1956. Print dress and blue pinafore. All original and tagged.

Meg, Little Women, 8", 1989. Pink dress, print apron.

**Littlest Kitten** — 8" vinyl, 1963, nude, clean, good face color .................................................. $125.00 up
    Dressed in lacy dress outfit with bonnet ........................................................................ $275.00 up
    Dressed in christening outfit .................................................................................................. $375.00 up
    In Sewing or Gift Set ............................................................................................................... $750.00 up
    Dressed in play attire ..................................................................................................................$175.00
**Little Thumbkins** — 8", #14532, Hans Christian Andersen Series, lavender/pink/yellow tiers..$60.00
**Little Victoria** — 7½" – 8", #376, 1953 – 1954 only (Wendy Ann).................................... $1,200.00 up
**Little Women** — Meg, Jo, Amy, Beth (Marme in sets when available)
    16" cloth, 1930 – 1936 ...........................................................................................$750.00 up, ea.
    7" compo., 1935 – 1944 (Tiny Betty) .................................................................$375.00 ea.
    9" compo., 1937 – 1940 (Little Betty) .................................................................$350.00 ea.
    13" – 15" compo., 1937 – 1946 (Wendy Ann)...................................................$375.00 ea.
    14" – 15" h.p., 1947 – 1956, plus Marme (Margaret and Maggie) .............. $450.00 ea., $2,200.00 set
    14" – 15" h.p., widespread fingers, ca. 1949 – 1952................................................$575.00 ea.
    14" – 15" h.p., BK, plus Marme (Margaret and Maggie) ........................... $450.00 ea., $2,200.00 set
    14" – 15", Amy with loop curls, must have good face color (Margaret) ...........................$600.00 ea.
    8", Amy with loop curls, 1991, #411......................................................................................$100.00
    7½" – 8" h.p., SL, SLW, all #609, 1955, plus Marme (Wendy Ann) ........... $450.00 ea., $2,300.00 set
    8" h.p., BKW, all #609, all #409, all #481, 1956 – 1959 (Wendy Ann)........ $350.00 ea., $1,600.00 set
    8" BKW, all #381, 1960 – 1963 (Wendy Ann)............................................. $250.00 ea., $1,200.00 set
        #781, 1966 – 1972 ............................................................. $125.00 ea., $650.00 set
        #7811 to #7815, 1973 .............................................................. $75.00 ea., $375.00 set
    8" straight legs, #411 – #415, 1974 – 1986 ............................................ $70.00 ea., $325.00 set
        #405 – #409, 1987 – 1990 ..................................................... $60.00 ea., $275.00 set
        #411 – #415, 1991 – 1992 .................................................... $60.00 ea., $275.00 set
        #14523 – #14528, 1995 ....................................................... $60.00 ea., $275.00 set
        #33375, #33380, #33385, #33386, 2002, Amy, Meg, Jo, Beth...................... $70.00 ea.
        #36120, Marme, 2003, brown plaid dress....................................................$80.00
        #36125, Laurie, 2003, brown three-piece suit .............................................$75.00
        #33375, #33380, #33385, #33386, 2004, Amy, Meg, Jo, Beth.........................$80.00 ea.
        #39070, 2004, Amy's Party Dress, long pink party dress with roses ...............$90.00
    Exclusive for FAO Schwarz (see FAO Schwarz under Special Events/Exclusives)
        #28140 – #28180, 2000 .................................................. $65.00 – $325.00 set
        #40325, #40320, #40335, #40330, 8", 2005 – 2006, Amy, Meg, Jo, Beth ......$75.00 ea.
    10", #14630 – #14633, 1996 ............................................................. $70.00 ea., $325.00 set
    10", #40315, 2005 – 2006, Jo Goes to New York, doll, extra clothes, 5-drawer trunk,
        bed with accessories........................................................................................$300.00
    10", #40265, 2006, Amy in Paris Trunk Set, three outfits, trunk.............................$325.00
    11½" – 12" h.p., jointed elbows and knees, 1957 – 1958 (Lissy) .............. $450.00 ea., $2,300.00 set
    11½" – 12" h.p., one-piece arms and legs, 1959 – 1968 (Lissy) ................. $250.00 ea., $1,300.00 set
    12" plastic/vinyl, 1969 – 1982 (Nancy Drew) ................................................. $65.00 ea., $325.00 set
    12" plastic/vinyl, 1983 – 1989, new outfits (Nancy Drew) .............................. $60.00 ea., $300.00 set
    12", 1989 – 1990 only (see Sears-Roebuck under Special Events/Exclusives)
    12", 1993 only, no Marme (Lissy) .......................................................................$100.00 ea.
    16", 1997 – 2000, plastic/vinyl, Little Women Journal Series (no Marme)........................$85.00 ea.
    16", 1999 – 2000, Marme, #28040, Little Women Journals ......................................$85.00
**Lively Huggums** — 25", knob makes limbs and head move, 1963..............................................$150.00
**Lively Kitten** — 14", 18", 24", 1962 – 1963, knob makes limbs and head move ..........$100.00 – 250.00
**Lively Pussy Cat** — 14", 20", 24", 1966 – 1969, knob makes limbs and head move .....$75.00 – 225.00
**Lola and Lollie Bridesmaid** — 7" compo., 1938 – 1940 (Tiny Betty)........................$350.00 up, ea.
**Lollie Baby** — rubber/compo., 1941 – 1942..........................................................................$100.00
**Lollipop Munchkin** — (see Munchkin Peasant)
**Looby Loo** — 15½" h.p., ca. 1951 – 1954...........................................................................$675.00 up
**Lord Fauntleroy** — 12", 1981 – 1983, Portrait Children (Nancy Drew) ...............................$70.00

**Lord Valentine** — 8", #140502, 1994 only (Wendy Ann) .................................................................$60.00
**Louisa** — (see Sound of Music)
**Love** — (see Collectors United/C. U. under Specials Events/Exclusives), 8", made for public in 1994
    (only differences on C.U. doll are gold locket, pearls set into cap, and gold metal braids
    on slippers, heart box) ...............................................................................................................$70.00
**Love Notes for Grandma** — 8", #36915, 2003 – 2004, red checked dress, notes .........................$75.00
    10", #35890, 2003, trick or treat, mask, bag with candy .............................................................$100.00
**Love to Be Loved** — 8", #40040, 2005 – 2006 (Asian) with panda.................................................$85.00
**Lovey Dove (Dovey)** — 19" vinyl baby, 1958 – 1959, closed mouth, molded or
      rooted hair, few are mistagged .......................................................................................$175.00
    19" h.p./latex, 1950 – 1951.............................................................................................................$175.00
    12" all h.p. toddler, 1948 – 1951 (Precious)..............................................................................$375.00 up
    1951, dressed as "Ringbearer".....................................................................................................$675.00 up
    "Answer Doll" with lever in back to move head ........................................................................$525.00 up
**Lucinda** — 12" plastic/vinyl, 1969 – 1970 (Janie) ...........................................................................$250.00
    14" plastic/vinyl, #1435, #1535, 1971 – 1982 (11-year production), blue gown (Mary Ann)....$65.00
    14", #1535, 1983 – 1986, Classic Series, pink or peach gown (Mary Ann) ...............................$75.00
**Luck of the Irish** — 8", #327, 1992 – 1993 only, Americana Series (Maggie Mixup) ................$65.00
    8", #38595, 2004 – 2005, with 5" leprechaun and pot of gold .....................................................$90.00
**Lucy** — 8" h.p., #488, 1961 only, Americana Series, strip cotton/poke bonnet (Wendy Ann) ..$1,800.00 up
    10", #26420, 2001 – 2004, Peanuts Gang, blue dress, includes backdrop..................................$45.00
    10", #33715, 2002, School Days Lucy (Peanuts), plaid coat, books .........................................$45.00
**Lucy and Ricky** — 9" set, Vitameatavegamin episode.....................................................................$200.00
**Lucy Bride** — 14" h.p., 1949 – 1950 (Margaret)..................................................................... $1,000.00 up
    18" h.p., 1949 – 1950 (Margaret) .............................................................................................. $1,100.00 up
    21" h.p., 1949 – 1950 (Margaret) .............................................................................................. $1,200.00 up
    21", #2155, 1955 (Cissy) pale pink gown, very red hair, heavily painted face.............. $10,000.00 up
    14" compo., 1937 – 1940 (Wendy Ann) ......................................................................................$450.00
    17" compo., 1937 – 1940 (Wendy Ann) ......................................................................................$600.00
    21" compo., 1942 – 1944, Portrait, extra make-up (Wendy Ann) ........................................$2,500.00
**Lucy Gets in Pictures** — 10", #31450, 2001, long pink gown, feather headpiece....................$160.00
**Lucy Locket** — 8" straight legs, #433, 1986 – 1988, Storybook Series.........................................$60.00
    14", #25501, 1995, Ribbons & Bows Series, purple floral skirt (Louisa) .................................$85.00
**Lucy Ricardo** — (see FAO Schwarz under Special Events/Exclusives)
    9", 1950s gingham dress, with bottle and spoon........................................................................$110.00
    21", #50003, 1996 Timeless Legends, black dress with black and white polka dot s ...............$350.00
    10", #14071, Shadow Polka Dot Lucy, 1998 – 1999 ...................................................................$150.00
    10", #15160, 1999 – 2000, Lucy's Italian Movie, peasant outfit, grape vat ...............................$150.00
**Lucy's Rhumba** — 10", #25760, 2001, Be a Pal episode, white dress, ruffles .............................$130.00
**Lullaby Munchkin** — (see Munchkin Peasant)
**Madame (Alexander)** — 21", 1984 only, one-piece skirt in pink .................................................$275.00
    21", 1985 – 1987, pink with overskirt that unsnaps .....................................................................$225.00
    21", 1988 – 1990, blue with full lace overskirt..............................................................................$225.00
    21", #79507, 1995, 100th Anniversary, pink with lace jacket, limited edition of 500 ...............$425.00
    8", 1993 only, introduced mid-year (see Madame Alexander Doll Co.
      under Special Events/Exclusives)
    8" in blue gown (see Doll & Teddy Bear Expo under Special Events/Exclusives)
    8", #79527, 1995, 100th Anniversary .........................................................................................$100.00
**Madame Alexander Celebrates American Design** — 10" h.p. (Cissette), 2000, pink gown. $125.00
**Madame Alexander Collector's Phonograph Album** — 1978, Madame's voice
    reading children's stories ...........................................................................................................$35.00
**M.A.D.C. (Madame Alexander Doll Club)** — (see Special Events/Exclusives)
**Madame Butterfly** — 10" (see Marshall Fields under Special Events/Exclusives)
    8" h.p., #22000, 1997 – 1998, shadow, kimono.........................................................................$85.00

Marme, 8", 1990, Little Women. Print dress.

Madame Alexander, 21", 1985 – 1987 (Jacqueline).

21", #22010, 1997, kimono over silk robe ............................................................................$325.00
**Madame de Pompadour** — 10", #25010, 1999 (Cissette), elaborate taffeta costume ..............$175.00
  10", #45630, 2006, Madame de Pompadour Spring, green dress..................................................$270.00
  10", #42095, 2006, Madame de Pompadour Winter, elaborate ball gown ...........................$270.00
**Madame Doll** — 21" h.p./vinyl arms, 1966 only, pink brocade (Coco) ...........................$2,300.00 up
  14" plastic/vinyl, #1460, #1561, 1967 – 1975, Classic Series (Mary Ann) ...............................$225.00
**Madame Pompadour** — 21" h.p./vinyl arms, #2197, 1970, pink lace overskirt
  (Jacqueline) ....................................................................................................................................$425.00
**Madame's Best** — 8", #38045, 2004, dress and pinafore .........................................................$85.00
**Madame X, John Singer Sargent's** — 10", #25300, 2000, long black gown .......................$100.00
**Madelaine** — 14" compo., 1940 – 1942 (Wendy Ann) .......................................................$650.00 up
  8" h.p., 1954, FAO Schwarz special...................................................................................$800.00 up
**Madelaine du Bain** — 11" compo., closed mouth, 1937 (Wendy Ann) .............................$500.00
  14" compo., 1938 – 1939 (Wendy Ann) ...........................................................................$600.00 up
  17" compo., 1939 – 1941 (Wendy Ann) ...........................................................................$675.00
  21" compo., 1939 – 1941 (Wendy Ann) ...........................................................................$950.00 up
  14" h.p., 1949 – 1951 (Maggie) ........................................................................................$950.00 up
**Madeline** — 17" – 18" h.p./jointed elbows and knees, 1950 – 1953 .................................$800.00 up
  18" h.p., 1961 only, vinyl head, extra jointed body, wears short dress, must be mint ........$750.00 up
  Ball gown 1961 only ..........................................................................................................$800.00 up
**Mad Hatter** — 8", #14510, 1995, Alice in Wonderland Series ...........................................$80.00
  8", #38880, 2004 – 2005, with teapot, cup, and mouse....................................................$85.00
**Madison, Dolly** — 1976 – 1978, first set Presidents' Ladies/First Ladies Series (Martha).......$125.00
**Madonna and Child** — 10", #10600, 1995, Christmas Series .............................................$100.00
  10", #39750, 2005, with baby Jesus and 12" stained glass window .......................................$180.00
**Maggie** — 15" h.p., 1948 – 1954 (Little Women only to 1956)...........................................$550.00
  17" – 18", 1949 – 1953....................................................................................................$650.00 up
  20" – 21", 1948 – 1954....................................................................................................$750.00 up
  22" – 23", 1949 – 1952....................................................................................................$800.00 up
  17" plastic/vinyl, 1972 – 1973 only (Elise) ........................................................................$150.00
**Maggie Elf** — 8", #14585, 1995, Christmas Series ............................................................$65.00
**Maggie Mixup** — 16½" h.p./vinyl, 1960 only (Elise body) ...............................................$400.00
  17" plastic/vinyl, 1961 only.............................................................................................$400.00
  8" h.p., #600, #611, #617, #627, 1960 – 1961, freckles....................................................$450.00
  8" Wendy Ann face, freckles ............................................................................................$650.00 up
  8" h.p., #618, 1961, as angel.............................................................................................$800.00
  8", #610, 1960 – 1961, dressed in overalls and has watering can........................................$800.00
  8", #626, 1960 – 1961, dressed in skater outfit .................................................................$750.00 up
  8", #634, 1960 – 1961, dressed in riding habit ..................................................................$550.00
  8", #593, 1960, dressed in roller skating outfit..................................................................$750.00 up
  8", #598, #597, #596, 1960, wearing dresses or skirts/blouses..........................................$475.00 up
  8", #31000, 1997 – 1998, Post Office commemorative, blue gingham....................................$50.00
**Maggie's Best Memories** — 8", #38905, 2004, plaid dress, scrapbook....................................$80.00
**Maggie Teenager** — 15" – 18" h.p., 1951 – 1953 .....................................................$475.00 – 650.00
  23", 1951 – 1953 ..............................................................................................................$650.00 up
**Maggie Walker** — 15" – 18" h.p., 1949 – 1953 .......................................................$400.00 – 650.00
  20" – 21", 1949 – 1953.....................................................................................................$600.00
  23" – 25", 1951 – 1953 (with Cissy face)...........................................................................$650.00 up
**Magnolia** — 21", #2297, 1977 only, many rows of lace on pink gown .................................$375.00
  21", #2251, 1988 only, yellow gown ................................................................................$275.00
**Maid Marian** — 8" h.p., #492, 1989 – 1991 only, Storybook Series (Wendy Ann) ...................$135.00
  21", 1992 – 1993 only, Portrait Series (Jacqueline)..............................................................$325.00
**Maid of Honor** — 18" compo., 1940 – 1944 (Wendy Ann) .............................................$700.00 up
  14" plastic/vinyl, #1592, 1988 – 1989, Classic Series, blue gown (Mary Ann)........................$90.00

10", #28645, 2001 – 2002, long pink dress, limited to 1,000 ......\$100.00
**Maimey Shadow Wendy** — 8", #38755, blue dress, white sweater, 2004 ......\$95.00
**Majorette** — 14" – 17" compo., 1937 – 1938 (Wendy Ann) ......\$850.00 up
**Majorette, Drum** — 8" h.p., #482, 1955 only (Wendy Ann) ......\$950.00 up
8", #314, 1991 – 1992 only, Americana Series, no baton ......\$55.00
**Making Friends on Sesame Street** — 8", #39086, #39085, 2004 – 2005 with Zoe,
Cookie Monster, and Elmo......\$150.00
**Making New Friends** — 8", #37225, 2003 – 2005, African-American, pink dress,
two dolls, #37226, Caucasian ......\$75.00
**Maleficent** — 10", black costume, staff with crow......\$125.00
**Mali** — 8", #11565, 1996 International, African-American print costume ......\$60.00
**Mama Kitten** — 18", #402, 1963 only, same as "Lively Kitten" but also has cryer box......\$125.00
**Mambo** — 8" h.p., #481, 1955 only (Wendy Ann) ......\$850.00 up
**Mammy** — 8", #402, 1989 only, Jubilee II set (black "round" face)......\$125.00
8" h.p., #635, 1991 – 1992 only, Scarlett Series (black Wendy Ann on Cissette body) ......\$100.00
10" h.p., #15010, 1997 – 1999 (black Wendy Ann)......\$100.00
8", #38825, 2004, checked dress, white apron, hat......\$85.00
8", #38825, 2005, gray dress, white apron, hat ......\$85.00
**Manet** — 21", #2225, 1982 – 1983, light brown with dark brown pinstripes (Jacqueline) ......\$225.00
14", #1571, 1986 – 1987, Fine Arts Series (Mary Ann)......\$65.00
**Marcella Dolls** — 13" – 24" compo., 1936 only, dressed in 1930s fashions......\$650.00 – 900.00 ea.
**March Hare** — cloth/felt, mid-1930s ......\$750.00
8", #42430, rabbit costume, teacup, pocket watch ......\$85.00
**Margaret Ann** — 15", #90100, 1999, blue dress, straw hat, porcelain......\$100.00
**Margaret (O'Brien)** — 14" h.p., nude with excellent color ......\$375.00
18" h.p., nude with excellent color ......\$600.00 up
14" h.p., in tagged Alexander boxed clothes......\$800.00
18" ......\$750.00 up
21" compo., tagged Alexander clothes ......\$1,300.00 up
**Margaret Rose** — (see Princess Margaret Rose)
**Margot** — 10" – 11" h.p., 1961 only, in formals (Cissette) ......\$500.00 up
Street dresses, bathing suit, 1961 only......\$425.00
**Margot Ballerina** — 15" – 18", 1951 – 1953, dressed in various colored outfits
(Margaret and Maggie) ......\$650.00 – 850.00
15" – 18" h.p./vinyl arms, 1955 only (Cissy) ......\$425.00 – 700.00
**Maria** — (see Sound of Music)
**Marie Antoinette** — 21", #2248, 1987 – 1988, multi-floral print with pink front insert
(Jacqueline) ......\$350.00
21" compo., 1944 – 1946, Portrait with extra make-up and in mint condition
(Wendy Ann) ......\$2,300.00 up
10", #40060, 2005, mauve court gown, fan ......\$170.00
**Marilla** — 10", #261-168, 1994, Anne of Green Gables Series......\$80.00
**Marine** — 14" compo., 1943 – 1944 (Wendy Ann as boy) ......\$800.00 up
**Marionettes/Tony Sarg** — 12" – 14" compo., 1934 – 1940 ......\$450.00 up
12" compo., Disney characters ......\$550.00 up
**Marionette Theatre** — by Tony Sarg, 1938......\$800.00 up
**Marley's Ghost** — 8", #18004, 1996, Dickens, silver chains ......\$55.00
**Marme** — (see Little Women)
**Marme Liza** — 21" compo., 1938 and 1946, extra make-up, mint condition (Wendy Ann)..\$3,200.00 up
**Marshall Fields** — (see Special Events/Exclusives)
**Marta** — (see Sound of Music)
**Martin, Mary** — 14" – 17" h.p., 1948 – 1952, wearing jumpsuit (Margaret)......\$700.00 – 1,000.00
14" – 17", 1948 – 1952, dressed in sailor suit or ball gown (Nell from South Pacific) ...\$750.00 – 975.00
**Mary Ann** — 14" plastic/vinyl, 1965, tagged "Mary Ann," in red/white dress......\$225.00

Margot Ballerina, 15", 1954, #1550 (Margaret). All original with hatbox of curlers and comb.

Marionettes, 12", composition, 1934 – 1940, Hansel and Gretel. Tony Sarg.

Mary-Bel, 16", 1959 – 1965, rigid vinyl. "The Doll That Gets Well."

| | |
|---|---|
| Dressed in skirt and sweater | $225.00 |
| Ballerina | $225.00 |
| 14" ballerina, 1973 – 1982 | $125.00 |
| 14", reintroduced #241599, 1994 only | $70.00 |

**Mary-Bel, "The Doll That Gets Well"** — 16" rigid vinyl, 1959 – 1965, doll only ............... $175.00
1959, 1961, 1965, doll in case ...................... $300.00
1960 only, doll in case with wardrobe ...................... $350.00
1965 only, doll with very long straight hair, in case ...................... $325.00
75th Anniversary, Mary-Bel Returns, 1998, #12220 ...................... $125.00

**Mary Cassatt Baby** — 14" cloth/vinyl, 1969 – 1970 ...................... $175.00
20", 1969 – 1970 ...................... $250.00
14" plastic/vinyl child, #1566, 1987 only, Fine Arts Series (Mary Ann) ...................... $75.00

**Mary Ellen** — 31" rigid vinyl, walker, 1954 only ...................... $650.00 up
31" plastic/vinyl arms, 1955 only, non-walker with jointed elbows ...................... $525.00 up

**Mary Ellen Playmate** — 16" plastic/vinyl, 1965 only, Marshall Fields
exclusive (Mary Ann) ...................... $350.00
12", 1965, in case with wigs (Lissy) ...................... $850.00 up
17", 1965, exclusive ...................... $350.00

**Mary Engelbreit Pink Flower Tea Set** — #33850, 2002 ...................... $35.00

**Mary Gray** — 14" plastic/vinyl, #1564, 1988 only, Classic Series (Mary Ann) ...................... $65.00

**Mary Had a Little Lamb** — 8", #14623, 1996 Nursery Rhyme, #11610, 1997 – 1999 ...................... $70.00

**Mary, Joseph, Baby Jesus in Manger** — 8", #19470, 1997 – 2000, Nativity set ...................... $225.00

**Mary Lennox** — 14", #1537, 1993 – 1994, Classic Doll Series ...................... $75.00
8" h.p., #13850, 1998 – 1999 (Secret Garden), plaid jumper, holds key ...................... $75.00

**Mary Louise** — 21" compo., 1938, 1946 – 1947, golden brown/burnt orange (Wendy Ann) . $2,700.00
18" h.p., 1954 only, Me & My Shadow Series, burnt orange and olive green (Cissy) .... $1,500.00 up
8" h.p., #0035D, 1954 only, same as 18", Me & My Shadow Series (Wendy Ann) ........ $1,200.00 up

**Mary, Mary** — 8" h.p., BKW, BK, #751, 1965 – 1972, Storybook Series (Wendy Ann) ........... $125.00
8" h.p., straight legs, #0751, #451, 1973 – 1975, marked "Alex" ...................... $70.00
8" h.p., straight legs, #451, 1976 – 1987, marked "Alexander" (1985 – 1987 white face) .......... $60.00
8", #471, reintroduced 1992 only (Wendy Ann) ...................... $60.00
8", #14556, 1996, floral dress, straw hat, #11600, 1997 – 1999, water can ...................... $60.00
8", #25930, 2000 – 2001 (Maggie), pink print dress, straw hat ...................... $60.00
14", #1569, 1988 – 1991, Classic Series (Mary Ann) ...................... $65.00
14", #241595, reintroduced 1994 only ...................... $85.00
8", #41125, 2006, print dress, straw hat ...................... $80.00

**Mary Mine** — 21" cloth/vinyl, 1977 – 1989 ...................... $125.00
14" cloth/vinyl, 1977 – 1979 ...................... $65.00
14", reintroduced 1989 ...................... $65.00

**Mary Muslin** — 19" cloth, 1951 only, pansy eyes ...................... $500.00
26", 1951 only ...................... $575.00
40", 1951 only ...................... $850.00

**Mary Poppins and the Penguins** — 10", umbrella and four penguins ...................... $135.00

**Mary Poppins Set** — 10" Mary, 5" Michael and Jane, 2004 – 2005, #38380 ...................... $220.00

**Mary, Queen of Scots** — 21", #2252, 1988 – 1989 (Jacqueline) ...................... $325.00

**Mary Rose Bride** — 17" h.p., 1951 only (Margaret) ...................... $850.00 up

**Mary Sunshine, Little** — 15" plastic/vinyl, 1961 (Caroline) ...................... $350.00

**Marzipan Dancer** — 10", #14573, 1995, Nutcracker Series (Cissette) ...................... $75.00

**Matthew** — 8", #26424, 1995, Anne of Green Gables Series ...................... $70.00

**Mayor of Munchkinland** — 8", #37125, 2004 – 2005, Wizard of Oz Series ...................... $80.00

**McElroy, Mary** — 1985 – 1987, fourth set Presidents' Ladies/First Ladies Series
(Mary Ann) ...................... $100.00

**McGuffey Ana** — 16" cloth, 1934 – 1936 ...................... $675.00 up
7" compo., 1935 – 1939 (Tiny Betty) ...................... $350.00

9" compo., 1935 – 1939 (Little Betty) ..............................................................................$375.00

15" compo., 1935 – 1937 (Betty) ....................................................................................$675.00

13" compo., 1938 (Wendy Ann) ......................................................................................$650.00

11", 1937 – 1939, closed mouth ......................................................................................$675.00

11" – 13" compo., 1937 – 1944 (Princess Elizabeth) ...........................................$625.00 – 750.00

14" – 16" compo., 1937 – 1944 (Princess Elizabeth) ...........................................$675.00 – 900.00

17" – 20" compo., 1937 – 1943 (Princess Elizabeth) .........................................$700.00 – 1,200.00

21" – 25" compo., 1937 – 1942 (Princess Elizabeth) .........................................$750.00 – 1,500.00

28" compo., 1937 – 1939 (Princess Elizabeth) ..............................................................$1,400.00

17" compo., 1948 – 1949 (Margaret) ..............................................................................$950.00

14½" compo., 1948, wears coat, hat, and muff ................................................................$950.00

18", 25", 31", 1955 – 1956, flat feet (Cissy) ...............................................$500.00 – 975.00

18" h.p., 1949 – 1950 (Margaret) ....................................................................................$900.00

21" h.p., 1948 – 1950 (Margaret) ..................................................................................$1,400.00

12" h.p. (rare doll), 1963 only (Lissy) ......................................................................$2,500.00 up

8" h.p., #616, 1956 only (Wendy Ann) ..........................................................................$750.00

8" h.p., #788, #388, 1963 – 1965 (was "American Girl" in 1962 – 1963) .........................$300.00

8", #496, 1990 – 1991 only, Storybook Series (Wendy Ann) ..............................................$70.00

8", #36710, 2005 – 2006, red plaid dress ........................................................................$50.00

29" cloth/vinyl, 1952 only (Barbara Jane) ......................................................................$650.00

15" porcelain, #90110, 1999 – 2000 ..............................................................................$150.00

14" plastic/vinyl, #1450, 1968 – 1969, Classic Series, plaid dress/eyelet apron

  (Mary Ann) ..............................................................................................................$90.00

14" plastic/vinyl, #1525, 1977 – 1986, Classic Series, plaid dress (Mary Ann) .........................$75.00

14" plastic/vinyl, #1526, 1987 – 1988, mauve stripe pinafore, Classic Series (Mary Ann) ........$75.00

14", #24622, 1995, red plaid dress, Nostalgia Series (Mary Ann) ......................................$75.00

**McKee, Mary** — 1985 – 1987, fourth set Presidents' Ladies/First Ladies Series (Mary Ann)..$100.00

**McKinley, Ida** — 1988, fifth set Presidents' Ladies/First Ladies Series (Louisa) .....................$100.00

**Meagan** — 14", #29990 or #30000, 1999.........................................................................$80.00

**Me and My Scassi** — (see FAO Schwarz under Special Events/Exclusives)

**Medici, Catherine de** — 21" porcelain, 1990 – 1991...........................................................$375.00

**Meg** — 8", #79530, 100th Anniversary, two-tiered blue gown with white and rose trim

  (also see Little Women) ..........................................................................................$100.00

**Melanie** — 21" compo., 1945 – 1947 (Wendy Ann) .....................................................$2,300.00 up

21" h.p./vinyl arms, 1961, lace bodice and overdress over satin (Cissy)...........................$1,500.00 up

21", #2050, 1966, blue gown with wide lace down sides (Coco) .....................................$2,200.00 up

  #2173, 1967, blue dress with white rickrack around hem ruffle (Jacqueline) .................$575.00

  #2181, 1968, rust brown dress and hat................................................................$650.00

  #2193, 1969, blue gown, white trim, many rows of lace, bonnet....................................$475.00

  #2196, 1970, white gown with red ribbon trim .......................................................$500.00

  #2162, 1971, blue gown, white sequin trim ...........................................................$450.00

  #2195, 1974, white gown, red jacket and bonnet.....................................................$450.00

  #2220, 1979 – 1980, white dotted Swiss gown with pink trim .....................................$300.00

1981, pink nylon with blue ribbon ................................................................................$300.00

#2254, 1989, all orange with lace shawl .......................................................................$275.00

10", #1173, 1968 – 1969, pink multi-tiered skirt (Cissette) .................................................$400.00

10", #1182, 1970, yellow multi-tiered skirt .....................................................................$450.00

8" h.p., #633, 1955 – 1956, green velvet (Wendy Ann)..................................................$1,300.00 up

12", 1987 only, Portrait Children Series, aqua green gown, brown trim (Nancy Drew) ..........$75.00

10", #1101, 1989 only, Jubilee II, royal blue dress with black trim (Cissette) ........................$100.00

8", #627, 1990, Scarlett Series, lavender/lace (Wendy Ann) ...............................................$85.00

8", #628, 1992, peach gown/bonnet with lace..................................................................$80.00

8", #25775, 2000, blue gown and hat trimmed in lace.......................................................$90.00

10", #16555, 1996, Melanie's Sewing Circle, blue dress .....................................................$100.00

Melanie, 21", #2220, 1979 – 1980 (Jacqueline). White dotted Swiss gown with pink ribbon.

10", #42275, 2006, white dress, straw hat, red sash .................................................................$130.00
**Melinda** — 10" h.p., 1968 – 1969, blue gown with white trim (Cissette) .....................................$425.00
    10" h.p., 1970, yellow multi-tiered lace skirt.............................................................................$400.00
    22", #1912, 1962 only, wears white organdy dress with red trim ........................................$350.00
    14", 16", 22" plastic/vinyl, 1962 – 1963, cotton dress .........................................................$275.00
    14", 16", 22" plastic/vinyl, 1963, party dress.........................................................$275.00 – 475.00
    14", 1963 only, as ballerina ..................................................................................................$300.00
**Melody and Friend** — 25" and 8" (see Madame Alexander Doll Co. under Special Events/Exclusives)
**Merlin** — 8", #13560, 1999, red velvet robe and crystal ball .......................................................$75.00
**Merry Angel** — 8" (see Spiegel's under Special Events/Exclusives)
**Metroplex Doll Club** — (see Special Events/Exclusives)
**Mexico** — 7" compo., 1936 (Tiny Betty) .....................................................................................$300.00
    9" compo., 1938 – 1939 (Little Betty) ...................................................................................$325.00
    8" h.p., BKW, #776, 1964 – 1965 (Wendy Ann) .................................................................$125.00
    8" h.p., BK, #776, 1965 – 1972 ...............................................................................................$95.00
    8" straight legs, #0776, 1973 – 1975, marked "ALEX" .........................................................$65.00
    8" straight legs, #576, #550, #520, 1976 – 1991, marked "Alexander" (1985 – 1987) ...............$60.00
    8", #11551, 1995 only (Maggie) ..............................................................................................$55.00
    8", #24100, 1997 – 1998, Mariachi outfit, guitar ..................................................................$70.00
    8", #38915, 2004 – 2005 (Wendy), white blouse, red skirt ...................................................$90.00
**Michael** — 11" plastic/vinyl, 1969 only (Janie) (Peter Pan set), with teddy bear .......................$375.00
    8", #468, 1992 – 1993, Storybook Series (Peter Pan set) (Wendy) ......................................$65.00
**Mickey Mouse and Minnie Mouse** — 8", 31601, 2003 – 2005, mouse ears, yellow shoes.....$100.00
**Midnight** — 21", #2256, 1990, dark blue/black (Jacqueline) ......................................................$300.00
**Midnight Angel** — 8", #33135, 2002 – 2003, black gown and fur wings ...................................$80.00
**Millennium Princess** — 8", #25810, 2000 only, lavender gown ...................................................$100.00
**Miller's Daughter** — 14" with 8" Rumpelstiltskin, #1569, 1992 only, limited to 3,000 sets. $300.00 set
**Milly** — 17" plastic/vinyl, 1968 only (Polly) ...............................................................................$375.00
**Mimi** — 30" h.p. in 1961 only, multi-jointed body, dressed in formal............................................$950.00
    Dressed in romper suit/skirt....................................................................................................$600.00
    Dressed in Tyrolean outfit .......................................................................................................$950.00
    Dressed in slacks, stripe top, straw hat ...................................................................................$675.00
    Dressed in red sweater, plaid skirt..........................................................................................$650.00
    21" h.p./vinyl arms, #2170, 1971, vivid pink cape and trim on white gown (Jacqueline) ......$575.00
    14", #1411, 1983 – 1986, Opera Series (Mary Ann) ..............................................................$65.00
**Minister, Little** — 8" h.p., #411, 1957 only........................................................................$3,200.00 up
**Miracle Santa** — 10", 1996, with street sign ..............................................................................$100.00
**Miracle Wendy** — 8", 1996......................................................................................................$90.00
**Miss America** — 14" compo., 1941 – 1943, holds flag............................................................$850.00 up
**Miss Eliza Doolittle** — 10", #20112, 1996 Classic...................................................................$100.00
**Miss Gulch with Bicycle, Toto** — 10", #13240, 1997 – 2001, Wizard of Oz Series................$125.00
**Miss Leigh** — 8", 1989, made for C.U. Gathering (see Special Events/Exclusives)
**Miss Liberty** — (see M.A.D.C. under Special Events/Exclusives)
**Miss Magnin** — (see I. Magnin under Special Events/Exclusives)
**Miss Mary Mack** — 8", #45205, 2006, black outfit.....................................................................$50.00
**Miss Muffet, Little** — 8" h.p., BK, #752, 1965 – 1972, Storybook Series (Wendy Ann) .........$100.00
    8" straight legs, #0752, #452, 1973 – 1975, marked "Alex".....................................................$75.00
    8" straight legs, #452, 1976 – 1986 (1985 – 1986 white face), marked "Alexander" (Wendy) ..$65.00
    8" straight legs, #452, 1987 – 1988 (Maggie) ........................................................................$60.00
    8", #493, 1993, Storybook Series, #140493, 1994....................................................................$60.00
    8", #13500, 1998 – 2000, comes with bowl, spoon, and pillow .............................................$75.00
    8", #38790, 2004 – 2005 (Wendy), with spider ......................................................................$75.00
**Miss Scarlett** — (see Belk & Leggett under Special Events/Exclusives)
**Miss Smarty** — 8", #17610, 1999 – 2001, Mary Engelbreit (Maggie), pink checked outfit.........$75.00

**Miss Unity** — (see U.F.D.C. under Special Events/Exclusives)

**Miss U.S.A.** — 8" h.p., BK, #728, 1966 – 1968, Americana Series (Wendy Ann) .....................$325.00

**Miss Victory** — 20" compo., 1944 – 1946, magnets in hands (Princess Elizabeth) .............$750.00 up

**Misterioso** — 10" h.p., #20119, 1996 Cirque du Soleil Series......................................................$80.00

**Mistletoe and Holly** — 10", #38555, 2004, long plaid dress, fur collar and hat .......................$125.00

**Mistress Mary** — 7" compo., 1937 – 1941 (Tiny Betty) .............................................................$375.00

**Molly** — 14", #1561, 1988 only, Classic Series (Mary Ann) ........................................................$70.00

**Molly Cottontail** — cloth/felt, 1930s ........................................................................................$650.00

**Mommy & Me** — 14" and 7" compo., 1948 – 1949 (Margaret and Tiny Betty) ..........$1,700.00 up, set

**Mommy & Me at Home** — 8", 10", h.p., #11009, 1997 – 1998, pink floral outfits ...................$125.00

**Mommy & Me On-the-Go** — 8", 10", h.p., #11010, 1997 – 1998...............................................$125.00

**Mommy's Pet** — 14" – 20", 1977 – 1986.........................................................................$50.00 – 175.00

**Mona Lisa, DaVinci's** — 8", h.p., 1997, #22140, green velvet dress ...........................................$75.00

**Monday's Child** — 8", #27770, 2001, pink dress, mirror ...........................................................$80.00

    10", #28860, 2001, print skirt, 10" goose.................................................................................$125.00

**Monet** — 21", #2245, 1984 – 1985, black and white checked gown with red jacket (Jacqueline)....$225.00

**Monique** — (see Disney Annual Showcase of Dolls under Specials Events/Exclusives)

**Monkeying Around** — 8", #38510, 2004 – 2005, comes with knit monkey .................................$85.00

**Monroe, Elizabeth** — 1976 – 1978, first set Presidents' Ladies/First Ladies Series

    (Mary Ann) ................................................................................................................................$125.00

**Moonlight Dance** — 10", #28900, 2001, blue tulle and brocade dress.......................................$125.00

**Moore, Annie** — 8", #39715, 2005, pleated long skirt, white blouse, straw hat, canvas bag........$85.00

**Mop-Top Annie** — 8", #14486, 1995, red dress with white dots...................................................$60.00

**Mop-Top Baby Girl** — 12", #29030, 1998, yarn hair, patchwork dress .......................................$50.00

**Mop-Top Billy** — 8", #140485, 1993 – 2000, Toy Shelf Series ....................................................$60.00

**Mop-Top Wendy** — 8", #140484, 1993 – 2000, Toy Shelf Series .................................................$65.00

**Morisot** — 21", #2236, 1985 – 1986 only, lime green gown with white lace (Jacqueline)...........$250.00

**Morning Glory** — 14", #25505, Ribbons & Bows Series, floral dress with lace (Mary Ann) .....$90.00

    8", #28476, 2001– 2002, lavender dress, bonnet with flowers ...............................................$75.00

**Morocco** — 8" h.p., BK, #762, 1968 – 1970 (Wendy Ann).........................................................$275.00

    8" h.p., #11559, 1996 International, belly dancer...................................................................$60.00

    8", #33510, 2002, Maroon belly dancer, plush camel .............................................................$70.00

**Moss Rose** — 14", #1559, 1991 only, Classic Series (Louisa) .....................................................$75.00

**Mother & Me** — 14" – 15" and 9" compo., 1940 – 1943, mint condition

    (Wendy Ann and Little Betty) ..........................................................................................$1,400.00 up

**Mother Goose** — 8" straight legs, #427, #459, 1986 – 1992, Storybook Series (Wendy Ann) ....$60.00

    8", #11620, 1997 – 1999, with goose and book of rhymes.......................................................$60.00

    10", #28860, 2001 – 2003, print dress with 10" goose .............................................................$125.00

**Mother Gothel and Rapunzel** — 8" and 14", #1539, 1993 – 1994, limited to 3,000 sets...$225.00 set

**Mother Hubbard** — 8", #439, #459, 1988 – 1989, Storyland Series (Wendy) .............................$60.00

**Mother's Day** — 8", #10380 – 10382, 1995, three hair colors, Special Occasions Series.............$60.00

    8", #30265, 2001, pink, white dress with porcelain flower box ................................................$80.00

    8", #45220, 2006, blue print dress, flowers ..............................................................................$55.00

**Mouseketeer** — (see Disney Annual Showcase of Dolls under Special Events/Exclusives)

**Mr. and Mrs. Frankenstein Set** — 8", 1996..........................................................................$250.00

**Mr. Monopoly** — 8", #25260, 2000, tails, top hat, comes with game .........................................$75.00

**Mr. O'Hara** — 8", #638, 1993 only, Scarlett Series (Wendy) ....................................................$150.00

**Mrs. Buck Rabbit** — cloth/felt, mid-1930s.............................................................................$750.00

**Mrs. Claus** — (see mid-year specials for Madame Alexander Co. under Special Events/Exclusives)

    14", #24607, 1995, Christmas Series .......................................................................................$100.00

**Mrs. Darling** — 10", 1993 – 1994, Peter Pan Series (Cissette).................................................$125.00

**Mrs. Fezziwig** — 8", #18005, 1996, Dickens, moiré gown.........................................................$60.00

**Mrs. Malloy's Millinery Shop** — 10" Portrette, #201167, 1995 only, trunk set

    with wardrobe and hats ............................................................................................................$250.00

**Mrs. March Hare** — cloth/felt, mid-1930s .................................................................$700.00
**Mrs. O'Hara** — 8", #638, 1992 – 1993 only, Scarlett Series (Wendy)........................$150.00
**Mrs. Quack-a-Field** — cloth/felt, mid-1930s .........................................................$625.00
**Mrs. Snoopie** — cloth/felt, 1940s .......................................................................$625.00
**Muffin** — 19" cloth, 1966 only ...........................................................................$100.00
   14", 1963 – 1977 .........................................................................................$75.00
   14" cloth, 1965 only, sapphire eyes ...........................................................$75.00
   14" black cloth, 1965 – 1966 only.............................................................$100.00
   14" cloth, 1966 – 1970, cut slanted blue eyes............................................$75.00
   14" cloth, eyes like sideways commas .........................................................$50.00
   12" all vinyl, 1989 – 1990 (Janie) ...............................................................$50.00
   12", 1990 – 1992, in trunk/wardrobe.........................................................$125.00
**Mulan** — 8", #36260, 2003, black wig, kimono, 2¼" Mushu.................................$90.00
**Munchkin Peasant** — 8", #140444, 1993 – 1995, Wizard of Oz Series...................$100.00
   Daisy, 8", #28770, 2001 – 2002, daisies on costume....................................$95.00
   Flower Bonnet, 8", #28775, 2001 – 2002, blue, white costume, ruffled flower-trimmed hat.....$85.00
   Herald, 8", #140445, 1994 – 1995, Wizard of Oz Series.............................$125.00
   Mayor, 8", #140443, 1993 – 1995, Wizard of Oz Series .............................$125.00
   Lollipop, 8", #14513, 1995, Wizard of Oz Series, pink/white striped outfit ...........$125.00
   Lullaby, 8", #14512, 1995, Wizard of Oz Series, white gown ......................$100.00
   Lullaby, 8", #13300, 1999 – 2001, pink dress and hat..................................$90.00
   Flower, 8", #27035, 2000 – 2001, Wizard of Oz Series................................$65.00
   Lullaby Munchkin, 5", #27070, porcelain, 2000 – 2002, pink costume ........$75.00
   Mayor of Munchkinland, 8", #37125, 2003, green coat, hat, watch..............$80.00
**My Boyfriend's Back** — 10", #42820, 2006, gray skirt, black leather jacket............$100.00
**My Doll House** — (see Special Events/Exclusives)
**My Favorite Ballerina** — 14", #25485, 2000, lilac, ballet outfit.............................$75.00
   14", #25480, 2000, pink, ballet outfit.........................................................$75.00
**My First Christmas Tree** — 8", #36875, 2002 – 2004, Spode ornament, green dress .............$85.00
**My First Christmas with Lenox Ornament** — 8", #34215, 2002........................$85.00
**My First Communion** — 8", #38575, 2005, blonde, with rosary, cross necklace....$85.00
   8", #38576, 2005 – 2006, Latin, with rosary, cross necklace........................$85.00
   8", #38577, 2005, brunette, with rosary, cross necklace...............................$85.00
   8", #38578, 2005 – 2006, African American, with rosary, cross necklace .....$85.00
**My Heart Belongs to Grandma** — 8", #36165, 2003 – 2004, pink dress, red heart .............$70.00
**My Heart Belongs to You** — 8", #35440, brunette, #35441, African-American, red dress, 2003.$65.00
**My Little Sweetheart** — (see Child At Heart Shop under Special Events/Exclusives)
**My New Friend Hello Kitty** — 8", #42680 (#42681 Asian), with mini Hello Kitty ...............$80.00
**Mystery Dance 1951** — 14", #26035, 2000, pink lace and tulle long gown...........$175.00
**Nana** — 6" dog with bonnet, #441, 1993 only, Peter Pan Series.........................$50.00
**Nana/Governess** — 8" h.p., #433, 1957 only (Wendy Ann) .............................$2,000.00 up
**Nancy Ann** — 17" – 18" h.p., 1950 only (tagged Nancy Ann).............................$975.00 up
**Nancy Dawson** — 8", #441, 1988 – 1989, Storybook Series (Maggie) ...................$60.00
**Nancy Drew** — 12" plastic/vinyl, 1967 only, Literature Series ...........................$450.00 up
**Nancy Jean** — 8" (see Belk & Leggett under Special Events/Exclusives)
**Nan McDare** — cloth/felt, 1940s .......................................................................$625.00
**Napoleon** — 12", #1330, 1980 – 1986, Portraits of History (Nancy Drew)..............$60.00
**Nashville Goes Country** — 8" (1995, see Collectors United/C.U. under Special Events/Exclusives)
**Nashville Skater** — #1 (see Collectors United/C.U. under Special Events/Exclusives)
   #2 (see Collectors United/C.U. under Special Events/Exclusives)
**Nat (Little Men)** — 15" h.p., 1952 (Maggie) ...................................................$850.00 up
**Natasha** — 21", #2255, 1989 – 1990, brown and paisley brocade (Jacqueline)..........$325.00
**National Velvet** — 12", 1991 only, Romance Series, no riding crop (Nancy Drew)...$80.00
   8", #10409, 1996, riding habit......................................................................$75.00

**Nativity Set** — 1997 – 2000, #19460, Mary, Joseph, Jesus, Angel, Créche,
    Three Wise Men, Shepherd, Drummer.................................................$950.00
    8" #38770, 2004 – 2005, Mary, Joseph, Jesus, Créche, donkey, lambs.............$300.00
**Nature Trail** — 8", #40000, 2005, print dress, wheelbarrow ...........................$75.00
**Neiman-Marcus** — (see Special Events/Exclusives)
**Nelson, Lord** — 12" vinyl, #1336, 1984 – 1986, Portraits of History (Nancy Drew)...................$60.00
**Netherlands Boy** — Formerly "Dutch" (Wendy)
    8" h.p., straight legs, #577, 1974 – 1975, marked "Alex" .........................$65.00
    8" h.p., straight legs, #577, 1976 – 1989, marked "Alexander" (1985 – 1987)............$60.00
**Netherlands Girl** — 8" h.p., #591, #525, 1974 – 1992 (Wendy) ...........................$60.00
**New Arrival** — 19", #30290, 2001, stork with Baby Kisses 8" doll.........................$50.00
**New England Collector Society** — (see Special Events/Exclusives)
**New Year's Eve** — 8", #42825, 2006, black dress, Chaos bear ...........................$120.00
**New Zealand Moon** — 8", #39805, 2005, with kiwi bird ...........................$85.00
**Nicole** — 10", #1139, 1989 – 1990, Portrette, black/off white outfit (Cissette) ............$80.00
**Nigeria** — 8", #11552, 1995 only (also in 1994 Neiman-Marcus trunk set as Kenya)...........$60.00
**Nightingale, Florence** — 14", #1598, 1986 – 1987, Classic Series ...........................$90.00
**Nightmare Before Christmas** — 8", #42645, 2006, black Halloween costume, ghost, and box...$75.00
**Nikki** — 9", #40865, 2005, red plaid skirt, black bag ...........................$30.00
**Nina Ballerina** — 7" compo., 1940 (Tiny Betty) ...........................$350.00
    9" compo., 1939 – 1941 (Little Betty)...........................$375.00
    14" h.p., 1949 – 1951 (Margaret) ........................... $575.00 up
    17", 1949 – 1951 ...........................$550.00
    15" h.p., 1951, came in various colors, all years (Margaret)...........................$725.00
    19", 1949 – 1950 ........................... $850.00 up
    23", 1951 ...........................$850.00
**1950s Cissette Trunk Set** — 10", #38740, 2004, hatbox, trunk, four outfits,
    BK Cissette...........................$300.00
**Nixon, Pat** — (see Presidents' Ladies/First Ladies Series) 14", 1994 only ...............$150.00
**Noah's Ark** — #33155, 2002, includes 8" Noah, wooden ark, pair zebras, camels,
    giraffes, resin doves...........................$250.00
**Nod** — (see Dutch Lullaby)
**Noel** — (see New England Collector Society under Special Events/Exclusives)
**Normandy** — 7" compo., 1935 – 1938 (Tiny Betty) ...........................$300.00
**Northern Lights Angel** — 10", #42240, 2006, white lace, organza...........................$150.00
**Norway** — 8" h.p., BK, #584, 1968 – 1972 (Wendy Ann) ...........................$100.00
    8" straight legs, #584, 1973 – 1975, marked "Alex"...........................$65.00
    8" straight legs, #584, 1976 – 1987, marked "Alexander" (1985 – 1987 white face) ........$60.00
    8" straight legs, #11566, 1996 International Viking costume...........................$65.00
    8", #35880, 2003 – 2004, red sweater, tweed skirt, troll...........................$95.00
**Norwegian** — 7" – 8" compo., 1936 – 1940 (Tiny Betty) ...........................$300.00
    9" compo., 1938 – 1939 (Little Betty) ...........................$325.00
**Now I Lay Me Down to Sleep** — 8", #28380, 2001– 2002, white gown, bonnet.............$80.00
**Nurse** — 16", 1930s, cloth and felt...........................$675.00
    7" compo., 1937, 1941 – 1943 (Tiny Betty) ...........................$375.00
    9" compo., 1939, 1942 – 1943 ...........................$400.00
    13" – 15" compo., 1936 – 1937 (Betty), all white outfit, Dionne nurse, mint in box .......... $950.00 up
    15" compo., 1939, 1943 (Princess Elizabeth) ...........................$550.00
    14" h.p., 1948 (Maggie and Margaret) ...........................$850.00
    8" h.p., #563, 1956 only, all white dress (Wendy Ann) ........................... $600.00 up
    8", #429, 1961, all white dress, comes with baby........................... $650.00 up
    8" BKW, BK, #329, #460, #660, #624, 1962 – 1965, wears striped dress, comes with baby....$525.00
    8", #308, all white uniform, Americana Series, 1991...........................$65.00
    8", #17620, 1999, World War II, brown, white costume with medicine bag ...........$65.00

Nurse, 8", BKW, #563, 1956.
All original.

# Scarlett O'Hara

Scarlett, 21", #2153, 1963 – 1964. In 1965 this outfit was made on a blonde doll and named Godey. Jacqueline doll.

Scarlett Bride, 21", #2258, 1990 – 1993 only (Jacqueline).

#27825, 2002 ................................................................................$85.00
#35955, 2003, Scarlett's Sash for Ashley, red and white dress................................$85.00
#38820, 2004, Matron of the Mansion, long red and white gown.................................$100.00
#38820, 2005 – 2006, Shadow Matron of the Mansion, red dress.................................$100.00
8" h.p., 1990, M.A.D.C. Symposium (see M.A.D.C. under Special Events/Exclusives)
8", 1993, mid-year issue (see Madame Alexander Doll Co. under Special Events/Exclusives)
21" h.p./vinyl arms, #2153, 1963 – 1964 (became "Godey" in 1965 with blonde hair) ... $1,500.00 up
21" h.p./vinyl arms, 1965, #2152, green satin gown (Jacqueline)................................. $1,900.00 up
  #2061, 1966, all white gown, red sash, and roses (also with plain wide lace hem;
    inverted "V" scalloped lace hem  –  allow more for this gown) (Coco) ............ $2,800.00 up
  #2174, 1967, green satin gown with black trim........................................................$675.00
  #2180, 1968, floral print gown with wide white hem................................................ $850.00 up
  #2190, 1969, red gown with white lace................................................................$675.00
  #2180, 1970, green satin, white trim on jacket ....................................................$525.00
  #2292, #2295, #2296, 1975 – 1977, all green satin, white lace at cuffs...........................$375.00
  #2110, 1978, silk floral gown, green parasol, white lace............................................$400.00
  #2240, 1979 – 1985, green velvet ...................................................................$325.00
  #2255, 1986 only, floral gown, green parasol, white lace............................................$325.00
  #2247, 1987 – 1988, layered all over white gown....................................................$350.00
  #2253, 1989, full bangs, all red gown (Birthday Party gown) .........................................$375.00
  #2258, 1990 – 1993 only, Scarlett Bride, Scarlett Series .............................................$375.00
  #2259, 1991 – 1992 only, green on white, three ruffles around skirt ...............................$325.00
21", #162276, 1994 (Jacqueline), tight green gown, three-layered bustle...............................$300.00
  #009, porcelain, 1991 only, green velvet, gold trim...................................................$350.00
  #50001, Scarlett Picnic (Jacqueline), floral gown ...................................................$300.00
  #15020, 1997, rose picnic dress, carries garden basket................................................$300.00
  #15170, Black Mourning Scarlett, 1999 ...............................................................$350.00
  #25765, 2000, Atlanta Stroll Scarlett, striped bodice................................................$375.00
  #28760, 2001, Peachtree Promenade, limited to 500, blue dress, black trim.....................$450.00
  #33475, 2002, Matron of the Mansion Scarlett, red velvet, limited to 250.......................$425.00
  #35950, 2003, Scarlett at the Mill, green plaid skirt, copper overdress, limited to 350 ....$375.00
10" h.p., #1174, 1968 only, lace in bonnet, green satin gown with black braid trim (Cissette).$450.00
  #1174, 1969, green satin gown with white and gold braid ............................................$425.00
  #1181, #1180, 1970 – 1973, green satin gown with gold braid trim..................................$350.00
  #1100, 1989 only, Jubilee II, burgundy and white .....................................................$125.00
  #1102, 1990 – 1991 only, Scarlett Series, floral print gown ..........................................$125.00
  #1105, 1992 only, Scarlett at Ball, all in black........................................................$100.00
  #161105, 1993,  1994, green velvet drapes/gold trim..................................................$125.00
  1994 – 1995, Scarlett in red dress with red boa ......................................................$125.00
  #16107, 1995 only, white sheath with dark blue jacket ...............................................$125.00
  #16654, 1996, mourning dress.........................................................................$100.00
  #16656, 1996, Scarlett and Rhett, limited set........................................................$200.00
  #15000, 1997 –  1998, Hoop-Petti outfit.............................................................$100.00
  #15040, 1997, mourning outfit .......................................................................$100.00
  #14980, 1998 – 2000, blue satin gown, lace shawl (Cissette), Portrait Scarlett ...............$125.00
  #25770, 2000, Sewing Circle Scarlett, white top, lavender skirt......................................$100.00
  #28755, 2001, Atlanta Stroll Scarlett, red/white striped dress .......................................$125.00
  #33470, 2002, Scarlett dressing gown and vanity set, limited to 500................................$325.00
  #36160, 2003, Sweet Sixteen Scarlett, white ruffle dress, red ribbon .............................$125.00
  #38815, 2004, Shanty Town Scarlett O'Hara, black trimmed gown .................................$150.00
  #39980, 2005, Scarlett O'Hara Visits the Mill, white dress, green jacket .........................$125.00
  #33910, 2006, Scarlett's Dinner with Rhett, black evening gown.....................................$150.00
12", 1981 – 1985, green gown with braid trim (Nancy Drew)..........................................$125.00
14" plastic/vinyl, #1495, 1968 only, floral gown (Mary Ann)..........................................$325.00

#1490, #7590, 1969 – 1986 (18-year production), white gown, tagged "Gone
with the Wind" (Mary Ann) ...................................................................$100.00

#1590, #1591, 1987 – 1989, blue or green floral print on beige......................$125.00

#1590, 1990, Scarlett Series, tiny floral print gown........................................$150.00

#1595, 1991 – 1992 only, Scarlett Series, white ruffles, green ribbon (Louisa, Jennifer)..$125.00

#16551, 1995 (see Peachtree Lane)

#1500, 1986 only, Jubilee #1, all green velvet (Mary Ann) ...........................$150.00

#1300, 1989 only, Jubilee #2, green floral print gown (Mary Ann) ................$125.00

16", #46865, 2006, Scarlett Picnic, print dress, extra outfit.........................$250.00

**Scheherazade** — 8", #42545, 2006, red, gold harem costume .........................$65.00

**School Girl** — 7" compo., 1936 – 1943 (Tiny Betty) .....................................$325.00

**Scorpio** — 8", #21400, 1998, scorpion costume, golden spear..........................$90.00

**Scotch** — 7" compo., 1936 – 1939 (Tiny Betty)...........................................$325.00

9" compo., 1939 – 1940 (Little Betty) .........................................................$350.00

10" h.p., 1962 – 1963 (Cissette).......................................................... $900.00 up

**Scots Lass** — 8" h.p., BKW, #396, 1963 only (Maggie Mixup, Wendy Ann)............$175.00

**Scottish (Scotland)** — 8" h.p., BKW, #796, 1964 – 1965 (Wendy Ann)................$150.00

8" h.p., BK, #796, 1966 – 1972 ....................................................................$100.00

8" straight legs, #0796 – 596, 1973 – 1975, marked "ALEX"..........................$75.00

8" straight legs, #596, #529, 1976 – 1993 (1985 – 1987 white face), marked "Alexander" ........$65.00

8" re-dressed, Scottish outfit with English guard hat, 1994............................$60.00

8", #28550, 2001 – 2002, Scottish costume, blue plaid, bagpipes ...................$70.00

**Scouting** — 8", #317, 1991 – 1992 only, Americana Series..............................$125.00

**Scrooge** — 14", #18401, 1996, Dickens (Mary Ann)......................................$85.00

**Sears-Roebuck** — (see Special Events/Exclusives)

**Season's Greetings Maggie** —8", #26840, 2001, green smocked dress.......................$75.00

**Season's Greetings Wendy** — 8", #26845, 2001, red smocked dress ......................$75.00

**Secret Garden, My** — (see FAO Schwarz under Special Events/Exclusives)

14", #24616, 1995, trunk and wardrobe (Louisa) ........................................$225.00

**See No Evil, Hear No Evil, Speak No Evil** — 8", #39835, 2005 – 2006, with bear, dog,
and cat ........................................................................................................$105.00

**Sense and Sensibility** — 10", #25340, 2000, long white gown with embroidery .....................$100.00

**September** — 14", #1527, 1989 only, Classic Series (Mary Ann) .........................$85.00

10", #1152, 1992, Portrette, royal blue/gold flapper......................................$100.00

**Serenade** — 10", #36170, 2003, long ball gown with triangle black sequin design on skirt ........$125.00

**Sesame Street, 1,2,3** — Trunk Set, 2004 – 2005, #39082, African-American ...........................$225.00

**Sesame Street, 1,2,3** — Trunk Set, 2004 – 2005, #39080, 8", Big Bird, etc.............................$225.00

**Setting Sail** — 8", #37960, Asian, #37961, Caucasian, 2004 – 2005, dress with stars..................$85.00

**Seven Dwarfs** — Compo., 1937 only, must be mint .........................................$550.00 ea.

**Seventies Strut Shadow Cissette** — 10", #38760, Caucasian, 2004 #38761, African-American,
black outfit...............................................................................................$225.00 ea.

**Seventy-Fifth Anniversary Wendy** — 8", #22420, 1998, pink outfit....................$100.00

**Shadow Madame Pompadour Spring** — 10", #45630, 2006, green dress.............................$270.00

**Shadow Madame Pompadour Winter** — 10", #42095, 2006, long gown..............................$290.00

**Shadow of Madame** — (see Doll & Teddy Bear Expo under Special Events/Exclusives)

**Shadow Stepmother** — 8", #14638, 1996 ...................................................$125.00

**Shaharazad** — 10", #1144, 1992 – 1993 only, Portrette (Cissette) ....................$80.00

8", #33520, 2002, navy blue suit, dim sum...................................................$80.00

**Shanghai** — 8", #33520, 2003, navy blue silk outfit, dim sum.............................$80.00

**Share Your Happiness** — 8", #40825, 2005, pink coat, hat ................................$85.00

**Shea Elf** — (see Collectors United/C.U. under Special Events/Exclusives)

**Sheer Charm** — 8", #40805, 2005, Asian, plaid dress.......................................$50.00

**Sheer Delight** — 8", #40815, 2005 – 2006, African American, print dress ..............$50.00

**Sheer Joy** — 8", #40800, 2005 – 2006, (Wendy), print dress, straw hat ................$50.00

Scarlett, composition, made in the 1930s and 1940s. Original dress and hat (see page 79).

Scarlett, 8", #625, tiny flower print dress.

**Sheer Warmth** —8", #40820, 2005 – 2006, Latin, print dress........................................................$50.00
**Shepherd and Drummer Boy Set** — 8", #19490, 1997 – 2000, Nativity Set..........................$200.00
**Shepherdess with Lamb** — 8", #20010, 1999 – 2000, red robe, headdress.......................$80.00
**She Sells Seashells** — 8", #14629, 1996, Nursery Rhymes Series (Maggie) ..............................$70.00
   8", #42470, 2006, sundress, umbrella, basket of shells..................................................$85.00
**Shimmering Dance** — 8", #30645, 2001 – 2003, ballerina, blonde..................................$70.00
**Shimmering 1930s Catherine** — 16", porcelain, long white gown...........................................$150.00
**Shirley's Doll House** — (see Special Events/Exclusives)
**Shoemaker's Elf** — 8", #33665, 2002 – 2003, purple costume, 8" shoe.............................$100.00
**Shoemaker's Elf Boy** — 8", #14637, 1996.......................................................................$65.00
**Shoemaker's Elf Girl** — 8", #14636, 1996......................................................................$65.00
**Sicily** — 8", #513, 1989 – 1990 (Wendy Ann) ................................................................$65.00
**Signature Red Hat Style Cissette** — 10", #42180, 2006, purple dress .................................$130.00
**Signature Wendy** — 8", #38865, 2004 – 2005, pink print dress, stationery ............................$90.00
**Signs of Spring** — 8", #45340, 2006, red print dress, straw hat......................................$100.00
**Silver Star** — 8", #28875, 2001, silver satin and tulle ...................................................$75.00
**Simone** — 21" h.p./vinyl arms, 1968 only, in trunk (Jacqueline)............................. $2,150.00 up
**Simply Sweet Flower Girl** — 8", #32985, pink dress, rose bouquet, 2002 .........................$75.00
**Sing a Song of Sixpence** — 8", #42460, 2006, pink dress, pie with birds .................................$70.00
**Sir Lapin Hare** — cloth/felt, 1930s ...............................................................................$700.00
**Sister Brenda** — (see FAO Schwarz under Special Events/Exclusives)
**Sitting Pretty** — 18" foam body, 1965 only, rare.............................................................$375.00
**60's Go-Go Beach Party** — 8", #42030, 2006, red dog.....................................................$50.00
**Skater's Waltz** — 15" – 18", 1955 – 1956 (Cissy) ....................................................... $650.00 up
**Skating Doll** — 16", 1947 – 1950 (untagged "Sonja Henie" after contract expired) .................$700.00
**Sky's the Limit Fairy** — 8", #40770, 2005, red-trimmed fairy outfit ....................................$90.00
**Sledding Wendy** — 8", #36015, 2003 – 2004, pink jacket, blue pants, sled..........................$75.00
**Sleeping Beauty** — 7" – 9" compo., 1941 – 1944 (Tiny Betty and Little Betty)..........$325.00 – 450.00
   15" – 16" compo., 1938 – 1940 (Princess Elizabeth) .................................................$475.00
   18" – 21" compo., 1941 – 1944 (Wendy Ann).............................................$650.00 – 950.00
   10", #1141, 1991 – 1992 only, Portrette, blue/white gown.........................................$85.00
   21", #2195, 1959 only year this head used, authorized by Disney, blue satin brocade,
      net cape, gold tiara...................................................................... $850.00 up
   16", #1895, same head as 21" on Elise body, authorized by Disney ...........................$650.00
   10" h.p., 1959 only, authorized by Disney, blue gown (Cissette) .............................$350.00
   14" plastic/vinyl, #1495, #1595, 1971 – 1985 (14-year production), Classic Series,
      gold gown (Mary Ann)...................................................................$80.00
   14", #1596, 1986 – 1990, Classic Series, blue gown (Mary Ann)...............................$85.00
   14", #87010, 1996, pink and gold ball gown (Mary Ann).........................................$85.00
   8", #14543, 1995, Brothers Grimm Series, blue with silver crown..............................$65.00
   8", #13600, 1997 – 2000, blue satin gown, spinning wheel ......................................$65.00
   16", #25325, 2000, gold and lilac long ballet costume ............................................$150.00
   8", #30680, 2001 – 2005, blue gown, lace and rose trim ........................................$80.00
   16", #25325, 2001, lilac ballerina costume ........................................................$150.00
   10", #36570, 2004, pink satin ball gown, three 2" fairy figures..................................$150.00
   9", #37820, 2005 – 2006, vinyl, pink satin dress .................................................$35.00
   8", #42435, 2006, long blue dress ..................................................................$85.00
**Sleeping Beauty's Prince** — 8", #13650, 1999 – 2000 (Wendy), bend knees, purple costume..$85.00
**Sleigh Riding Wendy** — 8", #35650, 2003 – 2004, plaid vintage costume, sleigh, plush horse ........$160.00
**Slumbermate** — 11" – 12" cloth/compo., 1940s................................................... $250.00 up
   21" compo./cloth, 1940s ......................................................................... $475.00 up
   13" vinyl/cloth, 1951 only ....................................................................... $250.00 up
**Slumber Party Chloe** — 14", #30065, 2001, pajamas, sleeping bag...................................$60.00
**Smarty** — 12" plastic/vinyl, #1160, #1136, 1962 – 1963 ..................................................$275.00

1963 only, "Smarty & Baby"................................................................$350.00

1963 only, with boy "Artie" in case with wardrobe.............................$950.00

**Smee** — 8", #442, 1993, #140442, 1994, Storybook Series (Peter Pan), wears glasses.................$60.00

**Smiley** — 20" cloth/vinyl, 1971 only (Happy).....................................$250.00

**Smokey Tail** — cloth/felt, 1930s........................................................$650.00

**Snap, Crackle & Pop Set** — 8", #12120, 1998 – 1999, Rice Krispies Dolls set.......................$200.00

**Snips and Snails** — 8", #31330, 2000 – 2002, sweater, jeans, dog.............$70.00

**Snoopy Beagle Scout** — 8" dog, #38810, 2004, with Woodstock ............$70.00

**Snowboarding in Aspen** — 8", #45475, 2006, snowboard .....................$90.00

**Snowflake** — 10", #1167, 1993 only, Portrette, ballerina dressed in white/gold outfit (Cissette).$75.00

**Snowflake Symposium** — (see M.A.D.C. under Special Events/Exclusives)

**Snow Queen** — 10", #1130, 1991 – 1992 only, Portrette, silver/white gown (Cisette) ...............$100.00

8", #14548, Hans Christian Andersen Series, white with gold trim ............................$70.00

8", #32150, 2000 – 2002, white gown, fur-trimmed robe .........................................$85.00

**Snow White** — 13" compo., 1937 – 1939, painted eyes (Princess Elizabeth) ...........................$475.00

12" compo., 1939 – 1940 (Princess Elizabeth) .....................................$450.00

13" compo., 1939 – 1940, sleep eyes (Princess Elizabeth) ........................$475.00

16" compo., 1939 – 1942 (Princess Elizabeth) .....................................$550.00

18" compo., 1939 – 1940 (Princess Elizabeth) .....................................$750.00

14" – 15" h.p., 1952 only (Margaret) ................................................$750.00

18" – 23", 1952 only....................................................$800.00 – 1,200.00

21" h.p., rare (Margaret) ...................................................$1,200.00 up

14", #1455, 1967 – 1977, Disney crest colors (Mary Ann) .......................$300.00

8" h.p., 1972 – 1977, Disney crest colors (Wendy) ................................$325.00

8", #495, 1990 – 1992 only, Storyland Series (Wendy)...........................$80.00

8", #14545, 1995, Brothers Grimm Series, crest colors but with red bodice, #13800, 1997 – 2005 .. $80.00

12", 1990 (see Disney Annual Showcase of Dolls under Special Events/Exclusives)

14" plastic/vinyl, #1455, #1555, 1970 – 1985 (15-year production), Classic Series,

    white gown (Mary Ann) ..........................................................$100.00

    #1556, #1557, 1986 – 1992, ecru & gold gown, red cape (Mary Ann, Louisa) .................$100.00

14", #14300, 1995, crest colors but red bodice (Louisa) ...........................$125.00

14", #87013, 1996, Snow White's Trunk Set (Mary Ann) .......................$125.00

10", Disney crest colors (see Disney Annual Showcase of Dolls under Special Events/Exclusives)

14", #28615, 2001, white gown, red cape.............................................$125.00

10", #35520, 2002 – 2004 (Cissette), Disney colors, gift set with seven 5" vinyl dwarfs .........$300.00

9", #37815, 2004 – 2006, vinyl, Disney colors .....................................$35.00

8", #42445, 2006, yellow skirt, red striped top .....................................$65.00

**Snow White's Prince** — 8", #14639, 1996.......................................$65.00

**Snow White Wedding** — 8", #30460, 2001 – 2002, white gown, red cape, flower coat.............$90.00

**So Big** — 22" cloth/vinyl, 1968 – 1975, painted eyes.............................$225.00

18", #30310, 2001, cloth, Mary Engelbreit .........................................$45.00

**Soccer Boy** — 8", #16350, sports outfit with soccer ball, 1997.................$60.00

**Soccer Girl** — 8", #16341, sports outfit with soccer ball, 1997 – 1998........................$60.00

**Sock Hop 1950** — 8", #17780, 1999, poodle skirt ...............................$85.00

**Soda Shop Coca-Cola** — 8", #38695, 2004 – 2005, with glass and chair...................$85.00

**Soldier** — 14" compo., 1943 – 1944 (Wendy Ann) ...............................$375.00

17" compo., 1942 – 1945 (Wendy Ann) ............................................$850.00

**So Lite Baby or Toddler** — 20" cloth, 1930 – 1940s.........................$375.00 up

**Sophie** — 10", #28301, 2002 – 2003, green checked dress, sweater ...............$40.00

10", #35815, 2003, Fun Loving, blue sweater.......................................$40.00

**Sorcerer's Apprentice** — 8", #42640, 2006, red cape, broom.....................$85.00

**Sound of Music** —

Large set, 1965 – 1970

    14", #1404, Louisa (Mary Ann) .............................................$275.00

# Sound of Music

12", #1107 Friedrich (Janie or Smarty) ........................................................$275.00
14", #1403 Brigitta (Mary Ann)........................................................$225.00
14", #1405 Liesl (Mary Ann)........................................................$275.00
12" Marta, 12" Gretl (Smarty or Janie) ........................................$225.00
17", #1706 Maria (Elise or Polly) ........................................$300.00
Full set of seven dolls........................................................$1,100.00
Small set, 1971 – 1973
12" Maria (Nancy Drew) ........................................................$325.00
8", #801 Gretl (Wendy Ann) ........................................................$175.00
8", #802 Marta, #807 Friedrich (Wendy Ann) ........................$225.00
10" Brigitta (Cissette)........................................................$200.00
10" Liesl (Cissette)........................................................$250.00
10" Louisa (Cissette)........................................................$275.00
Set of seven dolls........................................................$1,200.00
Dressed in sailor suits and tagged, dates unknown
17" Maria (Elise or Polly) ........................................................$500.00
14" Louisa (Mary Ann) ........................................................$500.00
10" Friedrich (Smarty) ........................................................$375.00
14" Brigitta (Mary Ann) ........................................................$375.00
14" Liesl (Mary Ann) ........................................................$375.00
10" Gretl (Smarty) ........................................................$350.00
10" Marta (Smarty) ........................................................$375.00
Set of seven dolls........................................................ $2,700.00 up
12", 1965, Brigitta in sailor suit (Lissy) ........................ $800.00 up
12", 1965, Brigitta in Alpine outfit (Lissy) ........................$650.00
All in same outfits: red skirt, white attached blouse, black vest that ties in front with gold cord,
very rare ........................................$500.00 – 800.00 ea.
Reintroduced 1992 – 1993
8", #390, #391, 1992 – 1993 only, Gretl and Kurt (boy in sailor suit)..............$125.00
8", #390, #392, 1992 – 1994, Brigitta ........................................................$100.00
8", #394, 1993 only, Friedrich dressed in green/white playsuit ........................$125.00
8", #393, 1993 only, Marta in sailor dress ........................................................$200.00
10", 1992 – 1993 only, Maria (Cissette)........................................................$125.00
10", 1993 only, Liesl........................................................$125.00
12", 1992 only, Maria Bride (Nancy Drew) ........................................................$125.00
10", Maria at Abbey, dressed in nun's outfit (Cissette), 1993 only ........................$125.00
Reintroduced 1998
8", #14060, Gretl Von Trapp (Wendy), green/gray sailor suit........................$100.00
8", #14050, Marta Von Trapp (Maggie), sailor suit ........................................$100.00
9", #14040, Brigitta Von Trapp (Wendy), sailor outfit........................................$100.00
10", #14030, Captain Von Trapp (Cissette), gray Tyrolean suit ........................$125.00
10", #13890, Maria at the Abbey (Cissette), navy dress, guitar ........................$125.00
10", #13870, Mother Superior (Cissette), black and white nun habit ........................$125.00
10", #13880, Maria Travel Ensemble (Cissette), pleated skirt, bolero........................$125.00
9", #14020, Friedrich Von Trapp (Maggie), blue and gray sailor suit ........................$100.00
10", #14160, Louisa Von Trapp (Wendy), blue/gray pleated sailor suit ........................$100.00
10", #14090, Kurt Von Trapp (Wendy), sailor uniform ........................................$100.00
10", #14170, Liesl Von Trapp (Cissette), blue and gray sailor outfit........................$100.00

**South American —** 7" compo., 1938 – 1943 (Tiny Betty)........................................$300.00
9" compo., 1939 – 1941 (Little Betty) ........................................................$325.00
**Southern Belle —** 10", #25985, 2000, long white gown with lace, limited to 2,000........$150.00
**Southern Belle or Girl —** 8" h.p., SLNW, 1953, white dress, straw hat with pink silk roses ..$850.00 up
8" h.p., #370, 1954 (Wendy Ann)........................................................ $1,000.00 up
8" h.p., #437, #410, 1956, pink or blue/white striped gown (Wendy Ann)........................ $1,100.00 up

84

8" h.p., #385, 1963 only (Wendy Ann) ...................................................$650.00

12" h.p., 1963 only (Lissy)........................................................... $1,600.00 up

21" h.p./vinyl arms, #2155, 1965, blue gown with wide pleated hem (Jacqueline) .............$1,600.00

21", #2170, 1967, white gown with green ribbon trim .......................................$450.00

10" h.p., #1170, 1968, white gown with green ribbon through three rows of lace (Cissette) ..$450.00

1969, white gown with four rows of lace, pink sash (Cissette) ................................$450.00

#1185, 1970, white gown with red ribbon sash (Cissette) ...................................$350.00

#1185 (#1184 in 1973), 1971 – 1973, white gown with green ribbon sash ...............$300.00

10" (see My Doll House under Special Events/Exclusives)

**Southern Flower Girl** — 8", #25980, 2000, long pink gown, basket, limited to 2,800 ...............$90.00

**Southern Girl** — 11" – 14" compo., 1940 – 1943 (Wendy Ann) ..................................$350.00 – 650.00

17" – 21" compo., 1940 – 1943 (Wendy Ann).............................................$700.00 – 950.00

**Southern Miss** — 8", #45275, 2006, pink organdy, straw hat ........................................$100.00

**Southern Symposium** — (see M.A.D.C. under Special Events/Exclusives)

**Spanish** — 7" – 8" compo., 1935 – 1939 (Tiny Betty) ..................................................$300.00

9" compo., 1936 – 1940 (Litte Betty) ...................................................................$325.00

**Spanish Boy** — 8" h.p., BK and BKW, #779, 1964 – 1968 (Wendy Ann)........................$275.00

**Spanish Girl** — 8" h.p., BKW, #795, #395, 1962 – 1965, three-tiered skirt (Wendy Ann) ........$125.00

8" h.p., BK, #795, 1966 – 1972, three-tiered skirt....................................................$90.00

8" straight legs, #0795, #595, 1973 – 1975, three-tiered skirt, marked "ALEX" ......................$60.00

8" straight legs, #595, 1976 – 1982, three-tiered skirt, marked "Alexander" ..............................$60.00

8" straight legs, #595, 1983 – 1985, two-tiered skirt ..................................................$55.00

8" straight legs, #541, 1986 – 1990, white with red polka dots (1986 – 1987 white face) ..........$55.00

8" straight legs, #541, 1990 – 1992, all red tiered skirt.................................................$55.00

8" h.p., #110545, 1994 – 1995, red, two-tiered polka dot gown.........................................$55.00

8" h.p., #24160, 1999 – 2000, red rose and black gown ...............................................$75.00

8", #35605, 2003 – 2004, red satin outfit, plush ball..................................................$90.00

**Spanish Matador** — 8", #530, 1992 – 1993 only (Wendy) .......................................$65.00

**Sparkle Fairy** — 8", #38615, 2004 – 2005, pink dress with wings ....................................$85.00

**Sparkling Sapphire** — 10", #32080, 2000 – 2002, long red and blue gown .............................$175.00

**Special Girl** — 23" – 24" cloth/comp., 1942 – 1946 ....................................................$500.00

**Speedy Service** — 8", #42105, 2006, red striped outfit, tray with food........................$85.00

**Spiegel's** — (see Special Events/Exclusives)

**Spring** — 14", 1993, Changing Seasons, doll and four outfits .......................................$100.00

5", #25850, 2000, porcelain, pink dress, straw hat ..................................................$60.00

**Spring Angel** — 10", #28370, 2001 – 2002, long gown, feather wings...............................$100.00

**Spring Bouquet** — 8", #30890, 2001 – 2003,  white ballet outfit, green top, blonde ...................$65.00

**Spring Break** — (see Metroplex Doll Club under Special Events/Exclusives)

**Spring Chick-A-Dee** — 8", #42265, 2006, yellow dress, baby chick.................................$85.00

**Spring Garden Flower Girl** — 8", #34390, 2002 – 2003, flower-trimmed dress .......................$85.00

**Spring Parade Lissy** — 12", #42050, 2006, coat, straw hat.........................................$100.00

**Spring Promenade** — 10", #27810, 2001, long white dress, straw hat ..............................$125.00

**Spring Splendor** — 8", #42830, 2006, pink dress, Chaos bear......................................$80.00

**Springtime** — (see M.A.D.C. under Special Events/Exclusives)

**Stardust Greetings Angel** — 10", #39930, 2005, red angel costume ................................$100.00

**Starlight Angel** — 10", #10790, 1999 – 2000 (Cissette), star-accented gown...........................$125.00

**Starlight, Starbright** — 8", #43020, 2006, pink dress with stars....................................$50.00

**Stars and Stripes** — 10", #33740, 2002, red striped overskirt .....................................$125.00

**Stars and Stripes Forever** — 8", #40625, 2005, with flag garland...................................$60.00

**Stepmother** — 8", 1997, #13820, velvet cape, satin dress .........................................$80.00

**Stick Piggy** — 12", 1997, #10030, sailor outfit .....................................................$90.00

**Stilts** — 8", #320, 1992 – 1993 only, clown on stilts...............................................$80.00

**Story Princess** — 15" – 18" h.p., 1954 – 1956 (Margaret, Cissy, Binnie) ..................$600.00 – 950.00

8" h.p., #892, 1956 only (Wendy Ann) ...................................................... $1,300.00 up

**Straw Piggy** — 12", 1997, #10020, plaid pants, straw hat ..............................................................$95.00
**Strolling Through London** — 8", #45450, 2006, Maggie, plush dog..........................................$85.00
**Stuffy (Boy)** — h.p., 1952 – 1953 (Margaret) ......................................................................$850.00 up
**Suellen** — 14" – 17" compo., 1937 – 1938 (Wendy Ann)..................................................$975.00 up
    12", 1990 only, yellow multi-tiered skirt, Scarlett Series (Nancy Drew)...................................$80.00
    8" pink bodice, floral skirt, apron, #160645, 1994 – 1995....................................................$75.00
    Special for Jean's Doll Shop (see Jean's Doll Shop under Special Events/Exclusives)
**Suellen O'Hara** — 8", #15200, 1999 ...............................................................................$100.00
**Suffragette 1910** — 10", #17730, 1999..............................................................................$100.00
**Sugar and Spice** — 8", #13530, 1998 – 1999, pink and white lace dress ...............................$85.00
    8", #32145, 2000 – 2002,  three rows of ribbon on skirt, lollipop ...........................................$60.00
**Sugar Darlin'** — 14" – 18" cloth/vinyl, 1964 only ...........................................$65.00 – 125.00
    24", 1964 only ....................................................................................................................$150.00
    Lively, 14", 18", 24", 1964 only, knob makes head and limbs move..........................$125.00 – 250.00
**Sugar Plum Fairy** — 10", #1147, 1992 – 1993 only, Portrette, lavender ballerina .....................$80.00
    8" (Wendy), 1999 – 2000, #12640, pink satin and tulle ........................................................$75.00
    16", #80780, 2000, long ballet costume from *The Nutcracker* ...........................................$150.00
**Sugar Tears** — 12" vinyl baby, 1964 only (Honeybea) ..........................................................$100.00
**Sulky Sue** — 8", #445, 1988 – 1990, marked "Alexander" (Wendy Ann) ...................................$60.00
**Summer** — 14", 1993, Changing Seasons, doll and four outfits .................................................$90.00
    5", #25855, 2000, porcelain, blue dress, straw hat .................................................................$60.00
**Summer Angel** — 8", #27640, 2001 – 2002, multicolored tulle, blonde.................................$85.00
**Summer Day Dreaming** — 8", #42835, 2006, with Chaos bear .................................................$90.00
**Summer Garden Vintage** — 8", #28915, 2002 – 2003, with basket of flowers, blue striped pinafore ..$75.00
**Summer of Cissette** — 10", #45230, 2006, navy dot dress, red hat .......................................$125.00
**Summer Sailing** — 8", #40640, 2005, white dress..............................................................$70.00
**Summer Smiles Fairy** — 8", #40765, 2005,  pink and green costume .......................................$90.00
**Summers Past** — 8", #40595, 2005, print dress ..................................................................$85.00
**Summer Sweetie Pie** — 8", #40450, Maggie, 2005, red checked dress....................................$75.00
**Sunbeam** — 11", 16", 19", 1951 only, newborn infant, clean and in fair condition........$100.00 – 225.00
    16", 20", 24" cloth/vinyl, 1950, Divine-a-Lite Series (reg. #573, #313), scowling expression .. $125.00 up
**Sunbonnet Sue** — 9" compo., 1937 – 1940 (Little Betty) .....................................................$300.00
**Sunday Best** — 8", #38845, 2004 – 2005, dress with flowers, hat...........................................$90.00
**Sunday's Child** — 8", #27800, 2001, angel costume ...........................................................$100.00
**Sunflower Clown** — 40" all cloth, 1951 only, flower eyes ...............................................$850.00 up
**Sun-Maid Raisin Girl** — 8", #26190, 2000, red costume........................................................$65.00
**Sunny** — (see Collectors United/C.U. under Special Events/Exclusives)
**Sunrise, Sunset** — 8", #45200, 2006, pink and blue dress ......................................................$50.00
**Susannah Clogger** — (see Dolly Dears under Special Events/Exclusives)
**Susie Q** — cloth, 1940 – 1942 ......................................................................................$700.00
    8", #14590, 1995, Toy Shelf Series, yarn braids and pink polka dot dress with green jacket ........$65.00
**Suzy** — 12" plastic/vinyl, #1150, 1970 only (Janie) ..........................................................$325.00
**Swan Lake** — 16", #22040, 1998, Odette in white tutu .......................................................$175.00
    10", #35870, 2003, white tutu, feathers..............................................................................$125.00
    10", #42075, 2006, Odette, white ballet outfit .....................................................................$90.00
    10", #42080, 2006, Odile, black ballet outfit........................................................................$90.00
**Swan Princess** — 10", #14106, 1995 only, Fairy Tales Series ................................................$85.00
    8", #33690, 2002, white dress, crown, limited to 1,000 ......................................................$125.00
    8", #40310, 2005 – 2006, long white dress, pink trim..........................................................$85.00
**Sweden (Swedish)** — 8" h.p., BKW, #392, #792, 1961 – 1965 (Wendy Ann) ..........................$125.00
    8" h.p., BK, #792, 1966 – 1972 ........................................................................................$100.00
    8" straight legs, #0792, #592, 1973 – 1975, marked "Alex".....................................................$75.00
    8" straight legs, #592, #539, #521, 1976 – 1989, marked "Alexander" ......................................$65.00
    8", 1986 ............................................................................................................................$60.00

Suzy, 12", #1150, made in 1970 only. All original.

8", #580, reintroduced 1991 only.................................................................$60.00

    BKW with Maggie.................................................................$150.00

8", #35980, 2003 – 2004, print dress, red hat, wooden horse.....................$80.00

**Swedish** — 7" compo., 1936 – 1940 (Tiny Betty).....................................$325.00

    9" compo., 1937 – 1941 (Little Betty)...........................................$350.00

**Sweet Baby** — 18½" – 20" cloth/latex, 1948 only...........................$75.00 – 150.00

    14", 1983 – 1984 (Sweet Tears)...................................................$65.00

    14", reissued 1987, 1987 – 1993 (1991 has no bottle) (Sweet Tears).........$75.00

    14", 1990 – 1992 only (1991 has bottle), in carry case...................$125.00

    14", reintroduced 1993 only, pink striped jumper or dress................$65.00

**Sweet Harmony Angel** — 8", #40290, 2005, lavender costume.............$90.00

**Sweetie Baby** — 22", 1962 only.......................................................$125.00

**Sweetie Walker** — 23", 1962 only..............................................$275.00 up

**Sweet Innocence** — 8", #41985, 2006, white dress, hat, tan bear..........$95.00

**Sweet Irish Dancer** — 8", #36495, red hair, green decorated dress, 2003 – 2004.....$65.00

**Sweet Kisses for Grandma** — 8", #36155, 2003 – 2004, white dress, red trim.........$65.00

**Sweet Sentiments** — 8", #41990, 2006, with Chaos bear....................$100.00

**Sweet Sixteen** — 14", #1554, 1991 – 1992 only, Classic Series (Louisa)....$100.00

    10", #21060, 1997, pink silk dress, lace stole............................$90.00

    8", #35985, 2004 – 2005, black velvet top, tulle skirt...................$85.00

**Sweet Tears** — 9" vinyl, 1965 – 1974..................................................$85.00

    9" with layette in box, 1965 – 1973......................................$175.00

    14", 1967 – 1974, in trunk/trousseau...................................$175.00

    14", 1965 – 1974, in window box.........................................$175.00

    14", 1979, with layette.................................................$150.00

    14", 1965 – 1982.........................................................$65.00

    16", 1965 – 1971.........................................................$75.00

**Sweet Violet** — 18" h.p., 1951 – 1954 (Cissy)................................$875.00 up

**Swiss** — 7" compo., 1936 (Tiny Betty)...............................................$325.00

    9" compo., 1935 – 1938 (Little Betty)...................................$325.00

    10" h.p., 1962 – 1963 (Cissette)........................................$825.00

**Switzerland** — 8" h.p., BKW, #394, #794, 1961 – 1965...........................$125.00

    8" h.p., BK, #794, 1966 – 1972..........................................$100.00

    8" h.p., straight legs, #0794, #594, 1973 – 1975, marked "Alex"..........$75.00

    8" h.p., straight legs, #594, #540, #518, 1976 – 1989, marked "Alexander".....$60.00

    8", #546, 1986...........................................................$60.00

    8", #518, 1988 – 1990, costume change....................................$60.00

    8" BKW, Maggie smile face................................................$150.00

    8", #25795, 2000, pink and white costume with watch......................$65.00

**Symposium** — (see M.A.D.C. under Special Events/Exclusives)

**Taft, Helen** — 1988, fifth set Presidents' Ladies/First Ladies Series (Louisa)...........$100.00

**Take Home Coca-Cola** — 8", #40310, 2005, white dress, coat and hat, six-pack Coca-Cola.....$90.00

**Tara** — #14990, 1998, two-sided home of Scarlett.............................$125.00

**Taurus** — 8", #21340, 1998 – brown and white bull costume.....................$90.00

**Team Canada** — 8", #24130, 1998 – 1999, hockey skater.........................$80.00

**Team Mates** — 8", #38885, 2004 – 2005, with dog, baseball, and bat..........$85.00

**Tea Rose Cissette** — 10", #22370 – 1998, floral silk cocktail dress.........$110.00

**Tea Time with Muffy** — 8", #39990, 2005, with Muffy bear, teapot, and cup.....$150.00

**Teeny Twinkle** — 1946 only, cloth with flirty eyes..........................$525.00

**Tennis** — 8" h.p., BKW, #415, #632 (Wendy Ann)...............................$450.00

**Tennis Boy** — 8", #16331, 1997...............................................$60.00

**Tennis Girl** — 8", #16320, 1997..............................................$60.00

**Tess** — 10", #28405, 2001, green, pink vintage gown..........................$125.00

**Texas** — 8", #313, 1991 only, Americana......................................$65.00

Sweet Tears, 14", vinyl, 1967 – 1974. Layette set.

Thank You, 8", #21110, 1997 – 1998. Comes with flowers and thank-you card.

**Texas Shriner** — (see Shriner's First Ladies' Luncheon under Special Events/Exclusives)

**Thailand** — 8" h.p., BK, #767, 1966 – 1972 (Wendy) ...............................................................$100.00

    8" straight legs, #0767, #567, 1973 – 1975, marked "Alex".........................................$75.00

    8" straight legs, #567, 1976 – 1989, marked "Alexander"...........................................$65.00

    8" straight legs, #39770, 2005, Asian, pointed hat.......................................................$85.00

**Thanksgiving** — 8", #35680, 2003, sweater, pumpkin print skirt, turkey....................$65.00

**Thank You** — 8", #21110, 1997 – 1998, comes with a thank-you card........................$60.00

**That Girl** — 10", #26345, 2000 (Cissette), navy blue suit ........................................$90.00

**"There's No Place Like Home" Doll House** — trunk set, #13260, 1997 – 1999................$150.00

**There Was a Little Girl** — 14", #24611, 1995, Nursery Rhymes Series (Mary Ann)...............$75.00

**Thinking of You** — 8", #21500, 1998 – 1999, print dress, straw hat.......................$65.00

**This Little Light of Mine** — 8", #39760, 2005, long beige dress, candle ...................$95.00

**Thomas, Marlo** — 17" plastic/vinyl, 1967 only (Polly) ......................................$650.00 up

**Three Blind Mice** — 8", #39945, 2005 – 2006, with three mice ...............................$85.00

**Three Little Kittens** — 8", #26970, 2000 – 2001, blue plaid dress, three kittens .......................$90.00

    8", #45445, Maggie, three plush kittens .....................................................$90.00

**Three Little Pigs and Wolf** — compo., 1938 – 1939, must be mint.............................$675.00 up, ea.

**Three Little Pigs Set** — 12", #10000, 1997, bricks, straw, and sticks Pigs.........................$275.00

    8", #33656, 2003, three pigs, each with house bank...............................................$150.00

**Three Wise Men Set** — 8", #19480, 1997 – 1999, Nativity Set...............................$400.00

**Thumbelina & Her Lady** — 8" and 21" porcelain, 1992 –1993, limited to 2,500 sets ...........$450.00

**Thursday's Child** — 8", #27785, 2001, comes with suitcase .........................................$90.00

**Tibet** — 8" h.p., #534, 1993 only.......................................................................$60.00

    8", #39815, 2005 – 2006, Asian, with yak ...............................................................$85.00

**Tierney, Gene** — 14" – 17" compo., 1945, must be mint (Wendy Ann) .............................$3,300.00 up

**Tiger Lily** — 8", #469, 1992 – 1993 only, Storybook Series (Peter Pan) (Wendy Ann) ..............$85.00

**Time Out for Coca-Cola Sock Hop** — 10", #26225, 2000.............................................$125.00

**Timmy Toddler** — 23" plastic/vinyl, 1960 – 1961.........................................................$150.00

    30", 1960 only.....................................................................................................$250.00

**Tinker Bell** — 11" h.p., #1110, 1969 only, Peter Pan Series (Cissette)...................$425.00

    Magic wand and wings, #13960 in 1998 – 2000........................................................$75.00

    14", #87009, 1996 (Mary Ann)...........................................................................$95.00

    8", #30675, 2001, pink/blue costume, lace wings, limited to 2,500 pieces...................$75.00

    8", #34100, 2002 – 2005, white costume, silver wand ..............................................$80.00

    5", #30455, 2002, porcelain, pink and blue costume ................................................$75.00

    10", #31750, 2003, green costume, shoes, gold wand................................................$125.00

    5", #38325, 2004, vinyl, petite, with wand .............................................................$25.00

    8", #42245, 2006, lavender dress, wand .................................................................$85.00

**Tinkles** — 8", #10400, 1995, Christmas Series ........................................................$60.00

**Tin Man** — 8", #13211, 1998 – 2006, Wizard of Oz Series, silver face and costume.....................$70.00

    5", #28685, 2001 – 2003, porcelain.....................................................................$75.00

    5", #36340, 2005, silver costume.........................................................................$25.00

    9", #39780, 2005 – 2006, silver costume...............................................................$35.00

**Tin Woodsman** — 8", #432 in 1993, #140432 in 1994 – 1995 .....................................$100.00

**Tiny Betty** — 7" compo., 1935 – 1942 ...................................................................$325.00 up

**Tiny Tim** — 7" compo., 1934 – 1937 (Tiny Betty) .....................................................$325.00 up

    14" compo., 1938 – 1940 (Wendy Ann) ..................................................................$625.00

    16" cloth, early 1930s ........................................................................................$700.00 up

    8", #18001, 1996, Dickens (Wendy Ann) ..............................................................$65.00

**Tiny Treasure** — 8", #41975, 2006, beige dress, green bow .....................................$100.00

**Tippi Ballerina** — (see Collectors United/C.U. under Special Events/Exclusives)

**Tippy Toe** — 16" cloth, 1940s ..........................................................................$600.00

**Toast to Madame Alexander** — 8", #36145, 2003, long pink dress with fur at neck and hem,

    champagne bottle ..............................................................................................$90.00

**Today I Feel Excited and Sad** — 8", #33685, 2002, cloth ..........................................................$35.00
**Today I Feel Silly** — 14", #80710, 2000 – 2004, dressed cloth doll with four interchangeable faces .$50.00
**Today I Feel Silly and Angry** — 8", #33680, cloth, includes cat................................................$35.00
**To Grandma's House** — 8", #42365, 2006, red coat, hat.............................................................$85.00
**To Market, To Market** — 8", #38775, 2004 – 2006, with pig, red pinafore................................$50.00
**Tommy** — 12" h.p., 1962 only (Lissy)......................................................................................$800.00
**Tommy Bangs** — h.p., 1952 only, Little Men Series (Maggie, Margaret) ...............................$875.00
**Tommy Snooks** — 8", #447, 1988 – 1991, Storybook Series .......................................................$55.00
**Tommy Tittlemouse** — 8", #444, 1988 – 1991, Storybook Series (Maggie) .............................$55.00
**Tom Sawyer** — 8" h.p., #491, 1989 – 1990, Storybook Series (Maggie Mixup).........................$60.00
**Tony Sarg Marionettes** — (see Marionettes)
**Tooth Fairy** — 10" Portrette, 1994 only ...................................................................................$75.00
    8", #10389 – 10391, 1995 only, Special Occasions Series, three hair colors ...............................$65.00
    8", #21550, 1999 – 2000, pink sparkling outfit, satin pillow .......................................................$70.00
    8", #30660, 2001 – 2002, lavender costume, silver bag, crown, white wings.............................$80.00
    8", #42735, 2006, pink costume, pouch, certificate ....................................................................$80.00
**To Oz Bear Set** — #33634, 2002, four 3" bears .................................................................$100.00 set
**To Oz Cowardly Lion** — 8", #33632, 2002, with 3" bear .........................................................$95.00
**To Oz Dorothy** — 8", #33630, 2002, with 3" plush bear.........................................................$100.00
**To Oz Scarecrow** — 8", #33633, 2002, with 3" plush bear .......................................................$95.00
**To Oz Tin Man** — 8", #33631, 2002, with 3" plush bear .........................................................$95.00
**Top O' the Morning** — 8", #39810, 2005, with green bear .....................................................$85.00
**Topsy-Turvy** — Compo. with Tiny Betty heads, 1935 only.................................................$325.00 up
    With Dionne Quint head, 1936 only...........................................................................................$350.00
    Cinderella — #14587, 1995 only, two-headed, one side gown; other side dress with apron ........$125.00
    Red Riding Hood — 8", #14555 (three-way) Red Riding Hood, Grandma, Wolf .................$125.00
    Wicked Stepmother — 8", #14640, 1996, evil witch, stepmother .............................................$125.00
**Toulouse-Lautrec** — 21", #2250, 1986 – 1987 only, black/pink outfit............................................$300.00
**Toy Box Wendy** — 8", #36270, 2003 – 2004, print dress, toybox with toys and books.............$100.00
**Toy Soldier** — 8", #481, 1993, #140481, 1994, #13210 – 1998, white face, red dots on cheeks....$70.00
**Train Journey** — 8" h.p., #486, 1955, white wool jacket, hat, red plaid dress...........................$550.00
**Trapeze Artist** — 10", #1133, 1990 – 1991, Portrette (Cissette)....................................................$75.00
**Treena Ballerina** — 15" h.p., 1952 only, must be near mint (Margaret)..............................$750.00 up
    18" – 21", 1952 only.............................................................................................$650.00 – 875.00
**Tree Topper** — 8" (half doll only), #850, 1992 only, red/gold dress............................................$100.00
    8" (half doll only), #852, 1992 – 1994, Angel Lace with multi-tiered ivory lace skirt (Wendy) . $100.00
    8" (half doll only), #853, 1993 – 1994, red velvet/gold and green (Wendy) .............................$100.00
    10" (half doll only), #854, 1993 – 1994; #54854, 1995, pink Victorian (Cissette) ....................$125.00
    8" (half doll only), #540855, 1994; #540855 – 1995, all antique white (Wendy)......................$100.00
    8", #84857, 1995 – 1996, Yuletide Angel dressed in red and gold (Wendy), #19600, 1997.....$100.00
    8", #84859, 1995 – 1996, Christmas Angel dressed in white and gold (Wendy) ......................$100.00
    10", #54860, Glorious Angel dressed in red and white, gold crown, #19590, 1997 – 1998 (Cissette).$100.00
    10", #19610, 1997 – 1998, Heavenly Angel, gold and ivory costume (Wendy).....................$100.00
    10", Glistening Angel, 1998 – 1999, #19700 (Wendy), silver brocade .....................................$100.00
    10", Winter Lights, #20000, 1999 – 2000 (Wendy), AC illuminated........................................$100.00
    10", Holiday Trimmings, 2000 – 2001, #2704 (Wendy), red plaid gown ................................$100.00
    10", Golden Dream, 2000, #27055, gold and white gown.......................................................$100.00
    10", Caroler, 2000, #27045, red jacket, fur muff.....................................................................$100.00
    10", Star, 2000, #26100, gold star, tassels..............................................................................$75.00
    8", Shining Bright fiber optic angel, #28265, 2001 – 2002, white,
        gold (Wendy), fur wings ......................................................................................$110.00
    10", Starburst Angel, #28535, 2001, red/gold gown (Wendy).................................................$100.00
    10", Peace on Earth, #33445, 2002 – 2003, red gown, feather wings.......................................$125.00
    8", Lighting the Christmas Tree, #35920, 2003, gold wings, white dress...................................$100.00

**Trellis Rose Flower Girl** — 8", #28650, 2001 – 2002, long white dress.......................................$80.00

**Trick and Treat** — (see Child at Heart Shop under Special Events/Exclusives)

**Trip to the Moon** — 8", #40385, 2005, Wendy, dog wearing space helmet ................................$90.00

**Triumphant Topaz** — 10", #32165, 2000 – 2002, black and gold ball gown............................$150.00

**Truman, Bess** — 14", 1989 – 1990, sixth set Presidents' Ladies/First Ladies Series (Mary Ann) ..$100.00

**Tuesday's Child** — 8", #27775, 2001, white dress, blue ribbon ......................................................$90.00

**Tunisia** — 8", #514, 1989 only, marked "Alexander" (Wendy).......................................................$65.00

**Turkey** — 8" h.p., BK, #787, 1968 – 1972 (Wendy)......................................................................$100.00

    8" straight legs, #0787, #587, 1973 – 1975, marked "Alex".................................................$70.00

    8" straight legs, #587, 1976 – 1986, marked "Alexander" ..................................................$65.00

    8", #42525, 2006, red dress and hat, felt twirl ....................................................................$90.00

**'Twas the Night Before Christmas** — 8", #27305, 2001, long white gown...........................$80.00

**Tweedledee & Tweedledum** — 14" cloth, 1930 – 1931 ......................................................$750.00 ea.

    8" h.p., #13080, 1998 – 1999, checked pants, red jackets, propeller caps ...............................$150.00

    (see Disney Annual Showcase of Dolls under Special Events/Exclusives)

**Twelve Days of Christmas** — 8", #35555, 2002 – 2005, with tree and ornaments,

        plaid dress, red pinafore .........................................................................................$100.00

    5", #31745, 2003 – 2004, set of 12 dolls, display box .........................................................$300.00

**20's Bride** — #14103, 1995, Nostalgia Series.................................................................................$125.00

**20's Traveler** — 10", #1139, 1991 – 1992 only, Portrette, M.A. signature logo on box (Cissette) . $150.00

**25th Anniversary** — (see Enchanted Doll House under Special Events/Exclusives)

**Twilight Angel** — 8", #10780 (Wendy), 1999 – 2000, white organza gown..............................$100.00

**Twinkle Toes** — 8", #36905, 2003 – 2005, ballerina, bear with tutu ............................................$80.00

**Twinkle, Twinkle Little Star** — 8", #11630, 1997 .................................................................$65.00

**Twirling Confetti** — 8", 2003, #35075, pink tutu, flower trimmed.....................................$50.00

**Twirling Rose** — 8", #33145, 2002 – 2003, long blue ballet costume............................................$70.00

**Tyler, Julia** — 1979 – 1981, second set Presidents' Ladies/First Ladies Series (Martha) .........$100.00

**Tyrolean Boy and Girl\*** — 8" h.p., BKW (girl – #398, #798; boy – #399, #799), 1962 – 1965

        (Wendy Ann) ....................................................................................................$150.00 ea.

    8" h.p., BK (girl – #798; boy – #799), 1966 – 1972 ...........................................................$100.00 ea.

    8" straight legs (girl – #0798; boy – #0799), 1973, marked "ALEX" ...................................$75.00 ea.

    8" BKW (Maggie Mixup)...................................................................................................$150.00 ea.

**U.F.D.C. Sailor Boy** — (see U.F.D.C. under Special Events/Exclusives)

**Ugly Stepsister** — 10" h.p., #13340, 1997 – 1998, Cinderella Series ........................................$85.00

**Ukraine** — 8", #34325, 2002 – 2003, cultural costume, with decorated egg, flower hat...............$70.00

**Ultimate Angel** — 21", #10770, 1999, blue silk and lace gown...................................................$525.00

**Uncle Henry** — 8", #39915, 2005, Wizard of Oz Series, #39915, 2006.........................................$60.00

**Uncle Sam** — 8", #10353, 1995 only (Wendy) ...............................................................................$70.00

    8" h.p., #24170, 1999 – 2000, astronaut costume, United States of America............................$80.00

**Union Officer** — 12", #634, 1990 – 1991, Scarlett Series (Nancy Drew)...................................$85.00

    Soldier, 8", #634, 1991 only, Scarlett Series..................................................................... $125.00

**United States** — 8" h.p., #559, straight legs, 1974 – 1975, marked "Alex" ................................$75.00

    8", #559, Alex mold, misspelled "Untied States".................................................................$100.00

    8" straight legs, #559, 1976 – 1987, marked "Alexander" ......................................................$65.00

    8", #559, #516, 1988 – 1992 (Maggie)................................................................................$60.00

    8", #11562, 1996, Statue of Liberty costume, #24000, 1997 – 1998 ......................................$75.00

**United States Air Force** — 8", #12000, 1998 (Wendy), uniform and flag............................$85.00

**United States Armed Forces Set** — four dolls, five flags, flag stand ....................................$350.00

**United States Army** — 8", #12010, 1998 (Wendy) ....................................................................$85.00

**United States Marines** — 8", #12030, 1998 (Wendy)................................................................$85.00

**United States Navy** — 8", #12020, 1998 (Wendy).......................................................................$85.00

**U.S.A.** — 8" h.p., #536, 1993 – 1994 (#110536) (also see Neiman-Marcus, Caroline's Adventures,

        under Special Events/Exclusives)..........................................................................$75.00

    Las Vegas, 8", #28565, 2001, silver costume..........................................................................$75.00

\*Became Austrian Boy and Girl in 1974.

Sacajawea, 8", #28575, 2001 – 2002,  includes papoose.................................................$85.00

**Valentine —** (see Lady Valentine & Lord Valentine)

**Valentine Kisses —** 8", #27050, 2000 – 2001, red and silver outfit................................$65.00

**Van Buren, Angelica —** 1979 – 1981, second set

    Presidents' Ladies/First Ladies Series (Louisa) ...............................................$100.00

**Velvet Party Dress —** 8" h.p., #389, 1957 only, very rare (Wendy Ann)............................ $2,000.00 up

**Vermont Maid —** 8" (see Enchanted Doll House under Special Events/Exclusives)

**Victoria —** 21" compo., 1939, 1941, 1945 – 1946 (also see Flavia)

    (Wendy Ann) ....................................................................................... $2,000.00 up

  20" h.p., 1954 only, Me & My Shadow Series (Cissy)................................. $2,000.00 up

  14" h.p., 1950 – 1951 (Margaret) .................................................................$900.00

  18" h.p., 1954 only, Me & My Shadow Series, slate blue gown (Maggie).......... $2,000.00 up

  8" h.p., #2030C, 1954 only, matches 18" doll  (Wendy Ann) ......................... $1,300.00 up

  14" baby, 1975 – 1988, 1990 – 1997 ..............................................................$80.00

  18" baby, 1966 only ......................................................................................$70.00

  18", reintroduced 1991 – 1993, 1997...............................................$50.00 – 125.00

  20" baby, 1967 – 1989 ..................................................................................$75.00

  20" 1986 only, dress, jacket, bonnet .............................................................$85.00

  18" vinyl, 1998, velour romper, #29420 white, #29423 African-American ...............$100.00

  14", "Mozart Music" Concertina, #26915, 2000, plays Mozart music ................$75.00

  18", "Mozart Music" Symphony, #26900, 2000, plays Mozart music ....................$115.00

  14" – 18", 2002 – 2005, variety of outfits...............................................$90.00 – 130.00

  14", variety of outfits, 2006...................................................................$75.00 – 105.00

**Victorian —** 18" h.p., 1953 only, pink taffeta/black velvet gown, Glamour Girl Series

    (Margaret) ....................................................................................... $1,500.00 up

**Victorian Bride —** 10", #1148, 1992 only, Portrette..................................................$100.00

  10", blue satin and lace gown .......................................................................$100.00

**Victorian Bride —** (see Debra)

**Victorian Catherine —** 16", #90010, porcelain, elaborate gown.................................$200.00

**Victorian Christmas —** 8", #19970, red velvet and lace...........................................$100.00

**Victorian Coca-Cola —**  8", #36020, 2003 – 2004, red vintage dress and hat, Coke glass..........$85.00

**Victorian Countess —** 10", #28885, 2001, long white dress with lace ......................$150.00

**Victorian Girl 1954 —** 10" h.p., 2000 (Cissette), remake of 1954 Victoria ..............$100.00

**Victorians —** 8" Adorable silk, #26875, 2000, flower adorned dress........................$100.00

  8" Charming silk, #25035, 2000 – 2001, white silk dress ...............................$100.00

  8" Innocent silk, #25045, 2000 – 2001, white lace trimmed silk dress.................$100.00

  8" Sophisticated silk, #26780, 2000 – 2001, lilac silk costume ..........................$100.00

  8" Sweet silk, #25040, 2000 – 2001, pink silk dress .......................................$100.00

  8" Marigold, #27805, 2001, short yellow dress, hat with lace...........................$100.00

  8" Sailorette, #33555, 2002 – 2003, pleated vintage costume .............................$75.00

**Victorian Skater —** 10", #1155, 1993 – 1994, Portrette, red/gold/black outfit (Cissette)..........$150.00

**Victorian Valentine —** 8", #30615, 2000 – 2003,  pink pleated dress, hat

trimmed with lace, valentine..........................................................................$75.00

**Vietnam —** 8" h.p., #788, 1968 – 1969 (Wendy Ann) ...............................................$225.00

  8", #788, 1968 – 1969 (Maggie Mixup) .........................................................$250.00

  8", #505, reintroduced in 1990 – 1991 (Maggie)..............................................$65.00

  8", #45210, 2006, Asian face, green pants, pink top.........................................$60.00

**Vintage Violet Silk Victorian —** 8", #30405, 2001 – 2002,  pink dress.....................$100.00

**Violet —** (see Sweet Violet)

**Violet —** (Nutcracker Ballerina) 10" Portrette, 1994 only........................................$70.00

**Violetta —** 10", #1116, 1987 – 1988, all deep blue (Cissette) .....................................$65.00

**Virgo —** 8", #21380, pink pleated outfit, gold helmet ................................................$85.00

**Visions of Sugarplums —** 8", #37805, 2003 – 2004, red and green dress, sunglasses, lollipop ..$80.00

**W.A.A.C. (Army) —** 14" compo., 1943 – 1944 (Wendy Ann)................................... $750.00 up

**W.A.A.F. (Air Force)** — 14" compo., 1943 – 1944 (Wendy Ann) ..................................... $750.00 up

**Waiting for Santa Boy** — 8", #37090, 2003 – 2004, red p.j.'s, plush bear, cookies, milk ...........$80.00

**Waiting for Santa Girl** — 8", #37085, 2003 – 2004, red p.j.'s, plush bear, cookies, milk ...........$80.00

**Walk in the Park** — 8", #42195, 2006, with three dogs ................................................$100.00

**Waltz** — 16", 1999, pink gown trimmed in marabou................................................$150.00

    8" h.p., #476, 1955 only (Wendy Ann) ............................................ $700.00 up

**Want** — (see Ghost of Christmas Present) (sold as set)

**Washington, Martha** — 1976 – 1978, first set Presidents' Ladies/First Ladies Series (Martha) .. $225.00

**Watchful Guardian Angel** — 10", #10740, 1998 – 1999, blue/white outfit................................$150.00

**Watchful Guardian Angel Set** — three dolls, bridge, gift card ................................................$300.00

**W.A.V.E. (Navy)** — 14" compo., 1943 – 1944 (Wendy Ann) ................................................ $750.00 up

**Wedding Rings Ring Bearer** — 8", #36280, 2003, blonde, green and white costume..............$75.00

**Wedding Wishes** — 16", #28455, 2001, white gown with lace around hem, bouquet with red roses.$175.00

**Weeping Princess** — 8", #11104, 1995 only, International Folk Tales (Maggie) ........................$65.00

**Welcome Home** — Desert Storm, 8", 1991 only, mid-year introduction, boy or girl

    soldier, black or white.................................................................................$50.00

    8", #38145, 2004, blue striped dress with "Welcome Home" banner .....................$75.00

**Wendy** — 8", 1989, first doll offered to club members only (see M.A.D.C. under Special Events/Exclusives)

    5", #30350, 2001 – 2003, petite, pink checked dress ........................................$20.00

**Wendy and Her Radio Flyer** — 8", #42360, with bear, blanket, wagon .........................$90.00

**Wendy and Muffy** — 8", #33635, 2004, bag with tiny bear ...................................... $150.00

**Wendy and the Yellow Brick Road** — 8", #38720, 2004 – 2005 (Wendy)..............................$85.00

**Wendy Angel** — 8" h.p., #404, 1954 (Wendy Ann) ........................................ $850.00 up

**Wendy Ann** — 11" – 15" compo., 1935 – 1948 ....................................$350.00 – 575.00

    9" compo., 1936 – 1940, painted eyes.................................................$375.00

    14", 1938 – 1939, in riding habit, molded hair or wig ..................................$425.00

    14", any year, swivel waist, molded hair or wig.........................................$450.00

    17" – 21" compo., 1938 – 1944........................................$600.00 – 1,100.00

    14½" – 17" h.p., 1948 – 1949.........................................$600.00 – 850.00

    16" – 22" h.p., 1948 – 1950 .........................................$575.00 – 975.00

    23" – 25" h.p., 1949 ......................................................... $850.00 up

    8", #79516, 1995, 100th anniversary, wearing dress, coat, and bonnet, limited production ....$100.00

**Wendy Ann Felt** — 12", #37945, 2004, molded felt doll, linen dress, special for the Toy Shoppe ....$300.00

**Wendy Ballerina** — 8" (Wendy), 1999, pink trim on white lace tutu .........................$70.00

**(Wendy) Being Just Like Mommy** — 8", #801, 1993, has baby carriage, #120801, 1994 ....$125.00

**(Wendy) Being Prom Queen** — #120808, 1994....................................................$65.00

**Wendy Bride** — 14" – 22" compo., 1944 – 1945 (Wendy Ann) ....................................$325.00 – 675.00

    15" – 18" h.p., 1951 (Margaret).........................................$525.00 – 875.00

    20" h.p., 1956 (Cissy)........................................................ $950.00 up

    8" h.p., SLW, #475, 1955 (Wendy Ann).........................................$650.00

**Wendy Builds a Snowman** — 8", #39925, 2005 – 2006, with snowman....................................$75.00

**Wendy Cheerleader** — 8", #16500, 1998, pleated skirt, red sweater ........................$65.00

**Wendy Elf** — 8", #12818, 1995, Christmas Series.........................................$65.00

**Wendy (from Peter Pan)** — 15" h.p., 1953 only (Margaret) ...........................................$550.00 up

    14" plastic/vinyl, #1415, 1969 only (Mary Ann) ...........................................$275.00

    8", #466 in 1991 – 1993; #140466 in 1994; Storyland Series, pom-poms on slippers (Peter Pan) $65.00

**Wendy Go Bragh!** — 8", #35435, 2002 – 2003, white dress, green shamrocks...........................$65.00

**Wendy Goes Camping** — 8", #42100, 2006, tent, raccoon, fire, bedroll.....................................$90.00

**(Wendy) Goes to the Circus** — 8", #12819, 1996 (Wendy Ann) ........................................$60.00

**(Wendy) Her Sundress** — #120804, 1994 .........................................................$60.00

**Wendy-Kin Baby** — 8", one-piece vinyl body with hard plastic Little Genius head, 1954 . $375.00 up

**Wendy-Kin Wood Silk Rose** — 8", #40795, 2005, green dress ..............................................$250.00

**(Wendy) Learning to Sew** — 8", #120809, 1994, in wicker case ............................................$100.00

**Wendy Learns Her ABC's** — (see ABC Unlimited Productions under Special Events/Exclusives)

**Wendy Loves Being Loved** — 8", 1992 – 1993 only, doll and wardrobe..................................$125.00
**Wendy Loves Clifford the Big Red Dog** — 8", #38730, 2004 – 2005, 3" dog........................$80.00
**Wendy Loves Curious George** — 8", #42575, 2006, yellow dress, monkey ............................$85.00
**Wendy Loves Donald and Daisy** — 8", 2004 – 2005, cloth Donald and Daisy ......................$95.00
**Wendy Loves Goofy and Pluto** — 8", #39565, 2004 – 2005 ...............................................$95.00
**(Wendy Loves) Her First Day at School** — 8", #120806, 1994 – 1995................................$65.00
**(Wendy Loves) Her Sunday Best** — 8", #120807, 1994 – 1995.........................................$75.00
**Wendy Loves Kermit** — 8", #42615, 2006, green dress, Kermit..........................................$80.00
**Wendy Loves Mickey and Minnie** — 8", #39555, 2004 – 2006, red dress ...........................$95.00
**Wendy Loves Mr. Rogers' Neighborhood** — 8", red jacket, trolley.....................................$85.00
**Wendy Loves Munchkinland** — 8", #40160, 2005, includes mini Dorothy doll ......................$90.00
**Wendy Loves Sunday School** — 8", pink dress, white sweater ..............................................$80.00
**Wendy Loves Tennis** — 8", #42110, 2006, pink and white tennis outfit...................................$80.00
**(Wendy Loves) the Country Fair** — 8", #802, 1993, has cow, #120802, 1994 ....................$75.00
**Wendy Loves the Lion King** — 8", #40340, 2005, Lion King dress, plush lion........................$85.00
**Wendy Loves the Red Hat Society** — 8", #40860, 2005, red hat, fur, and dress....................$80.00
**Wendy Makes It Special** — 8", #31050, 1997 – 1998, pink satin dress ...................................$75.00
**Wendy Plays Hopscotch** — 8", #40170, pink print dress .....................................................$70.00
**Wendy Salutes the Heartland** — 8", #39955, 2005 – 2006, with quilt and stand .....................$95.00
**Wendy Salutes the Olympics** — 8", #86005, 1996, Olympic Medal.......................................$125.00
**Wendy's Anniversary Trunk Set** — 8", #36130, 2003, trunk, clothes, shoes, accessories......$200.00
**Wendy's Doll House Trunk Set** — 8", #12820, 1996..........................................................$275.00
**Wendy's Fabulous Fifties Trunk Set** — 8", #37925, 2003 – 2004, hatbox trunk,
     three sets of clothes..........................................................................................$300.00
**Wendy's Favorite Fairy Tales** — 8", #35655, 2003 – 2004, pink dress with pinafore,
     rabbit, cape, book, etc.......................................................................................$100.00
**Wendy's Gift for You** — 8", #40465, 2005, pink-trimmed dress, gift box.............................$100.00
**Wendy Shops FAO** — (see FAO Schwarz under Special Events/Exclusives)
**Wendy's Puppet Show** — 8", #33780, 2002 –2003, four puppets and theaters .........................$180.00
**Wendy's Special Cheer** — 8", #16500, 1998 – 1999, cheerleading outfit ...............................$65.00
**Wendy's Surprise Party** — 8", #40605, 2005 – 2006, pink cake and Danger the Dog .........$110.00
**(Wendy) Summer Box Set** — #805, 1993; #120805, 1994 ..................................................$100.00
**Wendy's Wicked Ways** — 8", #42410, 2006, spider costume with monkey ............................$95.00
**Wendy Tap Dancer** — 8" h.p., #13930, 1998, white jacket, gold tap pants ...........................$80.00
**Wendy the Gardener** — 8", #31400, 1998 – 1999, sunflower outfit, watering can, sunflowers .$70.00
**Wendy Visits Grandma** — 8", #42200, 2006, green print dress, suitcase................................$85.00
**Wendy Visits the Museum** — 8", #40400, 2005, striped dress .............................................$80.00
**Wendy Visits the Statue of Liberty** — 8", #40395, 2005 – 2006, red pants, camera............$50.00
**Wendy Visits the Zoo** — 8", #39845, 2005 – 2006, with ostrich, leopard, snake, penguin,
     and monkey ....................................................................................................$85.00
**Wendy Visits World's Fair** — (see Shirley's Doll House under Special Events/Exclusives)
**(Wendy) Winter Box Set** — #120810, 1994, boxed doll and wardrobe ...............................$100.00
**Wendy Woodkin** — 8", #37910, 2004, jointed wooden doll with tiny wooden doll ...............$250.00
**Wendy Works Construction** — 8", #31420, 1998 – 1999, includes tools and toolbox ..........$80.00
**Western Riding** — 8", #39735, 2005 – 2006, riding outfit, horse .........................................$90.00
**Wharton, Edith** — 10", #42060, 2006, black vintage outfit ................................................$130.00
**Wheels on the Bus, The** — 8", #34135, 2002 – 2003, yellow checked dress, bus on skirt......$50.00
**Where Oh Where Has My Little Dog Gone** — 8", #35675, 2003 – 2004, blanket, dog .........$75.00
**Where's My Blankie Total Moves Wendy** — 8", #40460, 2005 – 2006..............................$50.00
**White Christmas** — 10", #10105, 1995 only, Christmas Series.............................................$80.00
**White Christmas Pair** — 10", #15380, Betty and Bob from the movie *White Christmas*.......$175.00
**White Hat Doll** — 8", #25315, 2000, Maud Humphrey design .............................................$75.00
**White Iris** — 10", #22540, 1999 – 2000 (Cissette), white lace and roses ...............................$100.00
**White King** — 8" h.p., #13020, 1997 – 1998, white suit, cape ...........................................$100.00

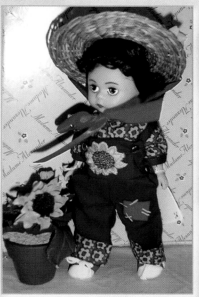

{ **Wendy the Gardener, 8", #31400, 1998 – 1999, came with watering can and flowerpot.** }

**White Rabbit** — 14" – 17" cloth/felt, 1940s .................................................................$500.00 – 750.00
    8", #14509, 1995, Alice in Wonderland Series.............................................................$125.00
    8", #14616, 1996, White Rabbit in court.....................................................................$90.00
**Wicked Stepmother** — 21", #50002, 1996, limited edition ............................................$325.00
**Wicked Witch of the East** — 10", #42415, 2006, black and orange costume with broom.......$130.00
**Wicked Witch of the West** — 10", #13270, 1997 – 2005 (Cissette), black witch costume, broom.$125.00
    21", #27760, 2000, long black costume with Dorothy globe, #42400, 2006............................$425.00
**Wilson, Edith** — 1988, fifth set Presidents' Ladies/First Ladies Series (Mary Ann)................$100.00
**Wilson, Ellen** — 1988, fifth set Presidents' Ladies/First Ladies Series (Louisa).......................$100.00
**Window Shopping** — 8", #37920, 2004, with store front, mannequin ......................................$95.00
**Winged Monkey** — 8" h.p. (Maggie), #140501, 1994 only.......................................................$100.00
    8" h.p. #25950, 2000 – 2002 (Wendy), blue jacket, hat, blue feather wings ...............................$75.00
**Winnie the Pooh** — 8", #38365, 2004 – 2006, with plush Pooh, Tigger, Piglet, and Eeyore.....$100.00
**Winnie Walker** — 15" h.p., 1953 only (Cissy)................................................................ $325.00 up
    18" – 25", #1836...................................................................................................$350.00 – 650.00
    1953 – 1954, in trunk/trousseau ...................................................................... $850.00 up
**Winter** — 14", 1993, Changing Seasons, doll and four outfits....................................................$100.00
    5" porcelain, #25865, 2000, fur-trimmed white coat and hat ................................................$60.00
**Winter Angel** — 10", #28365, 2001 –2004, blue costume, white fur wings ...............................$90.00
**Winter Fun Skater** — 8", #10357, 1995, Christmas Series ......................................................$65.00
**Winter Magic** — 8", #42040, 2006, blue outfit, Chaos bear .......................................................$90.00
**Winter Sports** — 1991 (see Shirley's Doll House under Special Events/Exclusives)
**Wintertime** — (see M.A.D.C. under Special Events/Exclusives)
**Winter Wonderland** — 10", #19990, 1999 – 2000, white satin, fur, jewels .............................$125.00
**Winter Wonderland (Nashville Skater #1)** — 1991 – 1992 (see Collectors United/C.U.
    under Special Events/Exclusives)
**Wishes Come True** — 8", #33315, 2002, ballerina outfit.........................................................$75.00
**Wishing Fairy** — 8", #36035, 2003 – 2004, pink costume, crystal snowflake.............................$80.00
**Wisteria Flower Girl** — 8", #30370, 2001 – 2002 (Maggie), lavender gown .............................$85.00
**Witch** — 8", #322, 1992 – 1993, Americana Series.................................................................$75.00
**Witches' Brew Wendy** — 8", #40620, 2005 – 2006, with black cat, green hat..........................$80.00
**Witch/Halloween** — (see Collectors United/C.U. under Special Events/Exclusives)
**Withers, Jane** — 12" – 13½" compo., 1937, closed mouth .................................................. $1,000.00 up
    15" – 17", 1937 – 1939.........................................................................................$850.00 – 1,300.00
    17" cloth body, 1939.............................................................................................$1,500.00
    18" – 19", 1937 – 1939.........................................................................................$1,500.00
    19" – 20", closed mouth .......................................................................................$1,400.00 up
    20" – 21", 1937.....................................................................................................$1,700.00 up
**With Love** — 8", #17003, 1996, pink gown, comes with a heart.........................................$65.00
    8", #17001, 1996, same as above except African-American .......................................$75.00
**Wizard of Oz** — 8", mid-year special (see Madame Alexander Doll Co. under Special Events/Exclusives)
    8", #13281, plaid pants, green tailcoat, 1998 – 2000...............................................$100.00
    8", #13280, 1998 – 2000, Wizard, with state fair balloon..........................................$150.00
    5", #38200, 2003 – 2004, set of four – Daisy, Lollipop, Coroner, and Town's Lady.................$100.00
    #38400, Wizard of Oz house trunk for 8" dolls .......................................................$150.00
    5", 2004 – 2005, Petite Set, Tin Man, Cowardly Lion, Scarecrow, Dorothy........................ $25.00 ea.
**Women, 1860s** — 10" h.p., 1990 (see Spiegel's, Beth, under Special Events/Exclusives)
**Wooden Wendy** — 8", #33820, 2003 – 2004, fully jointed wooden doll in pink dress ..............$275.00
**Workin' Out with Wendy 1980** — 8", #17810, 1999, BK, striped bodysuit............................$65.00
**Wynkin** — (see Dutch Lullaby)
**Yankee Doodle** — 8", #35945, 2003 – 2004, blonde, vintage patriotic costume ..........................$90.00
**Yellow Butterfly Princess** — 8", #25680, 2000 – 2001 (Maggie) ........................................$70.00
**Yellow Daffodil** — 10", #25620, 2000, long white and yellow gown ........................................$85.00
**Yellow Hat Doll** — 8", #25320, 2000, Maud Humphrey design...............................................$75.00

**Yes, Virginia, There Is a Santa Claus** — 8", #20200, 1999 – 2001, green dress with
lace collar and trim...................................................................................................$85.00
**Yolanda** — 12", 1965 only (Brenda Starr)...............................................$375.00 up
**Yugoslavia** — 8" h.p., BK, #789, 1968 – 1972 (Wendy)..................................$90.00
8" straight legs, #0789, #589, 1973 – 1975, marked "Alex" ........................$65.00
8" straight legs, #589, 1976 – 1986, marked "Alexander" ..........................$55.00
8", 1987 (see Collectors United/C.U. under Special Events/Exclusives)
**Yukon** — 8", #38610, 2004 – 2005, with sled and three dogs...........................$110.00
**Yuletide Angel** — (see Tree Topper)
**Zoe** — 10", #35821, 2003 – 2005 (Hannah), African-American, yellow dress, blue trim ...............$40.00
**Zorina Ballerina** — 17" compo., 1937 – 1938, extra make-up, must be mint condition
(Wendy Ann) ....................................................................................... $1,900.00 up

# Special Events/Exclusives

Shops and organizations are listed alphabetically.

**ABC Unlimited Productions**

Wendy Learns Her ABC's — 8", 1993, wears blue jumper and beret, ABC blocks
on skirt, wooden block stand, limited to 3,200.............................................$110.00

**Amanda Callahan's Susan's Dolls**

Amanda Sue — 8", #38120, 2004 (Maggie) limited to 250.......................................$100.00

**Ashton-Drake Galleries**

Apple of Grandma's Eye, The — 8", 2004, denim and red checked outfit, basket of cherries ..$90.00

Grandma's Little Honey — 8", 2004, yellow flower dress, straw hat .........................$90.00

Grandma's Little Sweetheart — 8", 2004, red print holiday outfit, gingerbread cookie...........$90.00

Some Bunny Loves Me, Grandma — 8", 2004, print dress and hat, with bunny ....................$90.00

Jacqueline Kennedy Bride — porcelain, 2004, taffeta wedding gown with rosettes of lace...$150.00

My First Christmas with Berta Hummel — 8", #39151, 2004, with ornament ........................$110.00

**Avon Products**

Party Dress Wendy — 8", #39150, 2004, pink dress.................................................$75.00

**Bay Area Alexander Doll Club**

Now I Am Ten — 8", #33855, 2002, white dress, pink trim ......................................$110.00

**Belk & Leggett Department Stores**

Miss Scarlett — 14", 1988 ...................................................................$150.00

Rachel/Rachael — 8", 1989, lavender gown.......................................................$65.00

Nancy Jean — 8", 1990, yellow/brown outfit .....................................................$60.00

Fannie Elizabeth — 8", 1991, floral dress with pinafore, limited to 3,000....................$85.00

Annabelle at Christmas — 8", 1992, plaid dress, holds Christmas cards, limited to 3,000 ......$125.00

Caroline — 8", 1993, limited to 3,600 .........................................................$100.00

Holly — 8", 1994, green eyes, freckles, red top with white skirt ..............................$85.00

Elizabeth Belk Angel — 8", #79648, 1996, red velvet............................................$175.00

**Bloomingdale's Department Store**

10", 1997, coral and leopard Cissette with Bloomie's big brown bag.............................$125.00

Golden Holiday Tree Topper — 1999, limited to 1,000 pieces, gilded gold and silver
embroidery on satin.......................................................................$150.00

Millennium Angel Tree Topper — 10", #27955, 2000, gold lamé dress with jewels.................$150.00

8", Angelic Tree Topper, #32035, 2001, burgundy velvet, limited to 300.........................$150.00

Snowflake Skater Sarah, #32030 ...............................................................$85.00

**Boscov's**

Bubbles — 8", #33815, 2003 (Wendy), pink outfit, limited to 500 ..............................$95.00

Frosted Dreams — 8", #35455, 2003, white outfit with fur......................................$100.00

**Celebrations Fantastic**

Let's Hop — 8", #33810, 2003, poodle skirt ...................................................$100.00

Dressed Like Mommy — 8", #39620, 2004, sunsuit, tulle petticoat ...............................$100.00

Lavender Fairy — 8", #33875, 2006, purple petal tutu..........................................$100.00

**Celia's Dolls**

David, the Little Rabbi — 8", 1991 – 1992, 3,600 made, three hair colors..............$65.00

**Cherished Friends Doll Shoppe**

Independent Traveler Coquette Jacqui — 10", #39490, 2004, zebra coat, fuchsia scarf.........$125.00

**Child at Heart Shop**

Easter Bunny — 8", 1991, limited to 3,000 (1,500 blondes, 750 brunettes, 750 redheads) .....$175.00

My Little Sweetheart — 8", 1992, limited to 4,500 (1,000 blondes, 1,000 brunettes with blue
eyes, 1,000 brunettes with green eyes, 1,000 redheads with green eyes, 500 blacks) ....$60.00

Trick and Treat — 8", 1993, sold in sets only (400 sets with red-haired/green-eyed "Trick" and black-haired/ black-eyed "Treat"; 1,200 sets with red-haired/green-eyed "Trick" and brunette/ brown-eyed "Treat"; 1,400 blonde/blue-eyed "Trick" and red-haired/brown-eyed "Treat") .. $175.00 set

## Christmas Shoppe

Boy and Girl, Alpine — 8" twins, 1992, in Alpine Christmas outfits, limited to 2,000 sets. .. $225.00 pr.

## Collectors United (C.U.)

## C. U. Gathering (Georgia)

Yugoslavia — 8", FAD, limited to 625 .......................................................................$70.00

Tippi Ballerina — 8", 1988, limited to 800 ...........................................................$300.00

Miss Leigh — 8", 1989, limited to 800 ....................................................................$80.00

Shea Elf — 8", 1990, limited to 1,000 ...................................................................$100.00

Ringmaster — 8", 1991, limited to 800 ...................................................................$75.00

Faith — 8", 1992, limited to 800 ...........................................................................$175.00

Hope — 8", 1993, blue dress (1910 style), limited to 900 ....................................$175.00

Love — 8", 1994, gold necklace and pearls on cap, limited to 2,400 ......................$75.00

Diane — 8", 1995, Back to the Fifties, limited to 800 .............................................$75.00

C.U. Varsity Sweater — white sweater, 1995, special event souvenir ........................$40.00

Olympia — 8", 1996, pants costume, with flag, limited to 800 .................................$90.00

Olympic Bag — 1996, special Alexander event souvenir ...........................................$40.00

C.U. Salutes Broadway — 8", 1997, burgundy theater outfit ..................................$110.00

Black Fur Stole — 1997, special Alexander event souvenir .......................................$30.00

Polynesian Princess — 8", 1998, print skirt and top ..............................................$175.00

Grass Skirt — 1998, special Alexander event souvenir ............................................$30.00

Fortune Teller — 8", 1999, red print costume trimmed in gold ..............................$125.00

Fortune Teller — 21", 1999, red print costume trimmed in gold...........................$1,050.00

Fortune Teller Accessories — 1999, scarves and bangle bracelets, special event ......$35.00

Carnival Queen — 16", 1999, pink or blue gown, limited to 24 .............................$300.00

Majestic Midway — 21", 1999, gold costume ...................................................... one-of-a-kind

Bonnie Blue Returns to Atlanta — 8", #31485, 2001, blue dress, limited to 500 ....................$125.00

Return to Tara — Scarlett, #32105, 2001, with Tara, limited to 100 ......................$225.00

Scarlett — 21", #31540, 2001, white dress, green sash .........................................$350.00

Greta — 16", #35530, 2002, orange checked dress, white straw bag, limited to 150 .............$175.00

Georgia Peach — 8", 2002, blonde or brunette, peach taffeta dress, straw hat.........................$75.00

Coca-Cola Cissy — #35160, 2002, red checked blouse, Coke bottle, straw hat....................$350.00

Coca-Cola Cissy — #35161, 2002, African-American, limited to 40 ......................$475.00

Sizzling Cissy — 21", #39195, 2004, limited to 150 .............................................$400.00

Sizzling Cissy — 21", 2004, African-American .....................................................$450.00

Candi Corn — 8", #40035, 2004, with kitty and game.........................................$100.00

Treats for Wendy – 8", #39250, 2004, orange dress, tulle skirt ...............................$80.00

April — 8", #31705, 2004 (Wendy), white dress, pansy trim, hat.............................$90.00

Wendy's Tea at the Waldorf — 8", pink dress, limited to 40 ..................................$150.00

## C.U. Nashville Winter Wonderland

Nashville Skater — 8", 1991, FAD, limited to 200 (Black Forest) ..........................$110.00

Nashville Skier — 8", 1992, FAD, limited to 200 (Tommy Tittlemouse) .................$100.00

First Comes Love — 8", 1993, FAD, limited to 200. .............................................$225.00

Captain's Cruise — 1994, with trunk and wardrobe, limited to 250......................$200.00

Nashville Goes Country — 8", 1995, western outfit with guitar.............................$125.00

Nashville Sunny — 8", 1996, yellow raincoat, hat.................................................$100.00

Miss Tennessee Waltz — 8", 1997, long ball gown, coat .......................................$125.00

C.U. Goes to Camp — 8", 1998 .........................................................................$100.00

Irish Cissy — 21", #27460, 2000, green gown, silver cape, limited to 200...............$500.00

Shannon — 8", #27255, 2000, green costume .......................................................$75.00

Lindsey — 8", #28920, 2001, print dress, straw hat, limited to 100........................$75.00

# Special Events/Exclusives

Autumn Splendor Coquette Cissy, 10", C.U., 2005. She wears pants and a jacket, and carries a tan purse.

Wendy Learns Nursery Rhymes — 8", #34520, 2002, with cardboard wardrobe and extra clothes.$125.00
Blue Danube — 21", #30685, 2001, blue gown ..................................................................................$250.00
21", African-American, limited to 36.................................................................................$350.00
8", #28211, blue gown, 2001 .............................................................................................$95.00
8", African-American, 2001, limited to 100......................................................................$125.00
Emily — 8", #38925, 2004, with doll, lavender coat, striped dress ....................................$85.00
Coquette N.Y., N.Y. — #40955, pink suit, velvet hat, limited to 60 .................................$150.00
City Shopper Wendy — 8", #40970, taffeta dress, straw hat .............................................$100.00
Cissy at Harvest Ball — 21", limited to 60 ....................................................................$375.00
Autumn Splendor Coquette — 10", 2006, pants, suede jacket...........................................$150.00
Autumn Wendy — 8", 2006, pants, velvet jacket..............................................................$100.00

## C.U. Greenville Show

Bride — 8", 1990, FAD, of Tommy Snooks, limited to 250 (Betsy Brooks) ..........................$100.00
Witch/Halloween — 8", 1990, FAD, limited to 250 (Little Jumping Joan) ..........................$100.00
Oktoberfest — 8", 1992, FAD, limited to 200.................................................................$100.00
C.U. Columbia, S.C. Camelot — 8", 1991, FAD (Maid Marian), limited to 400 ..................$125.00
C.U. Columbia, S.C., Homecoming Queen — 21", #28205, 2000, white gown, limited to 200..$325.00
C.U. Columbia, S.C., Homecoming Queen — 21", 2000, African-American, limited to 24....$600.00
C.U. Jacksonville — 8" Greta, 1996, black doll, blue sundress............................................$150.00

## C.U. Doll Shop Exclusives

Cameo Lady — 10", 1991, white dress, black trim, limited to 1,000....................................$125.00
Le Petit Boudoir — 10", 1993, FAD, limited to 700 .......................................................$175.00
America's Junior Miss — 8", 1994, white gown, medallion, limited to 1,200 ......................$70.00
Fitness — 8", 1995, tennis outfit .....................................................................................$60.00
Judge's Interview — 8", 1996, limited to 500.................................................................$70.00
Talent — 8", 1996, gold tuxedo jacket, black shorts .........................................................$65.00
Easter of Yesteryear — 8", 1995, comes with rabbit.........................................................$75.00
Sailing with Sally — 8", 1998, white dress, wooden boat..................................................$100.00
Gary Green — 8", 1998 ...................................................................................................$65.00
Christmas Morn — 8", 1999, #80130, nightgown, teddy bear, limited to 411 pieces.................$75.00
Sterling Light, Sterling Bright — 8", #30721, 2000, silver angel lighted tree topper..............$125.00
Katy — 8", #28925, 2000, printed dress, straw hat, limited to 100 ...........................................$85.00

## Colonial Southwest

Tanya — 8", 1999, honors M.A.D.C. former president Tanya McWhorter, limited to 550.....$200.00

## Colonial Williamsburg

Charlotte — 10", #26985, 2000, pink taffeta, eighteenth century dress........................$150.00
Colleen — 10", #31535, 2001, vintage cotton dress with panniers................................$150.00
Caroline — 8", #35230, 2002, eighteenth century cape, green costume .................$175.00
Catherine — 8", #33890, 2003, long satin dress, cape.......................................$100.00
Frances — 8", #41835, 2006, white gown, green cape.........................................$100.00
Anne (The Spring Season)— 8", #33891, 2004, basket of tulips ............................$100.00
    The Fall Season — 8", #39175, 2004, long green dress ...............................$100.00
    The Summer Season — 8", #33892, 2004, white shadow-striped dress ...........$100.00

## Disney Annual Showcase of Dolls

Cinderella — 10", 1989, #1, blue satin gown, limited to 250 .............................$600.00
Snow White — 12", 1990, #2, limited to 750 (Nancy Drew) ..............................$150.00
Alice in Wonderland/White Rabbit — 10", 1991, #3, limited to 750 .................$350.00
Queen of Hearts — 10", 1992, #4, limited to 500...........................................$350.00
Alice in Wonderland/Jabberwocky — 11" – 12" (Lissy), 1993, #5, limited to 500.................$325.00
Tweedledee & Tweedledum — 8", 1994, #6, wear beany hats with propellers,
    names on collar, limited to 750 ...................................................... $300.00 pr.
Morgan LeFay — 10", #797537, 1995, #7, limited to 500 ...............................$375.00
Bobby (Bobbie) Soxer — 8", 1990 – 1991 ....................................................$175.00
Mouseketeer — 8", 1991, blue skirt, white top .............................................$175.00

Roller Blades — 8", 1992, "Thoroughly Modern Wendy"...............................................$100.00
Round Up Cowgirl — 8", 1992, blue/white outfit................................................$150.00
Annette (Funicello) — 14" porcelain portrait sculpted by Robert Tonner, 1993, limited to 400 . $450.00
Monique — 8", 1993, made for Disney, limited to 250, lavender with lace trim....................$400.00
Snow White — 10", 1993, Disney crest colors.......................................................$175.00
Belle — 8" h.p., gold gown, 1994 ..................................................................$125.00
Cinderella — 14", 1994, Disney catalog, has two outfits, limited to 900 ..........................$200.00
   14", 1995, different gown, no extra outfits..........................................$175.00
Wendy's Favorite Pastime — 8", 1994, comes with hula hoop....................................$75.00
Sleeping Beauty — 14", 1995, waist-length hair, blue gown from movie and two other outfits. $200.00
Blue Fairy Tree Topper — 10", #79545, 1995 catalog exclusive (Cissette) ...........................$175.00
Snow White — 14", 1995............................................................................$150.00
Mary Poppins — 10", 1996, #79403 ................................................................$125.00
Alice — 14", 1996, catalog exclusive, limited to 1,500 ...........................................$150.00
Knave — 8", 1996, #8, wears two of Spades card, limited to 500 ...................................$150.00
Toto — 8", 1997, #9, comes with wooden basket, limited to 750 ....................................$125.00
Goldilocks and Baby Bear — 8", 1998, #10, purple print costume with Raikes bear.............$250.00
Mouseketeers — 8", 1999, Alex and Wendy as Mouseketeers, #11....................................$225.00
My Little Buttercup — 8", 2000, #12, yellow dress and hat trimmed in flowers and ribbons,
   #30320, limited to 200.............................................................$150.00
Sleeping Beauty — 8", 1999, pink satin gown, limited to 1,000 ....................................$125.00
Snow White — 8", 1999, Disney crest colors, limited to 1,000 .....................................$150.00
Ariel — 8", 1999, #25085, long red hair, green mermaid costume ...................................$100.00
Belle — 8", 1999, #25075, yellow ball gown with gold trim ........................................$125.00
Cinderella — 8", 1999, #25080, blue satin gown, limited to 1,000 .................................$125.00
Michael and Jane Banks — 8", 1999, #80450, 8" girl, boy limited to 200...........................$150.00
Jasmine — 8", 1999, #25095, lavender chiffon harem outfit.........................................$125.00
Belle Tree Topper — #31770, 2001.................................................................$175.00
Wendy's Wardrobe — 8", #31780, 2001, three dresses, cardboard wardrobe, limited to 170.$150.00

## Disney, Walt

Disney World Auction — 21", one-of-a-kind dolls ...................................... no prices available
   Sleeping Beauty — #1 in Series, 1989, 21", long blonde hair, in pink with rhinestones and pearls
   Christine (Phantom of the Opera) — #2, 1990, blue/white outfit with white mask (Jacqueline)
   Queen Isabella — #3, 1991, green/gold gown, long red hair (Jacqueline)
   It's a Girl — #4, 1992, comes with 8" baby in carriage (Cissy, Baby Genius)
   Emperor and Nightingale — #4, 1992, 8" winged Wendy Ann (23" Emperor bear by Gund)
   Women in the Garden — #5, 1993, four dolls (Cissette) dressed like 1867 Monet painting
   Cissy Bride — 1923 and 8" Flower Girl and Ring Bearer, #5, 1993
   Romeo and Juliet — #6, 21" h.p., 1994, using 1950s bald nude Maggie dolls, rewigged,
      dressed in blue, burgundy, and gold
   Sir Lancelot duLac — #7, 1995, 1950s doll dressed in burgundy and gold
   Queen Guinevere — #7, 1995, 1950s doll dressed in burgundy and gold
   Chess Set — 35 dolls from 8" to 21" on a satin chess board
   Mary Poppins and Children — 1999, 21" Mary Poppins, 14" Jane and Michael

## Doll & Teddy Bear Expo

Madame (Alexander) or Shadow of Madame — 8", 1994, in blue, limited to 500 first year...$150.00
Madame with Love — 8", #79536, 1995, has hat with "100" on top, limited to 750 .................$75.00
Maggie's First Doll — 8", 1996, pink cotton dress, carries cloth Alice doll............................$250.00
Miss Eliza Doolittle — 21", 1996, white lace dress, auction piece ................................... one-of-a-kind
Josephine Baker — 21", black Cissy, 1996, banana costume, auction piece.................. one-of-a-kind
Gingerbread — outfit only, for 8" doll ............................................................$50.00
Love Is in the Air — 8", Bride, 1999, limited to 100 ..............................................$125.00
Holiday Magic — 8", 1999, limited to 100, red and gold metallic gown................................$125.00
American as Apple Pie — 8", #27490, 2000, 100 pieces (Maggie)....................................$125.00

Shadow of Madame, 8", 1994, made for Doll & Teddy Bear Expo.

99

America the Beautiful outfit — 2000, with boots.....................................................................$75.00
Wild, Wild West — 8", #27495, 2000, limited to 100.........................................................$225.00
Wendy Visits the World's Fair — 8", #28905, 2002, red checked dress, limited to 100...........$100.00
Happy Birthday — 8", #35885, 2002, purple print party dress...............................................$85.00
Lifetime Achievement — 8", #36360, 2004, pink formal ....................................................$125.00
Lifetime Achievement — 8", #36365, 2004, African-American ............................................$125.00
Acceptance Speech Coquette Cissy — 8", #40150, 2004, Caucasian ....................................$150.00
Acceptance Speech Coquette Cissy — 8", #40155, 2004, African-American ..........................$150.00

### Doll Finders
Fantasy — 8", 1990, limited to 350 ...................................................................................$175.00

### Dolls and Ducks
Ice Princess — 8", 1999, silver gown and tiara ..................................................................$150.00

### Doll Market, The
Jacquetta Coquette, Jacqui — 10", #40105, 2004, blue silk dress ........................................$150.00

### Dolls 'n Bearland
Pandora — 8", 1991, limited to 3,600 (950 brunettes, 950 redheads, 1,700 blondes) .............$150.00

### Dolly Dears
Bo Peep — 1987, holds staff, black sheep wears man's hat, white sheep wears woman's hat
      (sheep made exclusively by Dakin) .............................................................................$225.00
Susannah Clogger — 8", 1992, has freckles, limited to 400 (Maggie) ..................................$200.00
Jack Be Nimble — 8", 1993, FAD, limited to 288..............................................................$100.00
Princess and the Pea — 8", 1993, limited to 1,000 .............................................................$100.00

### Dream Dolls and the Doll Peddler
Golden Elegance Coquette Cissy — 10", #41595, 2006, long gold gown ................................$150.00

### Elegant Doll Shop
Elegant Easter — 8", 1999, pink checked dress with bunny...................................................$125.00
Heart of Dixie — 8", 1999, red and lace outfit....................................................................$85.00

### Enchanted Doll House
Rickrack on Pinafore — 8", 1980, limited to 3,000.............................................................$275.00
Eyelet Pinafore — 8", 1981, limited to 3,423.....................................................................$275.00
Blue or Pink Ballerina — 8", 1983 – 1985, FAD, blonde or brunette doll in trunk
      with extra clothes.....................................................................................................$175.00
Cinderella and Trunk — 14", 1985, has glass slipper...........................................................$275.00
25th Anniversary (The Enchanted Doll) — 10", 1988, long gown, limited to 5,000 ...............$150.00
Ballerina — 8", 1989, blue tutu, limited to 360 .................................................................$125.00
Vermont Maiden — 8", 1990 – 1992, official Vermont Bicentennial doll, limited to 3,600
      (800 blondes, 2,800 brunettes).................................................................................$75.00
Farmer's Daughter — 8", 1991, limited to 4,000 (1,000 blondes, 1,500 redheads,
1,500 brunettes) ...........................................................................................................$85.00
Farmer's Daughter — 8", 1992, "Goes To Town" (cape and basket added), limited to 1,600.....$100.00

### Fashion Doll Quarterly
Cosmopolitan Coquette Cissy — 10", #40405, 2005, long black coat, with dog..........$150.00

### FAO Schwarz
Pussycat — 18", 1987, pale blue dress and bonnet.............................................................$100.00
Brooke  — 14", 1988, blonde or brunette (Mary Ann), with Steiff bear .....................$125.00
David and Diana — 8", 1989, in red, white, and denim, with wooden wagon ...... $225.00 set
Samantha — 14", 1989, white with black dots (Mary Ann) .........................................$125.00
Me & My Scassi — 21", 1990, dressed in all red, Arnold Scassi original (Cissy) .......$400.00
Sailor — 8", 1991............................................................................................................$125.00
Carnavale Doll — 14", 1991 – 1992 (Samantha).........................................................$125.00
Beddy-Bye Brooke — 14", 1991 – 1992 (Mary Ann) ...............................................$125.00
Beddy-Bye Brenda (Brooke's sister) — 8", 1992, sold only as set with 14" doll.... $225.00 set
Wendy Shops FAO — 8", 1993, red/white outfit, carries FAO Schwarz shopping bag....$125.00
My Secret Garden — 8", 1994, trunk with wardrobe................................................$300.00

**Farmer's Daughter, 8", 1991, limited to 4,000.**

Little Huggums — 12", 1994, red dress, bib and headband, has FAO logo horse ....................$65.00

Little Women — 8", 1994, dressed in outfits from movie, limited to 500 sets
      (five dolls) and 700 of each girl.......................................................... $125.00 ea., $750.00 set

Princess trunk set — 8", #79526, 1995 ...............................................................$300.00

Fun with Dick & Jane — 8", #70509, 1995, limited to 1,200 pieces...................$275.00 set

Lucy Ricardo — 8", limited to 1,200..................................................................$250.00

I Love Lucy — 8" Fred, Ethel, Lucy, and Ricky, sold as set only, limited to 1,200 ...........$675.00 set

Twilight Tango Cissy — 21", #35210, 2003, black and white gown, limited to 100 ................$350.00

Wendy Loves Patrick — 8", #37200, 2003, with dog Patrick ...................................$125.00

Chinoiserie Cissy — 21", #33335, 2003, long sheath gown ......................................$325.00

The Little Rascals — 8" Alfalfa, Darla, Spanky, Buckwheat, and dog, Petey, 1996,
      limited to 2,000 sets..............................................................$550.00 set

Singin' in the Rain — 8" Gene Kelly, Debbie Reynolds, with lamppost, 1996, 1952 film... $300.00 set

I Dream of Jeannie — 8", harem outfit, military uniform ......................................$250.00

Lucy and Ethel — 8", 1997, candy factory episode ...............................................$175.00

The Honeymooners — 8", 1997, Ralph and Alice Norton and Trixie, limited to 2,000 sets...$500.00

Grease — 1998, 10" Danny and Sandy in leather outfits ........................................$175.00

Fay Wray with Steiff King Kong — 1998, 10" doll...................................................$500.00

Silver Sensation — 16" Alex fashion doll, limited to 100........................................$250.00

Gallery Opening Alex —16", limited to 500.........................................................$300.00

Publisher's Meeting Alex — 16", limited to 200....................................................$150.00

Magnificent Mile Alex — 16", 2000, limited to 40 pieces........................................$550.00

Wendy Loves FAO — 8", #34580, 2003, with FAO bear .........................................$175.00

Star Wars — 8" Luke Skywalker, Han Solo, Leia, #35515, 2003, limited to 1,000 ................$400.00

Pinocchio and Blue Fairy — 8", #34035, 2003, limited to 160 .................................$175.00

80th Anniversary Wendy Trunk Set — 8", #35215, 2003..........................................$250.00

Lord of the Rings Set — 2004, 8" Frodo in green cape, 10" Coquette Arwen in purple gown,
      limited to 300.............................................................................$275.00

Dolly Dots Wendy-Kin Wood — 8", #39515, wood jointed doll, red dress .............................$250.00

Cute as a Button Trunk — 8", #39530, 2004, extra clothes, case that looks like a child's blouse.. $325.00

Elegant Attitude Coquette Cissy — 10", #39535, 2004, long black evening dress...................$150.00

Binah — 9", #39525, 2004, cloth doll, with raincoat, umbrella, and mouse .............................$50.00

Going to the Parade Wendy-Kin Wood — 8", #41260, 2005, blue coat, limited to 200...........$300.00

Cissy 50th Anniversary — 21", #41400, 2005, long silver gown ...............................$375.00

Pals Forever — 8", #41585, 2005, pink dress, Chaos bear ......................................$125.00

## First Modern Doll Club (N.Y. Doll Club)

Autumn in N.Y. — 10", 1991, FAD, red skirt, fur-trimmmed cape, hat, muff, and skates, limited to 260...$150.00

## GoCollect.com

Morning Ritual Cissy — 21", 2001, bathrobe, Yardley soap......................................$275.00

Afternoon Out — 16", #30315, 2001, red hair, sheath dress .....................................$200.00

Little Wendy Alexander — 8", #31920, 2001, pink gingham dress.............................$85.00

## Grant-a-Wish

Tour D'Jour — 16" Alex fashion doll, #34740, 2002, tweed coat, tan skirt, limited to 350 ....$175.00

Show Stopper Alex — faux fur coat, 16", 2002, red dress ............................................ one-of-a-kind

## Home Shopping Network

Blue Angel — 8", 1997, #19972, dark blue and gold dress and halo, resin wings, limited to 3,000.....$175.00

## Horchow

Pamela Plays Dress Up — 12", 1993, in trunk with wardrobe, limited to 1,250 (Lissy).........$325.00

Pamela Trousseau — 12", 1994, trunk and trousseau, limited to 265 .....................$400.00

14" trunk set, 1995 .....................................................................................$200.00

Mary Ann Dances for Grandma Trunk Set — 14", 1996........................................$225.00

## I. Magnin

Little Huggums (Imaginarium Shop) — 12", 1991, special outfits, bald or wigged,
      two wig colors .................................................................................$50.00

# Special Events/Exclusives

Little Huggums — 12" with cradle, 1992 ............................................................................$100.00
Cheerleader — 8", 1990, FAD, "5" on sweater ....................................................................$70.00
Miss Magnin — 10", 1991 – 1993, limited to 2,500 (Cissette) ...................................$150.00
Little Miss Magnin — 8", 1992, with tea set and teddy bear, limited to 3,600 ......................$200.00
Bon Voyage Miss Magnin — 10", 1993, navy/white gloves, has steamer trunk, limited
 to 2,500 .................................................................................................................$250.00
Bon Voyage Little Miss Magnin — 8", sailor dress, carries teddy bear and suitcase, 1993,
 limited to 3,500.......................................................................................................$225.00
Little Miss Magnin Supports the Arts — 8", 1994, pink painter smock, wears red ribbon
 for AIDS Awareness..................................................................................................$175.00

## Jacobsons
Wendy Starts Her Collection — 1994, has bear, limited to 2,400..............................$175.00
Little Huggums — 1995 ..............................................................................................$60.00

## Jean's Doll Shop
Suellen — 12", 1992, FAD ..........................................................................................$125.00
Wendy Walks Her Dog — 8", #79549, 1995, limited to 500 ......................................$75.00

## Lenox China Company
My Own Bell — 8", #27475, 2000, holiday dress with bell, limited to 1,000 ...........$125.00
Little Miss American Pride — 8", #34540, 2003, long white gown..............................$125.00
My Valentine — 8", #33725, 2003, red and white dress ..........................................$100.00
Snowflake Elegance — 8", #34525, 2003 ...................................................................$100.00
Christmas Holly — 8", #34535, 2003 ..........................................................................$85.00
Faith — 8", #31895, 2001, pink dress, basket .............................................................$95.00
Easter Lily — 8", #33750, 2003, lavender dress, limited to 1,000...............................$90.00
Lil' Sweetheart — 8", #36420, 2003, with heart ornament......................................$100.00
Little Miss Firecracker — 8", #36425, 2003, long dress, red hair ...............................$85.00
Miss Butterfly — 8", #36430, 2003, with Halloween ornament ...............................$100.00
Christmas Candy — 8", #36435, 2003 (Wendy), with ornament ...............................$100.00
Winter Rose — 8", #36440, 2003, long rose gown, with ornament...........................$100.00
Cherry Pie — 8", #31710, 2004, red checked dress .....................................................$90.00
Holiday — 8", #31725, 2004, burgundy dress..............................................................$85.00
Starlight Witch — 8", #31715, 2004, purple taffeta ................................................$100.00
Easter Joy — 8", #38160, 2004, lavender checked dress .........................................$100.00
Merrilee — 8", #40965, 2005, lace skirt, green top .....................................................$85.00
Easter Finery — 8", #39975, 2005, white organza, straw hat....................................$100.00

## Lillian Vernon
Christmas Doll — 8", #79630, 1996, green and gold holly print dress .......................$90.00
Miss Millennium — 8", 1999, #80580, blue ball gown, watch ................................$125.00
Christmas 2000 — 8", #27555, 2000, gown of white net with silver flecks, angel wings,
 silver crown, Christmas 2000 banner ......................................................................$75.00
St. Valentine's Day — 8", #26410, 2000, red and white outfit, limited to 2,000........$90.00
Easter — 8", #26150, 2000, white dress, plush bunny.................................................$90.00
Halloween Magic — 8", #27750, 2000, black velvet top ...........................................$80.00
Nutcracker — 8", #27560, 2000, Nutcracker outfit...................................................$100.00
1940s Christmas — 8", #31740, 2001, red velvet coat ...............................................$90.00
Autumn Fairy — 8", #32040, 2001, bronze and gold outfit........................................$75.00
Halloween — 8", #31465, 2001, black and orange cat costume ..................................$75.00
4th of July — 8", #33615, 2003, white dresss .............................................................$75.00
Peace Angel — 8", #35130, 2003, white gown .........................................................$125.00
St. Patty's Day — 8", #31695, 2003, green costume ...................................................$80.00
Trick or Treat Masquerade — 8", #33620, 2003, long black dress.............................$125.00
Valentine's Day — 8", #33620, 2003, red velvet.........................................................$80.00
Winter Wonderland — 8", #35120, 2003, red velvet, skates ......................................$80.00
Angel of Hope — 8", #37155, 2003, velvet costume ................................................$125.00

Easter Portrait — 8", #35205, 2003, lavender dress, rabbit ........................................$80.00
Happy Holidays to You — 8", #37150, 2003, red checked dress ...............................$75.00
He Loves Me — 8", #35145, 2003, valentine outfit................................................$75.00
Irish Eyes — 8", #35150, 2002, red hair, green outfit ........................................$75.00
Pumpkins for Sale — 8", #37165, 2003, with pumpkin cart....................................$100.00
Spiderella — 8", #37160, 2003, Halloween outfit................................................$85.00
Bedazzled Lil' Devil — 8", #33735, 2005, red tutu ...........................................$85.00
American Beauty — 8", #33865, 2005, long white dress trimmed in red....................$85.00

## Lord & Taylor
Victoria — 14", 1989 ..........................................................................$80.00

## Madame Alexander Doll Club (M.A.D.C.) Convention Dolls
Fairy Godmother Outfit — 1983, for 8" non-Alexander designed by Judy LaManna ...........$325.00
Ballerina — 8", 1984, FAD, limited to 360......................................................$225.00
Happy Birthday — 8", 1985, FAD, limited to 450..............................................$275.00
Scarlett — 8", 1986, F.A.D., red instead of green ribbon, limited to 625.................$250.00
Cowboy — 8", 1987, limited to 720..............................................................$375.00
Flapper — 10", 1988, FAD, black outfit instead of red, limited to 720...................$175.00
Briar Rose — 8", 1989, uses Cissette head, limited to 804 ................................$275.00
Riverboat Queen (Lena) — 8", 1990, limited to 925 ..........................................$225.00
Queen Charlotte — 10", 1991, blue/gold outfit, limited to under 900 ....................$375.00
Prom Queen (Memories) — 8", 1992, limited to 1,100 ........................................$125.00
Drucilla — 14", 1992, limited to 268..........................................................$225.00
Diamond Lil (Days Gone By) — 10", 1993, black gown, limited to 876 ....................$375.00
Anastasia — 14", 1993, FAD, available at convention, limited to 489 ....................$225.00
Navajo Woman — 8", 1994, comes with rug, sheep, and Hopi Kachina, limited to 835 .........$350.00
Flower Girl — 8", companion to 1995 souvenir doll, could be purchased separately.............$150.00
Folsom, Frances — 10", 1995 convention doll, #79517 (married Grover Cleveland) ...........$275.00
Showgirl — 10", 1996 convention doll, pink, blue, green, lavender, white feathers ...............$275.00
10", 1996 convention, black feather, limited to 20 pieces.........................................$500.00
A Little Bit of Country — 8", 1997, #79080, with guitar.......................................$225.00
Rose Festival Queen — 8", #79450, 1998, white gown, cape with roses .......................$200.00
Margaret O'Brien — 8", #79590, 1998 Convention Companion doll ...............................$175.00
Orange Blossom — 10", 1999, long peach dress and gold straw hat ...........................$125.00
Electra — 8", 1999, Convention Companion doll, silver costume...............................$75.00
Lilly Pulitzer — 21", 1999, Cissy Luncheon centerpiece doll, limited to 25 .........$1,400.00
Cissy Accessories — 1999, no doll, accessories for 21" doll .................................$60.00
Little Miss Bea — 2000, #26410, 8", honors Madame Bea Alexander, limited to 500............$225.00
Going to M.A.D.C.C. — 8", #26415, 2000 convention doll, black bodice, ecru tulle,
    limited to 700...........................................................................$250.00
Seaside Serenade Gala 2000 — 16" (Alex), long blue gown with rhinestones........................$350.00
Abigail Adams — 10", #31510, 2001 convention doll, blue and lavender dress (Cissette)......$175.00
Louisa May Alcott — 8", #31511, 2001, limited to 325, vintage blue and white gown...........$125.00
Aviatrix — 8", #31512, 2001, leather bomber jacket, khaki pants ............................$125.00
Aviatrix centerpiece — 8", 2001, African-American, limited to 52 ...........................$175.00
Evening at the Pops Cissy — 21", #31735, 2001, luncheon doll, lavender dress, hat ..............$275.00
Seaside Serenade Gala 2000 Centerpiece — 16", #27510, pink dressing gown (Alex) ...........$450.00
Charles River Regatta Alex — 16", 2001, navy linen pants, white top, limited to 310 ...........$275.00
Alex Regatta Ball — 16", #31650, 2001, limited to 52 .......................................$475.00
Cissy Gala — 21", 2000 luncheon doll, long blue and silver gown, limited to 300..................$450.00
Cissy Gala 2000 Centerpiece — 21", #27265, 2000, lavender dress, blonde ...................$700.00
Skating Into Your Heart — 8", #26250, 2000, Travel Party....................................$175.00
Little Miss USA — 8", 2001, short patriotic costume.........................................$85.00
Cissy Diva — #31730, 2001 centerpiece doll, fitted satin gown, faux fur, limited to 45..........$700.00
San Antonio Rose — 8", #34485, 2002, travel doll ..........................................$175.00

**Anastasia, 14", 1993 (Mary Ann). Cinderella's stepsister. Limited to 489. Special doll for M.A.D.C.**

Martha Jefferson, 8", #41785, 2006 M.A.D.C. Convention Doll. Limited to 480. Pink 1780s vintage costume. Represents wife of Thomas Jefferson.

Thomas Jefferson, 8", #41895, 2006 M.A.D.C. Convention at Williamsburg, Virginia companion doll. Limited to 300. 1780s period costume.

Princess Fairy — 8", #34455, 2002, All in a Row souvenir doll, gold star wand with hearts, limited to 230................................................................................$150.00

Navajo Boy — 8", #34480, 2002, travel doll centerpiece doll, limited to 45............................$350.00

Alice in Wonderland — 10", #35415, 2002, Welcome Breakfast centerpiece doll, comes with 8" plush bunny, limited to 65................................................................$275.00

Cissy Bridesmaid — 21", #34960, 2002, Cissy Luncheon centerpiece doll, pink lace over satin, limited to 40 ..............................................................................$600.00

Cissy Bride — 21", 2002, Cissy Luncheon doll, white lace over satin, #34955, June Bride ...$350.00

Sketchbook Cissy — 21", #34460, 2002, Banquet centerpiece doll, long pale pink gown, limited to 70................................................................................................$500.00

Sketchbook Cissette — 10", #34445, 2002, Kansas City Convention doll, limited to 450, matches 21" doll..................................................................................$250.00

Masquerade Alex — 16", #34470, 2002, Alex souvenir, limited to 285, long sleek lavender gown ..$175.00

Viva La Paris — 16", #34490, 2002 centerpiece, African-American, lavender feather showgirl costume, limited to 40..............................................................$275.00

Madame Sketchbook II — 8", #34465, 2002 companion, light pink dress.............................$65.00

White Rabbit — 10", plush, 2002 souvenir, blue dress, limited to 450 .....................................$20.00

M.A.D.C.C. Flapper — 21", red taffeta with beading, raffle (Cissy) ...........................one-of-a-kind

Georgia — 10", #37005, 2003 companion, white Victorian dress, lavender sash, limited to 200 ....$225.00

Savannah — 8", #36995, 2003 convention doll, trunk, basket, limited to 525...........................$200.00

Savannah Slumber Party — 8", #32456, gown, blue robe, panties, shoes in black stripe hatbox, outfit only..................................................................................$50.00

Wendy Visits Tybee Island — 8", #37040, 2003, travel doll, shorts, lavender top, pink bag, limited to 300............................................................................................$125.00

Billy Visits Tybee Island — 8", #37245, 2003, travel centerpiece, red top, shorts....................$200.00

Taylor Debutante Alexandra Fairchild Ford — 16", #37765, 2003, Alex centerpiece, white long dress, red curly wig, limited to 35.....................................................$325.00

Sweater Set — #32459, 2003, Savannah 20+ souvenir outfit, only for 8", pink knit sweater and hat in black striped box, limited to 60 ..............................................$50.00

Midnight Cissy — 21", #37015, 2003, Cissy event souvenir, black and white suit, hat, olive skintone, limited to 259.........................................................................$500.00

Mademoiselle Cissy — 21", 37010, 2003, Cissy event centerpiece, suit, hat, limited to 40......$600.00

Southern Belle Cissy — 21", 31105, 2003, banquet centerpiece, blue raw silk and lace antebellum dress, limited to 65................................................................$550.00

Yellow Rose of Texas — 8", #39180, 2004 souvenir doll, yellow and white bustle gown, silver boots and spurs, hat ............................................................................$225.00

Cinco de Mayo Cissette — 10", Cissette, event centerpiece, #34180, red satin dress, limited to 50 .$200.00

Mariachi Cissette — 10", #34220, 2004, souvenir doll, black jacket, skirt .............................$150.00

Quanah Parker — 8", #33930, 2004, breakfast centerpiece, Indian outfit, blanket, long feather headdress ........................................................................................$400.00

Blue Bonnet Maiden — 8", #34125, 2004, 20+ Event, Indian outfit, limited to 65 .................$350.00

Lone Star Wendy — 8", #34410, 2004, convention special, black checked shirt ....................$200.00

Billy Bob's Bronco Rider — 8", #33905, 2004, travel doll, red shirt, chaps ..........................$125.00

Chisholm Trail Cowgirl — 8", #34156, 2004, All in a Row, blue checked shirt ......................$150.00

Chisholm Trail Cowpoke — 8", #34255, 2004, All in a Row centerpiece, chaps....................$225.00

Texas Ranger Companion Doll — 8", #33900, 2004, brown suit, long black coat..................$100.00

Western Matinee Lissy Outfit — blue and white cowgirl outfit, blue boots .............................$85.00

1950s Lissy Cowgirl Centerpiece Outfit — red and brown outfit, brown boots.....................$200.00

Dance Hall Cissy — 21", 2004, 77 each of green, red, purple, and turquoise costumes..........$325.00

Silver Spurs — 21", #33970, 2004, Cissy centerpiece, denim pants, jacket, leather chaps......$650.00

Cattle Baron — 21", #33975, 2004, banquet centerpiece, black suit, hat ...............................$700.00

Hall of Fame Alex — 16", 2004, western outfit, suede coat ...................................................$225.00

Western Debutante — 16", #33990, 2004, striped top, western hat .......................................$175.00

Affair to Remember — 10", #37839, 2005 convention souvenir, Coquette, velvet top with

white full long skirt............................................................................$200.00
Miss California —8", #41035, 2005 companion doll, navy vintage swimsuit, limited to 275.....$85.00
California Poppy —8", #41100, 2005, Thank You doll, gold and green outfit ........................$100.00
Affair to Remember — 16", #41030, 2005, banquet centerpiece, Coco, black velvet top
   with full skirt....................................................................................$275.00
Traveling to Disneyland — 8", #41080, 2005, travel souvenir, Maggie, pink cotton dress
   decorated with Disney characters...........................................................$200.00
Traveling with Hannah —10", #37727, 2005, travel party centerpiece, denim pants, jacket,
   mouse ears hat, small plush Mickey Mouse .....................................................$70.00
Miss San Jose — 8", #41095, Maggie, 2005, breakfast centerpiece, red vintage bathing suit ....$125.00
Cissy Vixen — 21", #1110, 2005 Souvenir, pink or mauve taffeta dress with rhinestone
   bar accents, limited to 240....................................................................$500.00
Cissy Vamp — 21", 2005 Cissy centerpiece, beaded dress ....................................$1,100.00
Padre Sierra — 8", #41065, limited to 35, 2005, All in a Row centerpiece, brown hooded
   robe, cross, and Bible........................................................................$110.00
Mission Bride — 8", #41070, 2005 AIR souvenir, long white lace dress ........................$100.00
Little Miss California — 5", #37837, 2005, breakfast souvenir doll, vintage bathing suit .........$40.00
League of Her Own —8", #41115, 2005, blue vintage outfit with felt catcher's mitt..............$110.00
Hey Arnold —8", #41120, 2005, white suit, red striped coat and hat, tray of drinks .............$165.00
Tea with Sarah —8", #41045, 2005, 20+ souvenir, black 1800s costume ........................$225.00
Dance Hall Cissette — 10", #41085, 2005, purple saloon costume with aqua drape ...............$175.00
San Francisco Lady —10", Cissette centerpiece, #41090, long pink
   checked dress and hat, limited to 45 .........................................................$225.00
Celebration Jadde Lee, 16", #41050, 2005 Alex centerpiece, long red Chinese dress .............$275.00
Celebration Alexandra Fairchild Ford —16", #41060, black brocade Chinese gown..............$175.00
Martha Jefferson — 8", #41785, 2006 souvenir doll, pink and wine striped ball gown, cameo. $225.00
Thomas Jefferson — 8", #41895, 2006 Companion, green waistcoat, tan pants, black hat ......$85.00
Patsy Jefferson — 8", #41840, 2006 Travel Doll, blue vintage dress .....................................$125.00
Polly Jefferson — 5", 2006 Breakfast Souvenir...............................................................$35.00
Mrs. Hopkinson — 10", #41845, 2006 Travel centerpiece, pink print vintage design, straw hat ...$225.00
Sally Hemmings — 8", #43025, 2006 Special, African-American, print dress, apron, mop cap...$225.00

**Patsy Jefferson, 8", #41840, 2006 M.A.D.C. travel doll souvenir. Limited to 325.**

**Polly Jefferson, 5", 2006 M.A.D.C. Breakfast Souvenir. Limited to 480. Represents Thomas Jefferson's younger daughter.**

**Mrs. Hopkinson, 10", #41845 (Cissette), 2006 M.A.D.C. Travel Doll centerpiece. Limited to 75. Represents Patsy Jefferson's teacher.**

**Sally Hemmings, 8", #43025, African-American, 2006 M.A.D.C. Special Event doll, limited to 125.**

**Fife & Drum, 8", #41880, 2006 M.A.D.C. Companion centerpiece. Limited to 60.**

# Special Events/Exclusives

Kate Greenaway, 8", 2006
Special Event centerpiece at
M.A.D.C. convention.

Fife & Drum — 8", #41880, 2006, Companion Event centerpiece, red coat, white pants, drum....$175.00
Happy 20+ Day — 8", #41891, 2006 20+ doll, pink dress, straw hat, baby.............................$150.00
Virginia Dogwood — 8", #41905, 2006 Thank You doll, white petal skirt, wings, green tutu. $150.00
Kate Greenaway — 8", #45560, 2006 Let's Talk Dolls centerpiece, elaborate pink dress, straw hat ...$195.00
Alice in Wonderland — 10", #40508, 2006 Children's Event doll (Hannah Pepper), pig baby....$95.00
Mame — 10", #41061, 2006 Coquette souvenir, gold dress, black jewel coat .........................$150.00
Rosalind — 10", #40511, 2006 Coquette centerpiece, long red dress, fur trimmed, black gloves...$175.00
Sarah — 8", #41810, 2006 All in a Row souvenir, vintage silk dress, carpet bag.....................$125.00
Sophia — 10", #41815, 2006 All in a Row centerpiece, vintage long pleated silk dress, straw hat ...$225.00
Camille — 10", #41850, 2006 Cissette Event souvenir, leaf print dress, straw hat, umbrella..$200.00
Amelie — 10", #41855, 2006 Cissette centerpiece, long white dress with embroidery, umbrella....$225.00
Serving Wench "Lottie" — 10", #41875, 2006 Breakfast centerpiece, red dress, apron, mop cap..$185.00
Princess Royal Lissy — 12", #45360, 2006 Lissy souvenir, blue silk dress, crown .................$200.00
Royal Reception Lissy — 12", #45365, 2006 Lissy centerpiece, blue rose-trimmed party dress..$225.00
Classic Couture Alex — 16", #41805, 2006 centerpiece, pink Chanel type suit.......................$285.00
La Maison De Couture Alexandra — 16", #41800, souvenir, black lace long gown................$250.00
Morgan Le Fay — 21", #41865, 2006 Cissy centerpiece, limited to 60...........................$600.00
Lady of the Lake Cissy — 21", #41865, 2006 Cissy souvenir, blue and white flowing gown..$475.00
Governor's Ball Cissy — 21", #41703, 2006 Banquet centerpiece, limited to 23, purple
    1700s ball gown..........................................................................................$1,200.00
Governor's Ball Cissy —21", #41702, 2006 Banquet centerpiece, pink 1700s ball gown, limited to 23..$900.00
Governor's Ball Cissy — 21", 2006 Banquet centerpiece, blue 1700s ball gown, limited to 23.. $900.00
Governor's Ball Cissy — 21", 2006 Banquet centerpiece, green 1700s ball gown, limited to 23..$900.00

## M.A.D.C. Dolls, Exclusives (available to club members only)

Wendy — 8", 1989, in pink and blue, limited to 4,878..............................................................$150.00
Polly Pigtails — 8", 1990 (Maggie Mixup), limited to 4,896....................................................$100.00
Miss Liberty — 10", 1991 – 1992, red, white, and blue gown (Cissette)..................................$125.00
Little Miss Godey — 8", 1992 – 1993 ........................................................................$90.00
Wendy's Best Friend Maggie — 8", 1994 .....................................................................$65.00
Wendy Loves Being Best Friends — 8", name embroidered on apron, 1994.............................$65.00
Wendy Loves the Dionnes — 8", one-of-a-kind set of five dolls, made for 1994  convention.not available
Ultimate Cissy — 21", one-of-a-kind for 1996 convention ...............................................not available
Wendy Joins M.A.D.C. — 8", #79552, 1995 .................................................................$275.00
Wendy Honors Margaret Winson — 8", 1996 post-mistress outfit, honoring first
    M.A.D.C. president ................................................................................$75.00
From the Madame's Sketchbook — 8", 1997, replica of 1930s Tiny Betty ...........................$100.00

Alice in Wonderland, 10"
(Hannah Pepper), 2006
M.A.D.C. Children's Event
doll. Comes with pig baby
and blanket. Limited to 60.

Mame, 10", #45555, 2006
Cissy Coquette event
souvenir. Limited to 175.

Rosalind, 10", #45550,
2006 Cissy Coquette cen-
terpiece. Limited to 40.

Sarah All in a Row Traveler,
8", #41810, 2006 All in a Row
M.A.D.C. souvenir. Limited to 190.

Skate with Wendy — 8", 1998, plaid skating outfit, silver key ......................................$65.00
M.A.D.C. Boutique — 8", 1998 – 2002, frilly panties, white top.............................$40.00
Electro — 8", 1999 (Maggie), silver space costume, boy ..........................................$75.00
M.A.D.C. Angel — 8", 2000, pink gown, limited to 800 ........................................$150.00
M.A.D.C. Ballerina — 8", 2001, blue ballerina.....................................................$125.00
Springtime Darling — 8", 1999, blue dress, pink trim.............................................$75.00
Summer Blossom — 8", 1999, bikini, skirt, sandals.................................................$75.00
M.A.D.C. Story Princess — 8", #79550, 2002, rose gown, silver crown..................$175.00
Recipe for Contentment — 8", #37185, 2003, pink outfit........................................$75.00
Glamour Girl — 8", 2004, #35020, red print dress, club doll...................................$85.00
Signature Wendy — 5", 2005 Renewal Club doll, print dress, straw hat ..................$40.00
Victoria — 8", 2005, pink dress, black hat, club doll ..............................................$85.00
Blue Danube — 8", 2006 club doll, long blue print gown .......................................$88.00
Doll Collector's Day — 8", 2006 special, pink and blue checked dress....................$88.00

## M.A.D.C. Symposium/Premiere

Pre-Doll Specials (M.A.D.C. Symposium)
   Disneyworld — 1984 – 1985 (1984 paper doll) .................................................$60.00
   Wendy Goes to Disneyworld — #1 Sunshine Symposium, 1986, navy dress with polka
      dots, Mickey Mouse hat, pennant (costume by Dorothy Starling), limited to 100 ...$125.00

## M.A.D.C. Snowflake Symposium and Premieres

1st Illinois, 1986, tagged orange taffeta/lace dress, metal pail, and orange, limited to 200........$80.00
2nd Illinois, 1987, tagged, little girl cotton print dress (costume by Mary Voigt) ....................$80.00
3rd Illinois, 1988, tagged, gold/white print dress, gold bodice (created by Pamela Martenec) ..$80.00
4th Illinois, 1989, tagged, red velvet ice skating costume (created by Joan Dixon)..................$80.00
5th Illinois, 1990, bride by Linda's Bridal Shop (also Michelau Scarlett could be purchased).$85.00
   Scarlett — 8", 1990, #6, FAD (white medallion – Snowflake Symposium; red medallion –
      Premiere Southern Symposium), limited to 800 ...............................................$150.00
Springtime — 8", 1991, #7, floral dress, scalloped pinafore, straw hat, limited to 1,600 .........$125.00
Wintertime — 8", 1992, #8, all white, fur trim and hat (six locations), limited to 1,650..........$150.00
Homecoming — 8", 1993, #9 car coat with color trim (eight different colors, one for
   each location), limited to 2,000 .......................................................................$175.00
Setting Sail for Summer — 8" 1994, #10 (eight locations),  limited to 1,800 ..........................$125.00
Snowflake — 8", #79404, #11, 1995 (six locations), gold skater, limited to 1,200 ..................$150.00
Wendy Starts Her Travels — 8", 1996, #12 (three locations), trunk set, different color
   checked coat each location ..............................................................................$175.00

**Camille, 8", #41850, 2006 Cissette Event souvenir doll. From the painting** *In Monet's Garden*. **Limited to 275.**

**Sophia All in a Row Traveler, 10", #41815 (Cissette), 2006 M.A.D.C. All in a Row centerpiece. Limited to 80.**

**Amelie, 8", #41855 (Cissette), 2006 M.A.D.C. Cissette event centerpiece. From the painting** *In Monet's Garden*. **Limited to 75.**

**Princess Royal Lissy, 12", #45360, Lissy Event souvenir. Limited to 275.**

**Serving Wench "Lottie," 10", #41875 (Cissette), 2006 breakfast centerpiece. Limited to 80.**

Polly Pigtails, 8", 1990
Madame Alexander Club doll.

Bobby Takes a Picture — 8", 1996, California companion doll, limited to 215 pieces.............$250.00
Cheshire Cat — 8", 1996, Texas companion doll, limited to 215 pieces.................................$175.00
Wendy Tours the Factory — 8", 1996, New Jersey companion doll.....................................$150.00
Wendy's Tea Party — 8", #13, 1997 (four locations), pink organdy dress, tea set.................$150.00
Boo — 8", 1996, 150 pieces, ghost costume over Mother's Day doll, Illinois event.................$125.00
Diamond Pixie — 8", 1998, #14 (three locations), red Pixie costume .................................$200.00
Starlett Glamour — 10", 1999, #15, black evening gown.................................................$225.00
Millennium Wendy — 8", 2000, #25155, blue dress, straw hat, watch.................................$175.00
On the Town Alex — 16", 2001, gold dress and coat.......................................................$175.00
Evening on the Town Alex — 16", 2001, centerpiece doll, long black gown, stole.................$350.00
Spring Garden Party — 8", #34495, 2002 (Maggie), yellow dress ....................................$150.00
Spring Garden Party Centerpiece — 10", 2002, #34510 (Cissette), yellow outfit .................$125.00
M.A.D.C. March Winds, travel party outfit, red striped skirt ..........................................$50.00
Wendy Turns 50 — 8", #36220, souvenir doll, 2003, lavender satin dress, limited to 400.......$100.00
Wendy Turns 50 Centerpiece — 8", #36621, 2003, mint green satin dress, limited to 45........$150.00
Wendy Turns 50 Travel Outfit — 2003, red straw hat, red dot bathing suit.........................$40.00
Premiere Going Away Wendy — 8", #35801, 2004, white satin dress and hat ......................$125.00
Premiere Bride and Groom Centerpiece — 8", #36595, 2004, limited to 60 .........................$250.00
Premiere Bridesmaid Wendy Blue Companion — 8", #34920, 2004, limited to 110 ...............$175.00
Premiere Bridesmaid Wendy Violet Companion — 8", #34605, 2004, limited to 110 .............$175.00
Premiere Flower Girl — 5", #34369, 2004, pink satin dress ............................................$60.00
Wendy Attends the Ballet — 8", #31830, 2005, travel party, limited to 300..........................$125.00
Evening at the Ballet — 10", 2005, travel party centerpiece, limited to 50 .........................$250.00
First Recital Breakfast souvenir — 5", 2005, lion costume ............................................$50.00
First Recital Centerpiece — 8", 2005, lion costume......................................................$200.00
Wendy Loves the Ballet — 8", 2005, banquet centerpiece, limited to 60 ............................$175.00
Prima Ballerina — 8", 2005 souvenir doll, black and magenta costume ............................$125.00
Sugar — 8", 2006 souvenir doll, bend knees, pink dress.................................................$95.00
Everything Nice — 5", souvenir, matches Sugar ........................................................$40.00
Spice Cissette — 10", special doll, red dress .............................................................$150.00
Cissy Spice — 21", 2006 centerpiece, long red dress.....................................................$400.00
Puppy Dog Tails — 8", 2006 centerpiece, green outfit, plush dog.....................................$125.00

## M.A.D.C. Friendship Luncheon (outfit only)

Friends Around the Country — 1997, print dress and pinafore outfit ...............................$50.00
Wendy Plays Masquerade — 1998, pink butterfly costume ............................................$50.00
Wendy, Out and About with Friends — 1999, brown felt coat, leopard tam and purse ...........$50.00
Wendy Emcees Her School Play — 2000, pinafore, print dress, pink tam, standing
    microphone, limited to 700................................................................................$50.00
Wendy Starts Holiday Shopping — #31815, 2001, red and black dress and hat.....................$50.00
Thanksgiving at Grandma's — 2002, silk plaid dress....................................................$50.00
Thanksgiving at Grandma's Centerpiece — 8", braids, plaid dress (doll included)................$125.00
Hugs Wendy — 8", #36230, 2003, souvenir doll, black velvet top, white skirt with
    x's and o's, limited to 700................................................................................$75.00
Kisses — luncheon centerpiece, #36231, 2003 (Maggie), pink shirt with x's and o's .............$100.00
Special Kisses — Helper doll, 8", #36234, 2003 (Maggie), pink skirt, limited to 25 .............$125.00
Special Hugs — Helper doll, #36232, 2003, Wendy, special hairdo, limited to 20 .................$150.00
Hugs African-American — Helper doll, 8", #36233, 2003, white skirt, limited to 30.............$200.00
Wendy Goes Skating — 8", #38135, 2004, Asian face, limited to 40 ................................$175.00
Wendy Goes Skiing — 8", #38570, 2004, pink and blue outfit .......................................$75.00
Wendy Goes Sledding — 8", #38795, 2004, centerpiece, limited to 150................................$150.00

## Madame Alexander Doll Company

Melody & Friends — 25", 1992, limited to 1,000, designed and made by Hildegard Gunzel,
    1st anniversary dolls ................................................................................$700.00 up, set

Royal Reception Lissy, 12",
#45365, 2006 Lissy Event cen-
terpiece. Limited to 60.

Courtney & Friends — 25" and 8" boy and girl, 1993, second anniversary, limited to
   1,200, by Gunzel ..................................................................................$725.00 up, set
Rumpelstiltskin and Miller's Daughter — 8" and 14", #1569, 1992 only, limited to 3,000 ......$275.00
Special Event Doll — 8", 1994, organza and lace in pink with special event banner,
   ribbon across body, front of hair pulled back in curls ..................................$75.00
Wendy Makes it Special — 8", 1998, #31050, pink and white dress, hatbox ..........................$85.00
Wendy Salutes the Olympics — 8", #86005, 1996, Olympic medal ........................................$100.00
Maggie Mixup — 8", 1998, #31000, Post Office commemorative, blue gingham .....................$50.00
75th Anniversary Wendy — 8", #22420, 1998, pink outfit .......................................................$80.00
Wendy's Special Cheer — 8", #16510, cheerleader, 1999 ......................................................$70.00
George and Martha Washington — 8", 1999, limited......................................................$200.00 set
Mary McFadden Cissy* — 21", 1999, black and gold gown ..................................... one-of-a-kind
Isaac Mizrahi Cissy* — 21", 1999, gray skirt, red sweater ....................................... one-of-a-kind
Carmen Marc Valvo Cissy* — 21", 1999, long evening gown ................................... one-of-a-kind
Nicole Miller — 21", 1999, dress and fur coat ......................................................... one-of-a-kind
Diane Von Furstenberg Cissy* — 21", 1999, black dress, fur coat .......................... one-of-a-kind
Yeohlee Cissy* — 21", 1999, black skirt, long black coat ........................................ one-of-a-kind
Betsy Johnson Cissy* — 21", 1999, black short dress trimmed in pink ................... one-of-a-kind
Scaasi Cissy* — 21", 1999, white lace gown, red coat with feather ..............................$450.00
Jessica McClintock Cissy* † — 21", 1999, #22780, long gold ball gown .........................$475.00
Fernando Sanchez Cissy* † — 21", 1999, #22720, long white gown..............................$425.00
Josie Natori Cissy* † — 21", 1999, #22730 ....................................................................$450.00
Anna Sui Cissy* † — 21", 1999, #22590, has braids, brown dress, coat.........................$450.00
Linda Allard for Ellen Tracy Cissy* † — 21", 1999, brown skirt, long black coat............$475.00
Dana Buchman Cissy* † — 21", 1999, green dress, coat ...............................................$475.00
Donna Karan Cissy* † — 21", 1999, long black dress................................. one-of-a-kind
James Purcell Cissy* † — 21", 1999, long white gown with black circles .......................$400.00
Madame Alexander Celebrates American Design Cissy* † — 21", 1999, #22560...........$225.00
Badgley Mischka Cissy* † — 21", 1999, #22740, long evening gown ............................$450.00
Marc Bouwer Cissy* † — 21", 1999, #26125, African-American doll, long gown...................$550.00
Carolina Herrera Cissy* † — 21", 1999, #26121, red and white ball gown.......................$475.00
*An American Legend* book and doll in display box .........................................................$200.00
Charm and Cheer Lissy — 12", 2006, print dress, pink velvet coat, straw hat .............. one-of-a-kind
Silhouette Cissy — 21", #41570, 2006, limited to 30, Gene Convention Special, pink hat,
   blue and black dress........................................................................................$650.00

## Madame Alexander Doll Company Mid-Year Specials

Welcome Home — 8", 1991, black or white, boy or girl, Desert Storm soldier........................$50.00
Wendy Loves Being Loved — 8", 1992, doll and wardrobe.....................................................$100.00
Queen Elizabeth II — 8", 1992, 40th anniversary of coronation ............................................$125.00
Christopher Columbus — 8", 1992, #328, burgundy and brown costume .............................$125.00
Queen Isabella — 8", 1992, #329, green velvet and gold gown..............................................$125.00
Santa or Mrs. Claus — 8", 1993.................................................................................$125.00 ea.
Scarlett O'Hara — 8", 1993, yellow dress, straw hat...........................................................$150.00
Wendy Ann — 8", 1995, 100th anniversary, pink coat and hat..............................................$150.00
Sir Lancelot DuLac — 8", 1995, burgundy and gold knight's costume ..................................$125.00
Queen Guinevere — 8", 1995, burgundy and gold gown.......................................................$125.00
Wizard of Oz — 8", 1994, green metallic costume, black hat ...............................................$125.00
Dorothy — 8", 1994, emerald green checked dress ............................................................$225.00
Wicked Witch — 8", 1994, green face, black costume..........................................................$250.00
Little Miss USA — 8", 2002, red skirt, blue jacket, hat, baton, charity for 9-11 .....................$75.00
Tidings of Joy Ballerina — 2006, blonde (#41150), brunette (#41155), red (#41160),
   African-American (#41161), Asian (#41162), red and gold tutu ............................$90.00
The Spirit of New Orleans — 2006, purple Mardi Gras outfit.................................................$100.00

Sugar, 8", bend knees, 2006 M.A.D.C. Premiere souvenir.

Charm and Cheer Lissy, 12" hard plastic, 2006, one-of-a-kind.

*Cissy dolls made in limited editions for 1999. †1999 designer Cissy dolls were designed to be auctioned for Fashion Targets Breast Cancer.

### Marshall Fields
Avril, Jane — 10", 1989, red/black can-can outfit (tribute to T. Lautrec) (Cissette) ..............$125.00
Madame Butterfly — 10", 1990, blue brocade kimono, gold obi ................................................$150.00

### Matilda Company
Sweet Parfait Blonde — 8", #33590, 2003, silk outfit .................................................................$90.00
Sweet Parfait Red — 8", #33591, 2003, silk outfit ....................................................................$90.00
Sweet Parfait African-American — 8", #33592, 2003, silk outfit .................................................$90.00

### Metroplex Doll Club
Spring Break — 8", 1992, two-piece halter/wrap skirt outfit, limited to 400, beach bag.........$150.00
Victorian Tea — 8", #34000, 2002, blue pleated skirt, U.F.D.C. Luncheon ...........................$100.00

### Meyers 80th Year
8", "Special Event" doll with banner, 1994 .............................................................................$75.00

### Modern Doll Convention
Modern Romance Alex — 16", 2000, long strapless dress, limited to 200...............................$350.00
Modern Romance Alex centerpiece — 16", 2000, long strapless henna dress, limited to 20...$700.00
Up-to-the-Minute "Mod" Alex — 16", 2002, #35710, black gown, limited to 30....................$200.00
Up-to-the-Minute "Mod" Cissette — 10", 2002, #35711, centerpiece doll, black gown,
    limited to 55.......................................................................................................................$175.00
1871 Chicago Belle — 10", #36336, 2004, pink taffeta dress..............................................$200.00
Bella — 8", #36560, 2004, blue silk dress, limited to 50...................................................$150.00
Belle of the Ball Alex — 16", centerpiece, limited to 36 ....................................................$275.00
Fairy Godmother — 10" (Cissette), #40985, 2006, red cape, limited to 40 ............................$175.00
Celebration Minnie and Mickey — 8", #40740, Mickey faces, white outfits............................ $200.00

### M. Pancner's House of Collectibles
1920s Golden Girl — 10", #17740, 1999, limited to 25................................................$125.00
1950s Sock Hop — 8", #17780, 1999, limited to 50..................................................$75.00

### My Doll House
Southern Belle — 10", 1989, FAD, all pink gown with parasol and picture hat,
    limited to 2,300...................................................................................................$125.00
Queen Elizabeth I — 10", 1990, limited to 2,400.....................................................$125.00
Empress Elizabeth of Austria — 10", 1991, white/gold trim, limited to 3,600 (Cissette) ........$150.00

### Neiman-Marcus
Doll with four outfits in trunk — 8", 1990, called "party trunk," limited to 1,044...................$275.00
Caroline Loves Storyland — 8", 1993, trunk and wardrobe ...........................................$250.00
Caroline's Adventures — 8", 1994, trunk and costumes for USA, China, Germany, Kenya
    (Maggie)..............................................................................................................$225.00
Anne Series — 8", 1994, trunk set, character from Lucy M. Montgomery books...................$275.00
ABC Huggums — limited to 650 pieces ..................................................................$65.00
Miss St. John — 21", 1998, limited to 750 ..............................................................$550.00
Crayola Sets — 1999, dolls from regular line in ethnic sets .........................................$70.00
Holly Day — 8", #28195, #28196, #28197, 2000, red velvet dress....................................$100.00
Alex Zenra — 16", #31860, 2001, maroon dress, limited to 250 .....................................$130.00
Morning Dew Victoria — #28636, 2001, African-American .......................................... $85.00
Pink Bunny Huggums— #28961, 2001, African-American  ..........................................$65.00
Shopping for Mommy — 8", #40089, 2004, pink dress, shopping bag, limited to 75 ............$150.00

### New England Collector Society
Noel — 12", 1989 – 1991, porcelain Christmas doll, limited to 5,000...................................$225.00
Joy — 12", 1991, porcelain Christmas doll, limited to 5,000 ........................................$225.00

### New York Doll Club
Autumn in New York — 10", FAD, limited to 260...................................................$150.00

### Nordstrum's
Binah — 12", #39160, 2004, cloth .........................................................................$50.00
Nicole — 12", #39446, 2004, cloth ........................................................................$50.00
Charlotte — 12", #39448, 2004, cloth .....................................................................$50.00

Shopping for Mommy,
8", 2004, Neiman-Marcus
exclusive.

Amy — 12", #39444, 2004, cloth ..................................................................................$50.00
Grace — 12", #39447, 2004, cloth .................................................................................$50.00

**Oma's Doll Shop**
Victorian Seaside Wendy — 8", #35475, 2003, vintage bathing suit, limited to 1,000 .............$100.00
Baby Take a Bow — 8", #40960, red dotted cotton dress.........................................................$85.00

**Paris Fashion Doll Convention**
City Lights Alex —16", 2001, long white gown, limited to 200..................................................$700.00
City Lights centerpiece — 16", 2001, limited to 20 ................................................................$1,500.00
Festival Paris — 16", 2002, #34545, white dress, black velvet coat, limited to 50 .................$700.00
Festival Alex — 16", 2002, #34550, lavender 20s dress, limited to 50 ...............................$700.00
Alex — 16", #37690, 2003, Paris Festival souvenir, blue gown.............................................$400.00
10th Anniversary Alex — 16", 2004, silk halter dress, limited to 30.....................................$500.00
Evening in Paris Cissy — 21", #41330, taffeta dress, limited to 20.....................................$1,200.00
Evening in Paris Coquette — 10", #40035, 2006, taffeta dress, limited to 100........................$275.00

**Penney, J.C.**
At the Hop — 8", #27860, 2000, skirt with hoops..................................................................$85.00

**QVC**
Summer Cherry Picking — 8", #79760, 1998 (Wendy), cherry print dress, limited to 500 ....$225.00
Betsy Ross — 8", #79990, 1998 (Wendy), red striped dress, limited to 500..............................$95.00
Pilgrim Girl — 8", #79980, 1998 (Wendy), long blue dress, limited to 500 ...........................$100.00
Home for the Holidays — 10", #79800, 1998 (Cissette), limited to 400 ................................$125.00
A Rose for You — 8", 1999 (Wendy), lace-trimmed white dress with rose...............................$75.00
Lavender Rose — 10", 1999, lavender ball gown.....................................................................$125.00
Pollyana — 8", 1999 (Maggie), blue checked dress, straw hat, limited to 500..........................$75.00
Blossom — 8", 1999, pink print dress (Wendy), limited to 500 ...............................................$75.00
Little Bo Peep — 8", 1999, pink gown trimmed in lace, limited to 700 ..................................$80.00
Investigator Wendy — 8", 1999 (checked coat and hat), limited to 500....................................$90.00
Autumn Breeze — 8", 1999 .................................................................................................$80.00
Alice —  8", 1999.................................................................................................................$80.00
Kiss Me, I'm Irish — 8", 1999 (Maggie), green skirt, limited to 500........................................$80.00
Ladybug Garden — 8", 1999................................................................................................$75.00
Fun at Halloween — 8", 1999,  limited to 500 pieces (Maggie), yellow and black costume .....$80.00
Golden Light Tree Topper — 8", 1999, yellow and black costume, limited to 400 .................$125.00
Spring Flowers — 8", 1999, print dresss, basket of flowers (Maggie) .....................................$70.00
Fourth of July — 8", 1999..................................................................................................$75.00
Springtime Bride — 10", 1999, white slender dress, limited to 400........................................$125.00

**Robert Moore and Company**
Azalea Trail Maid — 8", #34555, 2003, long peach silk gown.............................................$150.00
Azalea Trail Green — 8", #35590, Tosca, #33591, brunette ....................................................$150.00
Pink Azalea Trail Queen — 10", #35095, long pink gown ....................................................$175.00
Pink Azalea Trail Queen Brunette — 10", #35096................................................................$175.00

**Saks Fifth Avenue**
Christmas Carol — 8", 1993, tartan plaid taffeta dress with velvet bodice...............................$150.00
Joy of Christmas — 1994, second in series, forest green taffeta dress .....................................$125.00
Book Tour Alex with Saks bag — 16", #31207, 2001 ...........................................................$125.00

**Savannah Doll Club**
Georgia State Day — 8", 2002, white dress with black trim, limited to 160 ............................$125.00

**Sears-Roebuck**
Little Women — 1989 – 1990, set of six 12" dolls (Nancy Drew) ......................................$600.00 set

**Shirley's Doll House**
Angel Face — 8", 1990 (Maggie Mixup), blue gown, white wings, limited to 3,500.................$90.00
Winter Sports — 8", 1991, FAD (Tommy Snooks), skates, tagged hat, limited to 975 ............$70.00
Wendy Visits World's Fair — 1993, 100th anniversary Chicago World's Fair, limited to 3,600...$85.00
Winter Angel — 1993, cape with hood, wings, holds golden horn, exclusive, limited to 1,000....$100.00

# Special Events/Exclusives

Maypole Dance — 8", 1994, shop's 20th anniversary doll, pink organdy dress and blue
    pinafore, limited to 3,000 (Wendy Ann)......................................................................$75.00
Grandma's Darling — 8", 1996, #79617, yellow dress, white blanket ......................................$80.00
Little Collector — 8", 1999, #79820, navy dress, straw hat, basket ........................................$80.00
Grandma's Girl — 8", #31545, 2001, brown dress with book, limited to 300............................$80.00
Once Upon a Time — 8", #31550, 2001, pink dress, crown......................................................$80.00

## Shriner's First Ladies' Luncheon
8" boy, 1993, wears fez, jeans, shirt, vest with Texas star on back, limited to 1,800 ...............$375.00

## South Carolina Chimney Sweep Guild
Lucky Dale — 8", #31975, 2001, top hat, tail, ladder ..............................................................$125.00

## Spiegel's
Beth — 10", 1990, 125th anniversary special, 1860s women, pink brocade gown..................$125.00
Christmas Tree Topper (also called Merry Angel) — 8", 1991, gold and red velvet angel costume.$150.00
Joy Noel — 8", 1992, tree topper angel, white satin/net with gold dots, gold lace, halo and
    skirt, limited to 3,000 ....................................................................................................$110.00
Mardi Gras — 10", 1992, elaborate costume of purple/gold/royal blue, limited to 3,000 ........$110.00

## Toy Shoppe, The
Springtime Silk Wendy-Kin Wood — 8", #40110, 2004, silk dress .........................................$275.00
Wendy Ann Felt — 12", #37945, 2004, cloth doll, blue dress ................................................$300.00
Midnight Elegance Coquette Cissy — 10", #39845, 2005, black satin dress...........................$150.00
Sapphire Symphony Coquette Cissy — 10", #41245, 2005, blue satin dress ...........................$150.00
Romance and Roses Coquette Cissy — 10", #41405, 2005, pink taffeta dress.........................$150.00
Wendy Shops at the Toy Shoppe — 8", #41410, 2005, pink jacket, white dress,
    mini Wendy, shopping bag..............................................................................................$95.00
Teatime with Teddy — 8", #41420, 2005, blue dress, tiny bear................................................$90.00
Edith the Lonely Doll Felt — 12", 2005, pink checked dress ..................................................$300.00
Wendy Loves Rudolph — 8", 2006, red checked dress, deer, doll, limited to 500 ....................$90.00

## Two Daydreamers
Whitney — 8", #34106, 2001, ribbon and jewel crown, limited to 120 ...................................$125.00

## U.F.D.C. – United Federation of Doll Clubs
Sailor Boy — 8", 1990, gray gabardine outfit, limited to 260..................................................$600.00
Miss Unity — 10", 1991, cotton eyelet dress, limited to 310 ..................................................$350.00
Little Emperor — 8", 1992, elaborate silk and gold costume, limited to 400...........................$375.00
Turn of the Century Bathing Beauty — 10", 1992, U.F.D.C. Region Nine Conference,
    FAD (Gibson Girl), old-fashioned bathing suit, beach bag, umbrella, limited to 300 ... $225.00
Columbian 1893 Sailor — 12", 1993 (Lissy) ..........................................................................$125.00
Gabrielle — 10", 1998 (Cissette), black suit, dressmaker's stand, limited to 400....................$225.00
One Enchanted Evening — 16", 1999, #80260, limited to 310 ................................................$350.00
Windy City Chic — 16", 2000, pink and black gown, limited to 350........................................$150.00
Susan — 8", #27465, 2000, doll, three outfits, case, limited to 400 .......................................$225.00
Yardley in Lavender — 21", 2001, sheath dress and jacket, with dog, limited to 150..............$300.00
Me & My Shadow Annette — 10", 2001, plum silk dress, limited to 360...............................$175.00
Me & My Shadow Annie — 8", 2001, plum silk dress, limited to 250.....................................$150.00
Eloise in Moscow centerpiece — 8", #27735, 2000, yellow coat, black hat.............................$100.00
The Love of Dolls Club Cissette — 10", #31960, 2001, long burgundy gown trimmed in fur ... $150.00
Buccaneer Bobby — 8", 2002, Denver luncheon doll, pirate sitting on shoulder, limited to 275 ... $125.00
Halloween — 8", 2002, centerpiece doll, #31465, black outfit .................................................$175.00
King Midas — 8", #33045, limited to 25, gold velvet robe, 2003 centerpiece doll ..................$250.00
Golden Jubilee Wendy — 8", #37130, 2003, limited to 210......................................................$125.00
Dolls and Kicks on Route 66 — 8", New Mexico Regional, jeans............................................$150.00
Belle — 8", #36470, pink striped clown outfit, limited to 90 ..................................................$150.00
Clara — 8", #39390, blue striped and polka dot clown outfit, limited to 190 ..........................$100.00
Dolls and Kicks on Route 66 — 8", #40630, 2006, blue pants, pink sweater............................$150.00